Holy Days and Holidays

THE OFFICIAL BLESSING OF PILGRIMS AND THEIR EQUIPMENT. From the illuminated thirteenth-century Ms. Latin 11560 of the Bibliothèque Nationale, Paris. *(Reproduced by permission.)*

Holy Days and Holidays

The Medieval Pilgrimage to Compostela

Horton and Marie-Hélène Davies

Lewisburg
Bucknell University Press
London and Toronto: Associated University Presses

© 1982 by Associated University Presses, Inc.

Associated University Presses, Inc.
4 Cornwall Drive
East Brunswick, N.J. 08816

Associated University Presses Ltd
27 Chancery Lane
London WC2A 1NS, England

Associated University Presses
Toronto M5E 1A7, Canada

Library of Congress Cataloging in Publication Data

Davies, Horton.
  Holy days and holidays.

  Bibliography: p.
  Includes index.
  1. Christian pilgrims and pilgrimages—Spain
—Santiago de Compostela—History.
  2. Santiago de Compostela (Spain)—Church
history. I. Davies, Marie-Hélène. II. Title.
  BX2321.S3D38   248.4'63'094611   80-69875
  ISBN 0-8387-5018-4   AACR2

Printed in the United States of America

For Dorothy Thomas

Contents

Illustrations

Acknowledgments

There were three ways of accomplishing a medieval pilgrimage: on foot, on horseback, or, luxuriously, in a litter. We modern pilgrims chose an equivalent of the third. Our first acknowledgment goes to M. and Mme. Lhoste, who provided us with a coughing, four-horsepower Renault, clad in blue-and-green plaid and Scotchly economical on gas. This car carried us over the French roads to Compostela, even though it occasionally had to be pushed and pulled, in thoroughly medieval fashion, by huffing and puffing villagers to the nearest car doctor.

We also wish to thank the assistant librarians of the Bodleian Library in Oxford, the British Museum in London, the Bibliothèque Nationale in Paris, the Firestone Library in Princeton, and the Dartmouth College Library in Hanover for their courteous assistance.

Last, Horton Davies wishes to extend his thanks to the Princeton University Research Committee in the Humanities and Social Sciences for two summer grants for travel and support.

H. and M.-H. Davies

Holy Days and Holidays

PART I
Motivations and Preparations

1

The Motivations of Pilgrimage

THE mystery and the complexity of motives that impelled men (and less commonly women) to go on pilgrimage in the Middle Ages are the subjects of this chapter. The mystery is undeniable because all human motives are difficult to fathom, particularly in the case of religion, where the most sublime intentions may accompany the most self-regarding aims.

The difficulty of probing the mystery is compounded because the vast majority of the many millions who thronged the roads or the seaways to the three distant shrines of Jerusalem, Rome, and Compostela were illiterate.[1] Hence the pilgrims were unable to *write* any account of their journey regardless of how often they might excitedly recount their experiences to their fellow travelers in the inns and hospices en route and to their friends on their return home. Furthermore, of the few travelers who could write few bothered to do so. Even then, writers rarely analyzed their motives. Finally, most accounts have probably perished.

Some few accounts that do survive and that cover the longest stretch of time inevitably deal with the supremely important Christian pilgrimage to Jerusalem.[2] No place could equal in holiness the site of the Passion and Resurrection of Jesus Christ. With the coming of the peace of the Church in A.D. 325 after the persecutions, Constantine the emperor had munificently honored the sacred sites by covering them with a magnificent basilica, in which the original cross of Christ found by Constantine's mother, Saint Helena, was exposed to the ecstatic veneration of the pilgrims, and a splendid rotunda covered the *anastasis,* or place of the Resurrection. The emperor also erected in Bethlehem a basilica commemorating the nativity of Jesus. Because of the different cultural environment and the deeper religious experience, Jerusalem pilgrims wrote up their travels more readily.

The records of the pilgrimage to Rome are even fuller. This too can easily be explained. In Rome were to be found the tombs of the martyred apostles Peter and Paul; here also was the seat of the papacy and the Curia—the headquarters of the Roman Catholic Church to which both bishops and important abbots repaired to receive their authorizations. Furthermore, while the historic center of the Roman Empire was from time to time invaded by pagans or heretical Christians, it never suffered the centuries-long domination by the Muslims as did the Eastern Church and Jerusalem. But even these pilgrimage records tend to be matter of fact and laconic; rarely if ever do they indulge in the type of brilliant self-analysis that we find in the *Confessions* of Saint Augustine of Hippo.

How much worse then is the case of persons who wish to investigate the reasons for which pilgrims traveled to Compostela, a place unheard of until the middle of the ninth century. It is located in a remote part of the inhabited world near Finisterre—"the end of the world"—and only became an important and popular shrine in the eleventh century.

There are a very few early and several late (fifteenth- and sixteenth-century) accounts of the itineraries taken by pilgrims to Compostela. The most important are the accounts of Nompar II, lord of Caumont, who went in 1417;[3] William Way, a fellow of the new College of Eton, a pilgrim in 1456;[4] Robert Langton, an ecclesiastical pluralist combining benefices in three English cathedrals;[5] Arnold von Harff, a nobleman from Cologne who was a pilgrim in 1499; and finally, the skeptical English doctor, Andrew Boorde, who reached Compostela in 1532.[6]

Otherwise, sources for the Compostela pilgrimage must be drawn from chronicles, wills, charters of religious houses, *vitae* of saints, canons of Church councils, and from the iconography of abbeys and cathedrals en route. Other sources are liturgical and paraliturgical services, supplemented by information drawn from other pilgrimage centers. Only thus can we learn about the motivation, preparation, routes, companions, stages on the way, hospitality, dangers, spirituality, amusements, and the triumphant arrival at the goal. Inevitably, historians have to deal with probabilities, sometimes indulging only in possibilities, and we can only hope that our guesswork is intelligent.

There is, however, one exception to this paucity of early information. It is the famous *Codex Calixtinus,* attributed wrongly to Pope Calixtinus (1119–24).[7] It is a primary and unexcelled source of information on the pilgrimage to Compostela and was produced about the middle of the twelfth century. We shall draw heavily from this source particularly in later chapters. It comprises five books. The fifth is an absorbing medieval *Guide Michelin* or Baedeker that lists the four major routes through France and across the Pyrenees into north and northwestern Spain to Compostela. It advises the pious traveler at which shrines en route he should stop to venerate the tombs or relics of the saints whose intercessions are efficacious. The second book is an invaluable compilation of the miracles attributed to the Apostle James. It was so renowned that Vincent of Beauvais summarized it in his *Historia generale* as did Jacobus de Voragine in his famous *Legenda sanctorum,* commonly if erroneously known as *The Golden Legend.* It functioned as a medieval equivalent of a modern neon-lit series of billboards or as the yellow pages in a telephone directory. It advertised the powers of Saint James as protector of pilgrims from many parts of the world, as a healer of many different diseases, and supremely as the *Matamoros*—slayer of infidel Moors and inspirer of the *reconquista,* or reconquest of Spain. The first book is liturgical in character: it comprises a collection of sermons, offices, and hymns, all honoring the apostle. The most fascinating sermon in the book for the historian is an extensive one, the *Veneranda dies,* occupying fourteen folios of the Compostela manuscript. It is virtually a treatise on pilgrimage, its aims and dangers. The entire book enables us to reconstruct the character of festal days in Spain in the mid–twelfth century. The third book gives an account of the legends on which the reputation of Compostela as a pilgrimage center was based, from the time of the supposed preaching of the apostle in Spain to the legend of the star-directed discovery of his tomb in Galicia. The fourth book of the *Codex* is a *chanson de geste,* or epic song, attributed to Turpin the warrior-bishop who accompanied Charlemagne on his campaigns. This legendary history of three of the Holy Roman emperor's campaigns beyond the Pyrenees records the epic deeds that took place on the *camino francés* and suggests the bonds between them and the pilgrimage, thus linking patriotism, pugnacity, and piety. The whole *Codex* was probably edited by Aymery Picaud of Parthenay-le-Vieux about 1139.

While the *Codex* is an unparalleled source of information on the Compostela pilgrimage, our researches require us to range not only along the four ways to Compostela through France, which we have in fact traveled, but much more widely to other pilgrimage centers. In addition we occasionally shall roam through many centuries before and after the Compostela pilgrimage was at its peak. In other chapters, however, we will concentrate on Compostela from about the mid–ninth to the end of the fourteenth century, and chiefly on the eleventh and twelfth centuries when the pilgrimage was most popular.

Although still undaunted, we proceed more hesitantly in our quest for motivations and inducements to pilgrimage because of the warning of Jonathan Sumption. He writes: "What considerations dictated a pilgrim's choice of a shrine is as much a mystery to us as it must have been to his contemporaries."[8] This mystery he rightly insists is partly due to several contingencies such as the pilgrim's baptismal name, his trade, mere fashion, and resorting to lots. To these we might add proximity to a particular shrine, or the enthusiastic report of a returned pilgrim and friend or relative, or good advertising from officialdom. While recognizing the element of the sheerly fortuitous, we must also take into account, as Sumption himself does later in his book,[9] the personal, legendary, political, judicial, and pecuniary factors that helped to account for the great popularity of pilgrimages in Christendom.

Our contention is that any attempt to be reasonably comprehensive in explaining the impulses to pilgrimage in the Middle Ages must take serious account of three sets of considerations. One is, as already indicated, the mixed motives of the pilgrims themselves. The second is the sinister delight in pilgrimages taken by those parasites who battened on the pilgrims, such as robbers, buccaneers, cheating innkeepers, unscrupulous shopkeepers, pardoners, and the like. Finally, account must be taken of the inducements to pilgrimage offered by the Church through encouraging sanctity or the sale of indulgences, and by princes appealing to patriotism, vengeance, and Christian courage all at once. Each of these sets of factors will be considered in turn.

First we turn to the mélange of pilgrims' motives. The skeptic may well insist that what is important is what the motive is mixed with, and it would be exceedingly uncharitable to imply that most pilgrims would undertake a long, inconvenient, and hazardous pilgrimage without some genuinely religious motivation. Without impugning the motives of any particular pilgrim, we shall attempt to construct a typology of motives from the highest to the lowest, assuming that the most golden motives are mingled with inferior lead, and that the most leaden are not without a gleam of gilt. The great range of motives is most concisely summed up by Bernal Diaz del Castillo, the Mexican conquistador, who said, "We came here to serve God and also to get rich."[10] Even the much-married Wife of Bath never gave up the hope of heaven and the intercession of the saints, or she would never for the mere sake of travel have undertaken many long pilgrimages:

> And thryes hadde she been at Jerusalem;
> She hadde passed many a straunge streem;
> At Rome she hadde been, and at Boloigne,
> In Galice at Seint Jame, and at Coloigne.[11]

Unquestionably the highest motive of the pilgrims was their quest for *sanctity*. With a different motive from the prodigal son in Christ's parable, [12] though with a similar ending, pilgrims left the familiar for the far place that they might at last find the way to their heavenly Father's home, with its many mansions of which their Lord had spoken[13] and where Christ kept high festival with all his friends the saints.[14] They counted the world well lost for Christ's sake. Peter the Venerable in

Liber de miraculis tells of a rich knight who, "touched by divine inspiration, prepared to renounce the world" and presented Cluny with gifts of clothing, horses, and large sums of money, and becoming poor sought Jerusalem.[15]

This quest was called by many terms and described by many metaphors. Its greatest name was perfection. The pilgrims intended to reconsecrate themselves to God and thus make a fresh start. For example, the Piacenza pilgrim to Palestine was tonsured and shaved his beard at Sinai as a symbol of the new dedication.[16] Other pilgrims at other holy places used the pilgrimage as a trial for entering monastic life.[17] The quest was to revivify the imagination and hence the devotion to Christ, the prophets, and the saints by visiting the places associated with their lives and particularly with their martyrdoms. This is made clear by a letter sent by Paula and Eustochium to Marcella about the holy places in Palestine about the year 382. They affirm that they are walking in the footsteps of many bishops, martyrs, and students of ecclesiastical history who have come to Jerusalem, "thinking themselves to be lacking in religion and in learning, and not to have received, as the saying is, a full handful of virtues, unless they had adored Christ in those very places from which the Gospel first shone forth from the Cross."[18] Moreover, wherever the indefatigable Egeria traveled in the Holy Land, whether at Sinai or Golgotha, she was particular to read the appropriate passage of Scripture, to offer a prayer, and to receive the Eucharist.[19]

The degree of rapture with which the sacred places were adored by one enthusiast was recorded by Saint Jerome in his Letter 108 to Eustochium, a memoir of Paula. Saint Paula "fell down and worshipped before the Cross, as if she saw the Lord hanging on it. On entering the Tomb of the Resurrection she kissed the stone which the angel moved from the sepulchre door; then like a thirsty man who has waited long, and at last comes to water, she faithfully kissed the very shelf on which the Lord's body had lain. Her tears and lamentations there are known to all Jerusalem—or rather to the Lord himself to whom she was praying."[20]

Saint Bernard of Clairvaux was moved to the sublimest flights of eloquence when he contemplated the Holy Land with its sacred associations: "The possession of patriarchs, the nurse of prophets, the teacher of apostles, the cradle of our salvation, the country of the Lord, the mother of faith, even as Rome is the mother of the faithful, chosen of God and sanctified, where stood the feet of the Lord, honoured by angels, frequented by every nation under heaven."[21] The Bible came alive again for those who trod in the very footsteps of Moses on Mount Sinai or traced the path of Jesus in Bethlehem, beside the sea of Galilee, and the end of the *via dolorosa et gloriosa* in Jerusalem in the Temple, the Garden of Gethsemane, Golgotha, and the Holy Sepulcher with its rotunda of the Resurrection. It not only increased their faith, but also augmented their charity and fortified their hope of everlasting life. All this and more was included in the pilgrim's search for sanctity.

Most simply, however, it was thought of as a quest for the soul's well-being. The pilgrim intended to serve God for a time and to live under his protection also. This was obedience to the Gospel precept— leaving behind one's self all that was dearest and turning one's back on the fatherland. There was then no other protection except God's.

Langland criticizes some aspects of pilgrimage, yet he makes his imaginary pilgrim point to the tokens he has brought back as souvenirs from many shrines, saying: "You can see by the signs in my hat how widely I've traveled—on foot and in all weathers, seeking out the shrines of the saints for the good of my soul."[22] Early or late Christian pilgrimages aimed primarily at amendment of life. A rite of the abbey of Sant Cugat del Vallès accompanies the consecration of the scrip or wallet of pilgrimage with this blessing: "In the name of Our Lord Jesus Christ, receive this scrip . . . so that, in perfect purity, security and amendment of life, you may deserve to reach the forecourt of the Holy Sepulchre, or of St. James or of St. Hilary [of Poitiers] or of any of the other saints which you desire to reach, and, your journey accomplished, you may return to us in perfect health."[23]

Another way of describing the quest for sanctity through pilgrimage would be to call it the imitation of Christ and of the imitators of Christ, the chief of whom had been martyred for their faith. Pilgrimage was thought of as a way of renunciation, of obeying the dominical command to "take up your cross and follow me"[24] for the sake of the beatitude of heaven. The cross on earth was to be endured for the crown in heaven. Bede described the holy vagabonds as "wishing to live as pilgrims on earth that they might be welcomed by the saints when they were called away from their earthly sojourn."[25] The imitation of Christ, however, was more than a radical interior change of motive and transvaluation of the paradoxical kind encouraged by the Master when he promises that "he that findeth his life shall lose it; and he that loseth his life shall save it."[26] Its very hardships recommended it as a means toward perfection. Saint Magdalveus traveled with great difficulties, *cum magna viarum angustia* in the eighth century.[27] The pilgrim was often sick en route and even occasionally died. He was, however, reminded that his life was one of risk and called for a deeper dependence on God as his only ultimate safeguard. It seemed particularly suited to penitents, who had to wipe away the guilt that soiled and sapped their lives.

The life of pilgrimage could be conceived as an imitation of Christ in a far more detailed way. There are many parallels between the life of Jesus and the life of the pilgrim. Jesus was born in poverty, and Mary and

Joseph could find no room for him in the inn at Bethlehem; and neither experience can have been unusual for many pilgrims. Wise men and kings came to offer their gifts to the Christ child, as pilgrims came to offer their gifts at the shrine of Christ or his friends the saints. The young Christ fled into Egypt because of the Slaughter of the Innocents, which made him and his parents wanderers. Christ, too, sought the desert as he considered the methods of his mission and chief purpose of his life; so did many a pilgrim (like the hermits before him) seek to contemplate in the desert and fight temptations there as did the Lord. The pilgrims as they crossed the deserts of northern Spain must often have been tempted to give up their pilgrimage. Saint-Guilhem-du-Désert (on the southern, or Provençal, route to Santiago) was an admirable center where lay the tomb of a general of Charlemagne who, with an iron will, wished to devote his remaining days to fighting the demons and curbing his passions in preparation for heaven without earthly distractions. Yet how many weaker-willed pilgrims must have been tempted to give up their pilgrimage in this formidably rocky wilderness? While several died on their way, those who survived must also have had their lesser imitations of the Passion, fighting off robbers, wolves, and the menacing Moors. And surely, as we have seen, they hoped for the reward of the righteous pilgrim in the ultimate *transitus* of death by resurrection and ascension like their Lord.

Furthermore, as we hope our studies of the iconography of the pilgrim routes to Compostela will make clear in chapter 5, there are many details in the biblical story that will make the pilgrim feel at home even while peregrinating. Those who rode on donkeys would surely recall the humble beast that bore the Blessed Virgin and the infant Christ, led by Saint Joseph, down to the safety of Egypt and away from the Slaughter of the Innocents foretold by the Magi. It would also remind them of the Prince of Peace, Jesus, riding triumphantly on Palm Sunday into Jerusalem. The weary, footslogging pilgrims would be comforted by the thought that the two unnamed and dejected disciples walking from Jerusalem on the road to Emmaus were indeed pilgrims, accompanied by a third person, the risen Christ himself, and that his incognito was penetrated in the eucharistic action of breaking the bread. They, too, found shelter (if they could afford it) in inns. Often, to be sure, they were not very salubrious ones, and the company was frequently as profane as it was godly. They, too, often met the risen Christ in the Sacrament of his Body and Blood, the refreshment of the soul. And these outward resemblances to the biblical saga did not make the journey less, in the words of the title of the famous treatise of Saint Bonaventure, an *Itinerarium in mentis Deum,* a mental journey to God.

The desire to visit the shrine of a saint and to see his or her relics is closely akin to hero worship, with the difference that the hero is

thought to be extraordinary by his own achievements, while the saint is
the ordinary become extraordinary through the help of divine grace.
The visitor to Stratford-upon-Avon shows his admiration for genius.
He usually attends a performance of the Royal Shakespeare Company
on the same evening that he has visited the parish church of Holy
Trinity where the dramatist's tomb lies. The visitor to Monticello
climbs the hill to see the home and memorabilia of Thomas Jefferson, a
man of all-round brilliance, statesman-lawyer, architect, diplomat, and
president. The visitor to Toledo visits El Greco's house in the hope of
finding some clue to the artistic genius whose elongated religious figures
spiral upward resembling the flamelike spirits of his mystical contemporaries Saint Teresa of Ávila and Saint John of the Cross. In short,
we visit the places of those whom we admire.

It was the same desire that sent the pilgrims to the distant shrines of
the saints of Christendom in the Middle Ages. Salzman[28] believes that it
was the sense of admiration (and, we might add, in the noblest pilgrims
the desire for emulation) and the associated fascination with relics that
made for the popularity of pilgrimages. The profound and genuine
respect for the lives of holy men and women led, so he asserts, to the
desire to "possess, or at least to see, objects which had belonged to
them—a comb, a pair of shoes, a girdle, or better still, a tooth or a bone
from their bodies."[29] Salzman's explanation is, however, too simplistic
to account for the combined causes that made pilgrimages attractive.
The examples of relics chosen are too trivial to be typical, though, as we
shall see later, some relics such as the breath of Christ in a bottle, or the
tears of the Virgin, or a feather of the Holy Ghost demand credulity of
the lowest order. For the most part, these examples are exceptions that
only point out the rule. There were, as we shall see in chapter 4, many
reasons for the growth of the popularity and the variety of relics and the
diverse uses made of them. Nonetheless Salzman provides an important
clue to the success of pilgrimages by suggesting that their magnetic
appeal was due to the relics at the shrines that were the goals of the
pilgrims. These holy bodies and even the fragments and mere ashes of
dead saints' bones were believed to be as effective as the saints had been
while they were on earth. In many cases, too, the miracle-working
powers of the saints were thought to be greater after their death than
before.

A pilgrimage in ancient or medieval times was for the devout a means
of grace. Austin Farrer, the former warden of Keble College, Oxford,
insisted that the parallel between relics on the one hand and sacraments
on the other was close. "Relics and monuments are on the natural
level," he wrote, "what sacraments are on the supernatural: they make
invisible things real."[30] Portraiture in fifteenth-century etchings and
nineteenth-century photography enabled the admirer to catch the

likeness of a famous person. The closest a medieval person could come to a defunct servant of God was either to visit the scenes of his or her labor or to see a relic.[31] How much deeper was the sense of the mental agony of Christ if one had visited the Garden of Gethsemane and imagined him awake while the disciples slept, begging that the cup of suffering might be spared him, and then praying, "Not my will, but thine be done."[32] How contorted his soul must have been, just like the writhing trunks of the olive trees in the garden! Similarly, if one thinks of the Marian pilgrimage that made Chartres so celebrated, one can imagine the wonderment with which the pilgrim, as early as the ninth century as well as in the twentieth, sees the pale blue tunic in which the Virgin is supposed to have heard the astonishing news of the Annunciation.

Neither for Jesus nor for his Mother could there be a body in a tomb as in the case of the saints, for the Scriptures affirm the bodily Resurrection of Christ, and tradition claims that Mary was physically assumed into heaven. In all other cases, especially those of saints who had died as martyrs, the bones were their most precious relics. Originally saints' bodies were buried beneath the altars of the church whose dedications they bore, and the faithful were able to touch the bones of the saint with their handkerchiefs through the *confessio,* or grille in the front of the altar. Later, the tomb of the saint would be placed in a crypt beneath the high altar of the church, and there would be steps leading down to the crypt from the nave and others egressing from the crypt to allow the flood of pilgrims to be uninterrupted. Finally, when the cult of relics became very popular, they were exhibited in chests of precious wood often covered with plates of gold and silver and placed on or behind the altar on the saint's feast day. Sometimes, as in the case of the famous head of Saint Foi of Conques, the relic was made into an enthroned replica of the saint.[33] If the relic were merely part of the body, it was made into a semblance, as in the famous gilded and begemmed foot of Saint Andrew in the treasury of the cathedral of Trier.[34] Holy places and holy relics stirred the imagination of the pilgrim and made sacrifices for the faith more credible and worthwhile.

The pilgrim's dominant desire for sanctity had to be more than a passing whim. It required determination to undertake so long, arduous, dangerous, and if his health was dubious, desperate a journey. But what gave him the confidence to undertake it was that, for the duration of the pilgrimage until his return home or his sepulture (if he did not return to his earthly home), he was virtually a member of a religious order. The Church in the West as well as the East has always highly honored its hermits, monks, and nuns by calling them "the religious" because in their various orders they have followed the path to perfection in chastity, poverty, and obedience. Pilgrims, not only in theory, but also in actuality in many cases, lived during the pilgrimage at a higher standard of Christian obedience, and many of them lived in poverty, trusting to divine providence. Quite literally many of them lived by the dominical counsel to "take no thought for the morrow,"[35] trusting to the charity of the abbeys and priories en route, as well as to the generosity of wealthier fellow pilgrims, or to the alms of the towns or villages through which they passed. Then as the pilgrimage routes grew more thronged because they became safer, the travelers could count on the hospices on the way to provide basic food and shelter. Many pilgrims also kept the vow of chastity on the way; others did not. Hence the proverb *Ir romera y volver ramera* ("Go a pilgrim, return a whore").

But it was their distinctive habit or dress (as well as the rectitude of their habits) that marked pilgrims out from ordinary wayfaring Christians, as the priest's tonsure differentiated him from laymen. The holy life-style of pilgrims was outwardly marked by an easily recognized uniform, as was that of the religious orders.[36] Pilgrims wore a long coarse tunic, a wallet or satchel made of linen or soft leather,[37] and a hat to protect from the scorching sun, needed especially on the three distant pilgrimages. The most distinctive part of their equipment was their staff with its rounded knob at the top and its metal tip. It was at once an insignia, a walking stick or crutch, and, if necessary, a weapon to ward off fierce animals and robbers.

By the first half of the twelfth century the pilgrim's equipment had already assumed a symbolical significance. The author of the remarkable sermon, *Veneranda dies*, after observing that the way of the pilgrim is the best yet the hardest, goes on to observe that the satchel or wallet has a small aperture and holds little in order to force the pilgrim to depend upon almsgiving, while the staff serves to repel wolves and dogs, the symbols of the snares of the devil, and is an additional leg for the pilgrim and the symbol of the Holy Trinity.[38]

Pilgrims returning home from the famous shrines wore a badge or emblem indicating where they had been. Those returning from the Holy Land wore the palm of Jericho, symbol of the newly springing life of regeneration or of the victorious lives of the martyrs. Those returning from Compostela wore cockleshells, which were plentiful on the neighboring seacoast of Iria where the body of Saint James, according to the legend, had first arrived in a rudderless stone boat from Palestine. Those returning from Rome wore the emblem of Saint Peter, the crossed keys.

Whether this symbolic significance was recognized by the pilgrims or their friends and relations or not, the fact remains that both the uniform and the tokens of the shrines they had visited were indications of the seriousness of their quest for sanctity and salvation. They were also reminders to the pilgrims themselves that they had been sent forth from their local church or neighboring abbey or cathedral after a special service in which their attire had been blessed and they had been commended to God.[39] Furthermore, the pilgrimage was like a novitiate: it did not commit one for life to an *angusta via* that might prove too hard to maintain. That was an additional advantage. Thus one became a temporary monk, nun, or friar. The conditional element introduced into consecration of life, however prudent, was a mixture of a little dross in the gold of the motive of sanctity.

A slightly larger element of dross was contained in the desire to die and be buried in holy ground, thus improving the chances of attaining eternal life. A contrite person who died on a pilgrimage was certain of reaching heaven.[40] This aim might be achieved by breathing one's last in a hospice en route or in a city church or remote abbey where, as a pilgrim, one might hope to be buried close to a saint's tomb, precisely because the saints are Christ's closest friends and will make intercession for those devoted to their cult. If it was shrewd earthly policy to have a friend in court, it was even shrewder to have a friend in the celestial court of Christ, the King of Kings and "ruler of the kings of the earth."[41] A famous pilgrim who received holy sepulture while on pilgrimage was William X, duke of Aquitaine.[42] He had been converted by Saint Bernard at the abbey of Parthenay in 1133 and, as a result, had founded the Hospital of Saint James for pilgrims not far from Bordeaux. During Lent in 1137 he expired while the Passion was being sung and was buried before the altar. He could surely count on the intercession of Saint James, as well as that of Saint Bernard of Clairvaux. Similarly, Hugues IV, the duke of Burgundy, had just concluded the pilgrimage to Compostela when he died in 1272.[43] It is of interest to learn that another devotee of Saint James of Compostela, King Louis IX, repeated the saint's prayer, *Esto Domine,* when dying, in the words: "Keep, Lord, thy people and sanctify them that fortified by the help of thy apostle, St. James, they may please Thee in their works and serve Thee with a quiet heart. Amen."[44] Saint James had after all, as was recorded in the Bible,[45] paid the supreme price of loyalty to Christ, being the first of the apostles to be martyred. Such fidelity to his liege Lord Christ was bound to make Saint James an influential intercessor for earthly monarchs.

Many went on pilgrimages to fulfill a vow made either by themselves or on behalf of another. Such a vow could be made in the case of recovery from a severe illness in which the intercession of the saint was believed to have restored one from the very brink of death. Or, again, one might have been in severe physical danger and promised to visit a shrine if one should be delivered from the peril. Such vows had a component of cupboard love in the religious motive if undertaken for oneself but could be of higher motivation if undertaken out of filial love for a parent or other relative, or out of charity for a friend, or as a member of a guild for other members. It was also possible to undertake a pilgrimage by proxy for money, for instance as a condition for gaining an inheritance, or as a part of one's professional duties, as, for example, an ambassador representing a prince simply in the line of duty. Such motives were less worthy than the search for sanctity. But in evaluating motives we are peregrinating on very slippery ground and in the dusk. For this reason some differing instances may illuminate the problem of mixed motives, combining sacred, sensible, and merely self-regarding considerations.

A famous pilgrim motivated by thanksgiving was the English King Richard Coeur de Lion, profoundly grateful for his freedom, who visited the shrine of Saint Thomas à Becket in Canterbury immediately after Richard's return to England from Palestine and the confines of an Austrian prison.[46] King Louis VII of France visited the same shrine of the Norman saint desperately beseeching the saint to preserve the life of his son, now despaired of, because he had been lost for four days in a boar hunt in the vast forest of Compiègne.[47] Another distinguished pilgrim was Aeneas Silvius Piccolomini who had led a dissolute life before becoming a priest and who wore the triple tiara as Pius II. Apparently, in fulfillment of a vow he made during a tempest (possibly on his crossing to Scotland in 1435), he walked barefoot on the frozen ground to White Kirk near North Berwick and on his return had to be carried rather than led by his servants.[48]

An interesting development, which also complicated the motives of pilgrims, was that of the vicarious or proxy pilgrimage. Many such pilgrimages were made after the death of the person to whom they referred. Such post-obit pilgrimages are frequently mentioned in wills from the twelfth to the sixteenth century. The earlier wills directed the proxy pilgrim to go to the distant shrines, while the later ones— possibly because of the increase of chantry chapels where priests would be financed to pray for the soul of the deceased in purgatory—required the vicarious wayfarer to go to domestic shrines. In 1466, for example, William Boston of Newark, a chaplain who was buried before the altar of Saint Stephen in the parish church, made a will ordering his tomb to be covered with a marble slab on which was to be placed a figure of his father and another of himself of the same precious stone. He also left twenty-six shillings and eight pence to be paid to a priest to make a pilgrimage for him to the shrines at Bridlington, Walsingham, Canterbury, and Hales.[49]

Proxy pilgrimages were also undertaken for the living, whether they happened to be sovereigns or humbler members of guilds. Kings sent their ambassadors on pilgrimage in their behalf. King Philip IV of Spain and his Queen Margaret sent Bishop Diego de Guzmán, later to be consecrated archbishop of Seville, to Compostela with gifts worthy of royalty, including wrought silver and rich Florentine textiles, to present to Saint James. Similarly, members of guilds made pilgrimages for the rest of the guild. In Lincoln the Guild of the Resurrection, founded in 1374, included in its regulations the following: "If any brother or sister of the guild wishes to make pilgrimage to Rome, Saint James of Galicia, or the Holy Land, he shall forewarn the guild, and all the bretheren and sisteren shall go with him to the city gate and each shall give him a half-penny at least."[50] So supportive of pilgrimages were some guilds, and equally anxious to share in the undoubted religious merits gained by pilgrims, that they kept a hostel for pilgrims at their own expense. The guild of merchants at Coventry, for instance, which was formed in 1340, maintained a lodging house with thirteen beds exclusively for the use of poor pilgrims crossing the country on their visits to holy shrines.[51]

One of the most powerful motives for going on pilgrimage was simply to get rid of an overwhelming sense of guilt, and penances often took the form of a pilgrimage prescribed by a priest. This is the chief motive recognized by the author of the *Veneranda dies* sermon, already referred to as a paradigm treatment, or treatise, on pilgrimage. The sermon includes the promise to sinners that if they are truly penitent, they will obtain through the influence and merits of Saint James the remission of their sins at his altar,[52] for Santiago retains the privilege granted by Jesus to his apostles that whosoever's sins are remitted the Lord will also remit. The *Book of the Miracles of Saint James*, also part of the *Codex Calixtinus*, stresses the importance of gaining absolution through a pilgrimage by recounting the story of an Italian visitor to Compostela: he had committed so grave a crime that even his own bishop did not dare to grant him pardon but ordered him to write out his crime on a sheet of paper and take it to the tomb of the Apostle James. There he arrived on July 30, and placed the note on the tomb where Bishop Theodomir found it when preparing to celebrate High Mass.[53] When it was opened it was entirely blank. The contrition of the penitential pilgrim had been accepted by Saint James and so the absolution was granted.[54]

The most dramatic act of mortification in the course of a penitential pilgrimage was that of King Henry II of England seeking absolution at Canterbury for his complicity in the murder of Thomas à Becket, archbishop of Canterbury, on December 29, 1170.[55] On July 12, 1174, the king, wearing the linen garment of a penitent, walked barefoot from Saint Dunstan's Church to the cathedral and descended to the crypt where the shrine then was. There, with his head pushed partly through one of the apertures through which Becket's coffin could be seen, he knelt to receive from each bishop and abbot present five strokes of the scourge and three from each of the eighty monks who were there. The punishment was accompanied with the charge: "As Christ was scourged for the sins of men, be thou scourged for thine own sins."[56] It is reported that Henry urged them to strike him harder to make his penance as real as his contrition was.

Penitential pilgrimages were first imposed in the sixth century by the Irish missionary monks. They thought them appropriate penances for the more heinous sins and crimes. Their penitentials disclose the origin of the distinction between "public" and "private" penance that the scholastic theologians of the thirteenth century defended with such vigor. Public penance, usually requiring pilgrimage, was imposed for private sins that had come to public knowledge or for openly scandalous behavior. The more public the figure, whether prince or priest, and the more spectacular the crime, the more necessary was it for the Church to require the evildoer to make his penance public and preferably of long duration. It was for such reasons that long pilgrimages were often required of personages. Saint Romuald recommended that Emperor Otto III walk barefoot to Mount Gargano where there was a shrine dedicated to the victorious leader of the angelic hosts, Saint Michael, because the emperor had murdered a Roman senator despite having promised him a safe-conduct. Similarly, Count Thierry, who murdered the archbishop-elect of Trier in 1066, was commanded to undertake a long pilgrimage. So was Raymond VI of Toulouse after his involvement in the death of the papal legate who died on the steps of the pilgrimage abbey of Saint-Gilles-du-Gard.[57]

Scandalous clergy received similar penances imposed upon them. Peter Damien, pronounced a doctor of the Church in 1828 by Leo XII, imposed pilgrimages to Tours, Rome, and Santiago on the refractory and corrupt clergy of Milan in the mid–eleventh century.[58] Rigaud, archbishop of Rouen, made it his custom during the visitations of his province to impose pilgrimage penances on both clergy and laity for sexual sins.[59] Guillaume de Nogaret, chancellor of Philip the Fair, king of France, who had dared in 1303 to attack Pope Boniface VIII at Anagni and imprison him there for three days[60] with the result that he died at Rome a month later, was ordered to visit Notre Dame de Vauvert, Rocamadour, Boulogne, Chartres, Saint-Gilles, Montmajour, and Compostela and to exile himself permanently in the Holy Land.[61]

In motive as in appearance, the penitential pilgrims were a group apart. They consisted to a large degree of high clergy and members of the religious orders who had committed serious crimes dishonoring their high calling. Such were those condemned for fornication, sodomy, bestiality, parricide or the murder of other close relatives or of clergymen, and for thefts from the Church's treasury. In consequence of the scandal they had created, they were made public examples. They made the pilgrimage on foot, with the very minimum of clothing, while clanking the chains that savaged their flesh. Viewing them as moral lepers and exiles, other pilgrims were aghast at their presence.[62]

It is interesting to note that those who committed venial sins or hid them went on pilgrimage as acts of personal piety but that their numbers increased from the end of the tenth century onward. This striking growth in the numbers of pilgrims and in the distances they went on pilgrimages is also correlated with a high increase in the number of monastic foundations. One most intriguing and largely convincing hypothesis to account for these phenomena is offered by Jonathan Sumption. He explains that they "may have been caused by a radical change in the role of the sacrament of penance."[63] Going behind the requirements of the Irish penitentials and thereby reverting to the practice of the early Church, the Carolingian reformers demanded that penances should be strictly superintended by the confessor imposing them and that only when they had been completed should absolution be given. From the end of the tenth century, however, there was a serious deviation from this practice. It now became common to differentiate between the sin, which could be absolved on confession, and its punishment, which still had to be paid off in purgatory. So while the penitent was reconciled to the Church by confession, he was still required to make satisfaction for his sins.[64] This created an increased fear of the Great Assize at the end of history, on Judgment Day, so formidably depicted on the tympana of Romanesque abbeys, such as that of Conques and Beaulieu, or cathedrals, such as that of Autun, so that the sense of guilt also increased proportionately. This in turn helped to lead to the belief that one could by performing good deeds commute the postmortem penalties in purgatory.

There were two ways to do this if one had led a dissolute life or was overly scrupulous. One way was to enter a monastery to seek the perfect life of the Christian athlete or warrior (both images were commonly used), of those who sought the prize of eternal life or the trophy of victory over the sins of the spirit and the flesh.[65] The other way to reduce the pains of vastly prolonged years in purgatory was to get generous indulgences, which were given out at the shrines of pilgrimage for those who had completed particularly arduous and distant journeys, or who had come on Jubilee years.

Indulgences if a late development[66] were a magnetic attraction for pilgrims. Although it might be said that the reconciliation given to public penitents was an anticipation of indulgences, it was only in the middle of the eleventh century that general indulgences were offered by the Church to all the faithful. They were available to those who satisfied a number of conditions: pilgrimage, almsgiving, presence at the consecration of a church. These were granted independently of the nature of the guilt. The first indulgences were only partial, remitting a quarter or half of the penalty, and, at the end of the twelfth century, the penalty was remitted to a year and forty days. Soon afterward plenary indulgences appeared, with the exception that some such may have been granted during the eleventh century in connection with the conquest of Spain. The first example authenticated is a bull of Urban II offering Crusaders the full remission of their penalties in 1095.

From this time a double evolution took place. Indulgences multiplied and the conditions necessary for obtaining them became less and less onerous. A notable indulgence was obtained by Stephen Langton, archbishop of Canterbury, in 1220, on the occasion of the translation of the relics of Saint Thomas à Becket on the fiftieth anniversary of the saint's "passion." This is regarded as the first "jubilee" indulgence granted by any pope. It became general in 1300 when Pope Boniface VIII solemnly and universally declared a full remission of sins and penalties to all making the pilgrimage to Rome in that year. Originally jubilee indulgences were supposed to be celebrated every hundred years, then it was reduced to fifty, and finally to twenty-five years.

Even so, wars, the division of Christianity as a result of the Great Schism, and other vicissitudes made it difficult for many Christians to benefit by Roman jubilees. Thus it was that many other sanctuaries of pilgrimage claimed and obtained the benefits of plenary indulgence and the jubilee. Notre-Dame du Puy, the great Marian sanctuary, obtained a jubilee indulgence each time Good Friday coincided with the day of the Annunciation, as on March 25, 1407, and later in 1418 and 1429. Saint James of Compostela gained its jubilee in 1434. Such jubilees made pilgrimages extremely attractive to persons who wanted remission of sins on easy terms. They ended in discrediting pilgrimages altogether.

Just as the search for relics materialized the protection of God and the saints, so did the indulgences on easy terms make religion a crude form of barter between the Church and the pilgrims. How crude it became can be seen from the verses, hardly poetry, of an English rhymester of the fourteenth century. His record of a pilgrimage to Italy is devoted almost exclusively to the thousands of bodies of martyrs[67] he had visited and the thousands of years of purgatorial pains they can remit to those who visit them. His crudely conceived and expressed advice is:

> Gif men wuste, grete and smale,
> The pardoun that is at grete Rome.
> Thei wolde tellen in heore dome [in their opinion]
> Hit were no neod to mon in cristiante
> To passe in to the holy lond over the see.
> To Jerusalem, ne to Kateryne.[68]

The same author indicates that the indulgences are proportionate to the difficulty, the distance, and therefore to the benefits to be acquired:

And thou that passest over the see
Twelve thousend yer is graunted to the.[69]

Clearly, the self-regarding element in a motive for pilgrimage is powerful if not predominant when it is undertaken less for the sake of enjoying heaven than for avoiding hell—and when with a miniscule tincture of love of God and of humanity there is mixed a large quantity of fear and guilt. The egocentric element is even more evident in the next set of motives we are to study. These impel the pilgrim to the shrine of a saint simply and solely to obtain a benefit of some kind.

One is bound to ask why there was such a desperate search for the intercession of the saints. Was it, as has often been suggested, that the figure of Christ as the Good Shepherd who went out to seek the lost sheep and brought it back on his shoulder rejoicing—so often depicted in the earliest Christian art[70]—had been forgotten and that it was replaced by the stern Christ of judgment? Hence, it is argued, the Gothic introduction of the Virgin Mary as intercessor[71] restored the balance and reintroduced the mercy that had been lost. Such a view has some truth in it, but as an explanation it is far too simplistic.[72] It should be emphasized, first, that at the very time—the thirteenth century—that we find vernacular Bibles being produced, which coincides with the development of Gothic to its height, we would also expect a renewed appreciation of the tenderness of Christ as revealed especially in the Gospel of Saint Luke and in the pericope *de adulteria*[73] in Saint John's Gospel. Furthermore, it seems just as likely to us that two factors accounting for the increased popularity of the cult of the Virgin are the monastic sublimation of the sexual instinct, especially as the popularity of monasticism was also increasing in these years, and a feudal attitude that one did not approach the most august earthly personages except through intermediaries.

But why were other saints besides the Virgin besieged with pilgrim intercessors? We suggest that the saints were like celestial courtiers—they had access to the King of Kings and the Queen Mother of heaven.[74] What is more natural than to approach God the Father or God the Son through his friends and associates, especially when as unusually holy persons—martyrs or confessors—they have proved their loyalty to Christ?

Besides, many of the saints were regional or local and thus familiar in the sense that their relics were kept in local abbeys and priories and cathedrals—either they had been the first bishops of the area evangelizing the pagans, as in the case of Saint Martial of Limoges, or had chosen to be available locally by permitting their relics to be removed to another locality, as in the case of Saint Mary Magdalene, whose body was supposed to have been brought from Provence to Vézelay's great basilica. Surely a local saint would be more friendly than a distant one because familiar with the life of his or her devotees and petitioners.

On the very simplest and most easily explicable level there were two reasons based on the authority of the Word of God in the New Testament to believe in the efficacy of the intercession of the saints. Had not Saint James in his Epistle insisted that "the supplication of a righteous man availeth much,"[75] so if the prayers of a living man while on earth are efficacious, will they not be much more so if they are the petitions of a proven saint who, through canonization, is in the immediate entourage of Christ in heaven?[76] And who can be as powerful if not more powerful than Christ—the phrase is deliberately chosen[77]—than his apostles? For Christ had promised that his apostles would perform even greater miracles and signs in his name than he had done.[78] And the Acts of the Apostles confirmed the promise by recounting miraculous healings, exorcising of demons, and even resurrections from the dead. One needs only to add that as reports of miracles were spread from one pilgrimage sanctuary to another, some of the later saints were believed to have at least as great power as the apostles. But part of the attraction of Saint James of Compostela was because he was the first apostle to be a martyr, as well as being one of the three who were closest to Christ, along with saints Peter and John the Evangelist.

For all these considerations,[79] then, it is hardly surprising that the saints' shrines were eagerly and expectantly visited in the hope of some important benefit previously withheld. This motive was probably the lowest in the religious scale, but, of course, some requests were cruder than others.[80]

In general, the nonvicarious pilgrims sought, apart from holiness, or religious education, or burial in holy ground, four kinds of non-pecuniary boons. There were restoration of physical health, exorcism from demonic possession, release from prison, and the gift of children for infertile couples. For family and friends, however, the distraught often sought for the miracle of restoration to life from death. Each of these kinds of requests at the shrines will be considered in turn.

It is hard for us, with the vast improvements of modern medicine, to conceive how desperately medieval persons sought the aid of the thaumaturgical saints. The *Book of the Miracles of Saint Foi* recounts, for example, how a young paralytic of Reims walked through what is today Belgium, France, Germany, Brittany, Italy, and Spain (including Compostela), whence he returned via Toulouse to Saint Foi at Conques, where at last he recovered the use of his limbs thanks to her.[81] Raymond Oursel also retells the story of Lord Geoffrey of Sémur-en-Brion who had tried all the sanctuaries in Burgundy without avail in the hope of finding a saint who would cure him of his almost intolerably blinding migraines. Finally, after three long weeks of petitions to Saint

Benedict in his priory at Percey-les-Forges, his prayers were answered.[82]

So important were these anticipations of modern Lourdes that in the twelfth century all the great saints in France on the routes to Compostela were healers. This is true of Saint Eutrope of Saintes, Saint Front of Périgueux, Saint Julien of Brioude, Saint Gilles-du-Gard, and even of Saint Mayeul, the former abbot of Cluny, who was honored at Souvigny. Toward the end of the Middle Ages, however, we see the beginnings of medical specialization on the part of the healing saints, for Saint Hilary of Poitiers and later Saint Anthony of the Desert are both invoked by those suffering from ergotic poisoning, while Saint Lazarus of Autun becomes the patron of lepers in their lazar houses because he was resurrected by Christ when his body had decomposed for four days.[83] Saints Sebastian and Roch preserved one from the plague, and saints Clair and Foi from illnesses of the eyes.[84]

It would not seem at all strange in a Christian civilization that the saints should engage in healing activities or in the liberation of the imprisoned. In this they were only following the example of their Lord as reported in the Gospels, and of his apostles as reported in the Acts of the Apostles. Had not Jesus enabled the lame to walk, the paralytic to regain the use of his limbs, the blind to see, the dumb to speak, the deaf to hear, and raised the dead to life? Furthermore, Christ had promised his apostles that they would receive the same power through their intercession: "Whatsoever ye shall ask of the Father in my name, he may give it to you."[85] That promise was honored, for the very first miracle performed by the apostles after their empowerment at Pentecost was the healing of a beggar who had been lame from birth, who after Saint Peter's invocation, "in the name of Jesus Christ of Nazareth, walk," did so with such vigor that he leaped as he praised God.[86] It would, indeed, have been curious if the saints had not been implored to fulfill the miraculous ministry of healing, for such was the sign of the divine approval of the mission of Christ and of his Church, and his friends, the Virgin and the saints, were believed to be the supreme intercessors for the faithful. Furthermore, as the Turners remind us, sickness and spirituality were correlated in the medieval mind, since many thought illness was a penalty sent by God for sin.[87]

What might surprise the modern observer would be the vast crowds of pilgrims, their noisy ululations, and the superabundance of ex-votos in the sanctuaries of the healing saints. The onlooker's eyes would be attracted by the many representations of various limbs and organs of the human body, made of gold, silver, and lead, or even of wax, symbolizing the gratitude of those whose limbs or organs had been healed, together with tablets expressing their thankfulness to the saint. There would also be the images of those who had been or desired to be helped by the saint.[88] The onlooker's ears would be battered by the moans and groans, the shrieks and cries, interrupted occasionally by outbursts of joy, the begging and beseeching in prayer of the crowds of pilgrims swarming into the sanctuaries to find relief for every kind of ailment. A pathetic, straggling procession would pass before his eyes (so different from the liturgical processions with their appropriate pomp and circumstance on Church festivals) comprising the chronically weak and fevered, the halt, the lame and the blind, the deaf and the dumb, and the skeletally thin together with those swollen with hideous excrescences, like goiters, or enormously inflated, with elephantiasis, almost all as emaciated or deformed as one might expect to see later in the paintings of Pieter Brueghel the Elder.

Although the thaumaturgical achievements of the saints were best advertised in the books of miracles attributed to them,[89] a popular collection of hagiographies such as the so-called *Golden Legend*[90] provided enough examples of cures of all kinds to inspire in pilgrims the hope that a cure would be efficacious in their own case if they visited a sanctuary where the relics of such a saint were to be found. Saint Martin of Tours is said to have kissed and healed a leper.[91] Saint Benedict, honored alike by the Cluniac and the Cistercian abbeys and priories, is credited with curing a child brought to him swollen with elephantiasis.[92] Saint Gilles in Provence had the remedy for those bitten by serpents and also for those enfeebled by fevers.[93] Saint Mary Magdalene whose relics were translated from Aix-en-Provence to the basilica of Vézelay, helped a childless pagan ruler and his wife to have a son.[94] Saint Bartholomew the Apostle, part of whose relics were obtained from Benevento in Italy and translated in the early twelfth century to the Augustinian priory of Bénévent-l'abbaye in the Creuse,[95] was successful at restoring the demon-possessed to sanity,[96] as was the Apostle James the Great.[97] Saint Hilary of Poitiers helped the moribund to a quiet death and like so many of the saints restored a dead child to life.[98] Saint Benedict similarly resurrected a young novice,[99] and Saint James of Compostela revivified a suicide.[100] Saint Léonard of Noblat, *salvator captivorum et confractor carcerum,* according to the anthem of his office was the chief patron of prisoners and was especially successful in obtaining release for Christian prisoners in the hands of the Saracens. Naturally, from his sanctuary walls were suspended vast quantities of handcuffs, fetters, and chains of liberated prisoners and those cured of mental illness who had been chained.[101]

As we have seen, the religious motives for pilgrimage descend from the most austere and purest intention of the imitation of Christ and of his followers, the saints, and the desire to belong at least for a time to a third order, with higher standards of Christian obedience than were usual for the laity, down to the cupboard love that fulfills a vow or hopes to get a gift in return for a gift.

Even so, we are far from having exhausted the motives for pilgrimage, for some appeared to be exclusively secular, difficult as that may seem in the context of a religious civilization. Even if it is thought improbable that there could be exclusively secular motivation for pilgrimages, it must at least be admitted that a heavily secular component could be and was, in fact, "mixed in" with the religious motivation. The sheer popularity of pilgrimages, the mixture of sinners and saints, and the delightful by-products of pilgrimage—travel, new faces and lands, escapism, snobbish emulation of the famous and the successful, loneliness, and the eagerness for a good company—all played their part, as we shall see. Furthermore, we have to take account of juridical, political, and proxy pilgrims, not to mention the camp followers and tricksters, like Chaucer's Pardoner whose relics consisted of "pygges bones" and his friend the Summoner, and the ignoble army of buccaneers, jugglers, dancers, minstrels, fiddlers, peddlers, and "professional" pilgrims, who often exploited and occasionally cheered the dominantly religious pilgrims on their way.

Certainly we must allow sheer curiosity to have been a powerful secular factor in the motivation of pilgrims as they sought new faces and new scenes. There were, especially in the fourteenth century when pilgrimages on safe roads became immensely popular, mere holiday-makers and pleasure-seekers on the roads, accompanied by the rag, tag, and bobtail of camp followers battening on the bounty or credulity of the well-to-do.[102] Long before the Reformation the abuses of pilgrimage were criticized in prose or satirized in verse. Langland, for example, in his *Piers the Plowman*, objected to the false hermits on palmers' way, near the shrine of Walsingham:

> Eremytes on an hep . with hokede staves,
> Wente to walsyngham . and hure [their] wenches after;
> Grete lobies and longe . [that] loth were to swynke,
> Clothede hem in copis . to be knowe fro othere,
> And made hem-selve eremytes . hure eise to have.[103]

A Lollard brought before Arundel, archbishop of Canterbury, for questioning in 1407, admitted that he had preached against the contemporary passion "to seek and visit the bones or images . . . of this saint and of that" that had become so dominating that "ofttimes divers men and women of these runners thus madly hither and thither into pilgrimage, borrow hereto other men's goods (yea, and sometimes they steal men's goods hereto), and they pay them never again."[104] In his deposition, Thorpe added that these were merely holidays for many pilgrims, thus nothing was forgotten that might add to their enjoyment. Hence, "finding out one pilgrimage, they will ordain beforehand to have with them both men and women that can well sing wanton songs; and some other pilgrims will have with them bagpipes; so that every town they come through, what with the noise of their singing, and with the sound of their piping, and with the jangling of their Canterbury bells, and with the barking out of dogs after them, they make more noise than if the king came their way, with all his clarions and many other minstrels."[105] One is reminded that Chaucer's Miller played the bagpipes loudly and that the Monk's bridle jangled "as loude as dooth the chapel belle." The Chaucerian pilgrims told tales, chattered noisily, argued passionately, and enjoyed themselves,

> For trewely, comfort ne myrthe is noon
> To ryde by the weye doumb as a stoon.[106]

Perhaps the most curious of all visitors to Christian shrines was the diplomat, al-Ghazzali, who was sent by Abdurrahman II on a mission to the king of the Normans soon after 844. On his return the poet turned aside to visit Saint James, in the company of the Norman ambassador.[107] After the antagonism between Christians and Moors in Spain, one is delighted to learn that the Sufi mystic, intending to visit Compostela for a few days, remained for two months. Probably the warrior-like aspect of the *Boanerges,* or Thunderer, had not yet developed in the cult of Saint James, which enabled him to become for Spain what Saint George was for England, or, we can only suppose that it was played down.[108]

A second and predominantly secular motive for pilgrimage was the desire for community and good fellowship. Victor Turner has shown the importance of this in a study of pilgrimages in different countries and among different religions, Hindu, Muslim, and Buddhist as well as Christian.[109] *Communitas,* which he believes all pilgrims seek, is, as he defines it, "a direct immediate confrontation or 'encounter' between free, equal, levelled, and total human beings. . . . It means freedom, too, from class or caste affiliation, or family and lineage membership."[110] This sense of *communitas* was, of course, particularly strong among members of any medieval guild, and their rules often provided for a member to go on pilgrimage to fulfill a vow, while at the same time allowing the other members of the guild to share in his merit. The Guild of the Virgin of Hull, founded in 1357, included in its rules the following: "If any brother or sister of the guild wishes, at any time, to make the pilgrimage to the Holy Land, then in order that all the guild may share in his pilgrimage, he shall be fully released from his yearly payment until his return."[111] Certainly a great deal of the joy in pilgrimage must have come from the temporary liberation from loneliness and the admission to a community transcending differences of status, class, and social role.

Closely allied to the desire for acceptance in a new community, and a wish to satisfy one's curiosity, was the longing for escape from the drudgery and monotony of daily life, as well as from duties, taxation, and trying domestic circumstances. Once pilgrimages became popular, as a consequence of safety in traveling, then they were a very convenient escape hatch in a sea of trouble. Laymen and laywomen were free from all legal taxes and other claims, except that of ecclesiastical law. Priests on pilgrimage continued to earn their full stipends, provided they did not stay away longer than three years.[112] Laborers, tired of their masters, left under the pretext of undergoing distant pilgrimages and willingly laid down their staffs at the door of a master who would give them higher wages.[113] A new vocation was discovered in some cases, that of the professional pilgrim[114] who eked out his livelihood by going as a mendicant and receiving free bread and board on the pilgrimage routes, with a little extra from any generous or credulous people who would listen to his traveler's tales embroidered by the imagination. These stories or persons were no more to be relied upon than pardoners and palmers on the roads, of whom Langland wrote:

> Pilgrimis and palmers . plyghten hem to-gederes
> To seche saint Iame . and seyntes of rome,
> Wenten forth in hure way . with meny un-wyse tales
> And haven leve to lye . al hure lyf-tyme.[115]

Another basis of the desire to escape was to go on pilgrimage just to flee famine or the plague, which became all too common a need in the later Middle Ages. Plagues and famine were considered manifestations of divine wrath and a pilgrimage was thought to be a sure way of appeasing God's indignation.[116]

Another secular motive, and a powerful one for pilgrimage especially in the earlier and less safe days, was a love of adventure and risk. This was more probably present in a distant than in a local and domestic pilgrimage. Part of the importance and the attraction of the pilgrimage to Compostela was that it traveled through kingdoms in northern Spain that were or had recently been under Muslim suzerainty and that it was therefore a perilous undertaking and was genuinely regarded as an alternative to the Crusades. The sea journey to Compostela, Rome, or Jerusalem involved the dangers of tempests and pirates, while the land journey involved the hazard of bandits and capture by the Saracens.

Nor were the precipitous Alps and Pyrenees easy to scale. Only the most daring or desperate must have undertaken such journeys in the earliest days of pilgrimage. Moreover, at all times there were risks for the weak, aged, and handicapped. Indeed, an essential element in pilgrimage was that of difficulty. That would be amply provided by the hundreds of miles to be covered between one pilgrimage shrine and another, all of the way on unmade roads, and much of it through areas that were unpopulated or sparsely populated, through thickly grown woods, marshes, flooding rivers, and menacing rocks and slippery scree in the mountains, not forgetting the wild beasts that threatened safety, from the wolf to the serpent. Then, as if this were not enough to daunt anyone but the most heroic or foolhardy or saintly traveler, there was always the possibility of the outbreak of war that could isolate pilgrims and shrines for months or even years.[117] Pilgrimage was a journey to test both sinews and souls.

Finally, the nadir of secular motivation in pilgrimage was reached when pilgrimages were imposed by law for political purposes or for the reparation of injuries, that is, for judicial causes. Here, indeed, the pilgrim is motiveless—it is society that imposes its view on him, for his intentions are irrelevant. For this reason we shall give this matter minimal consideration.

An early example of political pilgrimage—and many could be found from the fourteenth century onward[118]—was a treaty signed at Arcques near Saint-Omer in 1326 on Christmas Eve between the king of France, Count Louis of Flanders, and the Flemish cities. It stipulated that three hundred persons of Bruges and Cambrai had to go on pilgrimage, one hundred to Saint James, one hundred to Saint-Gilles, and one hundred to Rocamadour.[119]

Judicial pilgrimages to one or several shrines were regarded as fairly light penances for persons suspected of heresy, and it saved the Inquisition the cost of imprisonment. This mode of punishment was taken over from canon law by civil law in the thirteenth century. An early penal pilgrimage to Jerusalem in the ninth century required three brothers to go there because they had killed a priest who happened to be their uncle. Their bishop in southern Italy sentenced them "to make iron chains and bind them tightly on their arms and then make the circuit of the holy places in dust and ashes until such time as God accepted their penance."[120] The journey took them three years, but that was preferable to the alternative: permanent exile. The state copied the Church, as we see in the *Paix aux clercs* of Liège, a set of ecclesiastical laws as its name implies, issued in 1207, which demanded that assaults inside churches be punished by the imposition of pilgrimages. Only two months afterward a code of civil law was issued that declared that pilgrimage was to be the penalty for all assaults resulting in mutilation. Liège's example

was followed by almost every city in the Low Countries in the thirteenth century, and by the fourteenth it was established in France and
Italy.[121]

Thus we have considered motives that were highly religious as well as
crudely secular. Religious motives included the quest for sanctity and
for the imitation of the notable imitators of Christ, the saints, as well as
the desire to live at a higher standard of Christian obedience such as a
temporary third order membership offered the pilgrim who became a
monk for the interim and fought for the faith pacifically as the Crusader
did militarily. At a lower level, but still religious in motivation, was the
desire to be buried on holy ground and to make sure of salvation by
going on pilgrimage, or the quid pro quo attitude of giving thanks to a
saint at his or her shrine for a favor received or for a favor hoped for, or
simply to undertake a pilgrimage as a means of getting rid of one's guilt.
The highest secular motives appear to be a desire for community, a
sense of wonder and curiosity, a delight in the excitement of danger,
and, less worthy, a wish for escape from monotony or responsibility, or
the fulfilling of a judicial imposition or of political requirement.

Here, then we have a rich mixture of motives, and part of the genius
of the Roman Catholic Church has been that it has inspired the saint as
well as refusing to despise the man in the street. It has catered to both
the spare, austere diet of the anchorite and monk and the ampler fare
needed by the Wife of Bath. For the one group the stimulus of pilgrimage was the opportunity of visiting the shrines of the saints on the eves
of their vigils, on holy days; for the more typical pilgrim the lure was
that of combining holy days (in moderation) with holidays galore.

Though it was an oversimplification, Peter, a western Christian, the
abbot of Josselin, was not far from the truth in recognizing that there
were three sorts of pilgrims with three different motives: "the first of
those who seek the holy places for the sake of piety; the second of
penitents on whom a pilgrimage has been imposed as a penance, or who
undertake it of their own free will; the third of those near death who
desire sepulture in holy ground."[122] Equally perceptive was an oriental
Christian, Eutychius, a tenth-century bishop of Alexandria, who wrote
in *The Book of the Demonstration* about the aims of pilgrims in their
visits to sacred sites:

> By these relics and places . . . Christ gave us, all joined in one, a blessing, a
> sanctification, an approach to him, pardon for sins, feasts in which men
> come together in his name, spiritual joy without end and witnesses
> confirming the Scriptures.[123]

NOTES

1. Beryl Smalley points out in *The Study of the Bible in the Middle Ages* (Oxford: Clarendon Press, 1941), p. xiv, that it was only in 1300 that illiteracy in the higher classes was beginning to diminish and that vernacular Bibles were then being produced. Of course, the higher clergy, many abbots, and monks were very literate since they were the main recipients and transmitters of knowledge.

2. The chief pilgrimages described were the following: the Bordeaux pilgrim (A.D. 337), the nun Egeria (about fifty years later), Saint Paula (387), the Piacenza (ca. 570), Arculf, bishop of Gaul (between 679 and 688), Saint Willibald (between 724 and 730), Bernard the Monk (ca. 870), and Lethbald of Autun (described by Glaber in his *History of His Own Time*, completed in 1044). The liveliest account is unquestionably that of the Piacenza pilgrim. All other accounts used by John Wilkinson in *Jerusalem Pilgrims before the Crusades* (Warminster: Aris & Phillips, 1978), are secondhand sources in guidebooks, biographies, topographical surveys, or poems, with only incidental references to the Jerusalem of the Christian pilgrims. Apart from the Bordeaux pilgrim and Egeria (both before his book begins), Wilkinson has eighteen extracts occupying a total of one hundred pages, less twenty-three devoted to maps of the journeys described with a few blank pages.

3. See P. A. Sigal, *Les marcheurs de Dieu* (Paris: Colin, 1974), p. 116, and in the admirable bibliography.

4. The ms. of his *Itineraries* is in the Bodleian Library, Oxford. It was printed by the Roxburghe Club in 1857.

5. See *The Pilgrimage of Robert Langton*, translated and annotated by E. M. Blackie (Cambridge, Mass.: Harvard University Press, 1924).

6. An excerpt of his skepticism about the legends of Compostela is included in J. S. Stone, *The Cult of Santiago* (New York: Longmans, 1927), p. 345.

7. The most careful modern study of the manuscripts of the *Codex Calixtinus*, or *Liber sancti Jacobi*, has been made by Father Pierre David. The most important mss. are Ms. *Codex Compostellanus* in Compostela; Ms. Latin 12 in the Bibliothèque Nationale in Paris; Ms. C. 128 in the Biblioteca Vaticana in Rome; Additional Mss. 12213 in the British Museum in London; Ms. O. 634 y P. 120–4305 in the Biblioteca Real de Madrid; Ms. 99 of the abbey of Ripoll, Spain; and the Alcobaca Ms. in Portugal. The work is dated between 1139 and 1165. Fr. David's studies appeared in part in *Bulletin des études portugaises* and were later published in four volumes, with the general title of *Etudes sur le livre de saint Jacques attribué au pape Calixte II*, 4 vols. (Lisbon: Institut Français des études portugaises, 1946–49). Jeanne Vielliard has produced an annotated translation from the Latin into French of the famous Book V, as *Le guide du pèlerin de saint Jacques de Compostelle* (Mâcon, 1950; reprint 1963). Walter Muir Whitehill transcribed the entire five books in a work entitled *Liber sancti Jacobi, Codex Calixtinus, texto transcripcion*, which was published in two volumes in Compostela in 1944. In 1971 a facsimile of the Compostela ms. appeared as the first volume of a series, *Medievalia hispania*, entitled *Libro de la peregrinación del codice Calixtino*, published by Joyas Bibliográficas, Madrid, and edited by Carlos Romera de Lecca. An early and useful publication of Book V (which it erroneously termed Book IV) was *Le codex de saint Jacques de Compostelle* (Paris, 1888), edited by F.-J. Fita and J. Vinson. Hereafter the abbreviation *C.C.* will be used for the entire *Codex Calixtinus*, and "Guide" or "Guía" will refer to Book V. A Spanish translation of Book V (which also reproduced the Latin original) is the Marqués de la Vega Inclán's *Guía del Viaje a Santiago* (Madrid: Real Academia de la Historia, 1927).

8. *Pilgrimage: An Image of Mediaeval Religion* (London: Faber & Faber, 1975), p. 147.

9. Ibid., pp. 149, 161 (on mixed motives), 278, inter alia.

10. Samuel Eliot Morison, *The European Discovery of America: The Southern Voyages* A.D. *1492–1616* (New York: Oxford University Press, 1974), preface.

11. Geoffrey Chaucer, *The Canterbury Tales*, Prologue.

12. Luke 15:11–32.

13. John 14:2a.

14. This strain of medieval piety was superbly expressed in Bernard of Cluny's poem *De contemptu mundi*, which is the source of the famous hymn "Urbs Sion aurea," finely Englished by John Mason Neale as "Jerusalem the Golden." There is an inextinguishable longing for "radiancy

of glory" and "bliss beyond compare," for unity with the throng of martyrs and angels in the "halls of Sion conjubilant with song" and especially for the victorious end of the struggle against evil, for

> There is the throne of David, and there from care released,
> The shout of them that triumph, the song of them that feast,
> And they who with their Leader have conquered in the fight
> Forever and forever are clad in robes of white.

There is incomparable serenity, peace, splendor, and supernal joy in "the home of God's elect" that only "eager hearts expect."

15. Migne's *Patrologia Latina*, 189: 883: *Dum esset nobilis et dives in saeculo tactu divino spiritu ac mundo renuntiare disponens prius equos ac vestes multi pretii magnumque argenti pondus et omnia pene sua Cluniacum direxit, et sic pauper atque peregrinus Hierosolytam petiit.*

16. Wilkinson, *Jerusalem Pilgrims*, p. 87.

17. Ibid., p. 52; Bernhard Kötting, *Peregrinatio religiosa: Wallfahrten in der Antike und das Pilgerwesen in der alten Kirche* (Regensburg, Münster, 1950), p. 301.

18. *Palestine Pilgrims' Text Society* I (London, 1897), p. 9.

19. John Wilkinson, *Egeria's Travels* (London: S.P.C.K., 1971), pp. 94, 135–36.

20. This letter written to Paula's daughter was translated by John Wilkinson in his *Jerusalem Pilgrims*, p. 40.

21. *Liber ad milites templi* (V,11), translated in *Palestine Pilgrims' Text Society* VI (London, 1894), p. 4.

22. William Langland, *Piers the Ploughman*, trans. J. E. Goodridge (Harmondsworth and Baltimore, Md.: Penguin, 1959), p. 115.

23. The original reads: *In nomine Domini nostri Ihesu Christi, accipe hanc sportam habitum peregrinationis tue, ut bene castigatus et bene saluus atque emendatus pervenire merearis ad limina Sancti Sepulchri, aut Sancti Iacobi, aut Sancti Il [arii] vel aliorum sanctorum quo pergere cupis, et peracto itinere suo ad nos incolumis reuertere merearis* (*Rituale monasticum* of San Cugat del Vallès, Ms. 72, fols. 23–24, now in the Archivo de la Corona de Aragon). For other instances of a sea storm motivating a pilgrimage, see Samuel Eliot Morison, *Admiral of the Ocean Sea* (Boston: Little, Brown, 1942), pp. 327, 338, 597, 619.

24. Matthew 10:8.

25. Cited in Sidney Heath, *Pilgrim Life in the Middle Ages* (Boston and New York: Houghton Mifflin, 1912), p. 251.

26. Matthew 10:30.

27. See the eleventh-century *Vita* in *Acta sanctorum* (Antwerp: Johannes Meurisus, 1643–), II (October), p. 513. An English canon law of the late tenth century states: "It is a deep penitence that a layman lay aside his weapons and travel far barefoot and nowhere pass a second night and fast and watch much and pray fervently, by day and by night and willingly undergo fatigue and be so squalid that iron come not on hair or on nail" (B. Thorpe, *Ancient Laws* [London: English Record Commission, 1840]).

28. L. F. Salzman, *English Life in the Middle Ages* (London: Oxford University Press, 1926).

29. Ibid., p. 274.

30. *The Brink of Mystery* (London: S.P.C.K., 1976), p. 152.

31. Stone, *Cult of Santiago*, pp. 214–15.

32. Matthew 26:36–46; Mark 14:32–42; Luke 22:39–46.

33. The treasury of Saint Foi de Conques in Rouergue is incredibly rich in medieval reliquaries. First, there is the hieratic image of Saint Foi herself—the majesty with the ivory eyeballs that give the effect of staring eyes—and this may have been deliberate because of a famous case of healing attributed to her of a man whose eyes were torn out by the roots. There is also a golden reliquary of the arm of Saint George, a Pepin reliquary, the A-shaped jewel of Charlemagne, and the coffer covered in leather and enamels that once contained the relics of Saint Foi. For illustration and the history and provenance of these treasures, see *Rouergue roman* by G. Gaillard, M.-M. S. Gauthier, L. Balsan, and A. Surchamp (Yonne: Zodiaque, 1963), pp. 135–44, plates 38–68 and 2 in color. See also Louis Balsan, *Conques et son trésor* (Rodez: Editions de la cité, 1956).

34. This is reproduced in L. Grodecki, F. Mütherich, J. Taleron, and F. Wormald, *Le siècle de l'an mille* (Paris: Gallimard, 1973), p. 283. The reliquary is attached to the cover of a gilded chest. Trier cathedral treasury also has a reliquary of the Holy Nail, which is reproduced ibid.

35. Matthew 6:25–26.

36. See Sumption, *Pilgrimage*, p. 136: "This feeling of belonging to an initiated caste of holy men as formal in its own way as the monastic order itself the pilgrim expressed by wearing a distinctive uniform and by receiving at his departure the blessing of the Church."

37. The scrip as it appears on the tympanum of Autun, in the superb sculpture of Gislebertus on the shoulders of two pilgrims, suggests that between 1140 and 1170 it was a satchel, possibly made of linen or perhaps of leather. By 1200, however, the pouch of soft leather was attached to a belt around the waist (Sumption, *Pilgrimage*, p. 171). The Autun pilgrims wore hats that looked like helmets, but by 1350 the broad-brimmed hats had become the usual headgear of pilgrims (ibid., and G. R. Owst, *Literature and Pulpit in Medieval England*, 2d rev. ed. [Oxford: Blackwells, 1961], p. 104).

38. *Codex Calixtinus* I, xvii (pp. 152–53 in the Whitehill transcription) reads: "*Quod pera angustus saculus sit, significat quia paruam et modicam expensam peregrinus in domino confisus debet secum deferre. Quod de corio bestie mortue facta sit, significat quia ipse peregrinus debet mortificare carnem suam cum uiciis et concupiscentiis, in fame et siti, in ieiuniis multis, in frigore et nuditate, in contumeliis et laboribus multis. Quod non uinculis alligata sed ore semper aperta est, significat quod ipse prius cum egenis propria debet expendere, et exinde paratus ad accipiendum, et paratus ad dandum debet esse. Per baculum quippe quem quasi pedem tercium ad sustentacionem suman orator accipit, fides sancte Trinitatis in qua perseuerare debet insinuatur. Baculus defensio est contra lupum et canem. Canis contra hominem usus est latrare, et lupus ouem deuorare. Per canem et lupum generis humani insidiator diabolus designatur.*" See chapter 4 for fuller exposition of the symbolism.

39. See *Codex Calixtinus* I, xvii, Whitehill transcription, p. 151. See also, J. Wickham Legg, ed., *The Sarum Missal Edited from Three Early Manuscripts* (Oxford: Clarendon Press, 1916), *Pro iter agentibus*, pp. 451–53. Also Heath, *Pilgrim Life*, pp. 121–22. For an English translation see *The Sarum Missal in English*, Part II (London: De la More Press, 1911), "Order of Service for Pilgrims," pp. 166–73.

40. Raymond Oursel, *Les pèlerins du moyen âge: les hommes, les chemins, les sanctuaires* (Paris: A. Fayard, 1963), p. 29.

41. A title used for the *Rex tremendae majestatis* of the Book of Revelation sometimes known from its Greek title as the Apocalypse. See 1:5.

42. Georgiana Goddard King, *The Way of Saint James*, 3 vols. (New York: Putnam, 1920), I, p. 109.

43. Ibid., p. 110.

44. Ibid., p. 111.

45. The Acts of the Apostles 12:1–2: "Now about that time Herod the King put forth his hands to afflict certain of the church. And he killed James the brother of John with the sword." For other major references to Saint James in the New Testament, see Matthew 4:21, 20:23, referring to the calling of James and the request of the mother of James and John to Jesus that her sons might have the preeminent positions of rulership in the kingdom of God, and the accounts of the Transfiguration of Jesus of which James was one of the witnesses. The latter experience is recorded in Mark 9:2–8, Luke 9:37–42, and Matthew 17:1–8. The title *Boanerges* —sons of Thunder— attributed to both James and his brother John the Evangelist derives from the incident in which they urged Jesus to call thunder down from heaven on the Samaritans because the latter were unwilling to offer Jesus hospitality in their village, hearing that he was returning to their rival cultic city of Jerusalem. This incident is recorded in Luke 9:51–55.

46. J. J. Jusserand, *English Wayfaring Life in the Middle Ages*, rev. ed. (London: Unwin, 1925), p. 349. A similar desire to express gratitude for a safe return from the Holy Land by Juan, the lord of the Nettles (Sieur des Orties), to his home near Zalduendo, found a different mode of expression. In the latter case he built a chapel in thanksgiving to Saint Nicholas of Bari, a popular patron saint of travelers, which is now the shrine of Saint Juan himself in the parish church of Saint Nicholas (King, *Way of Saint James*, I, p. 298).

47. Jusserand, *English Wayfaring Life*, p. 349.

48. Ibid., p. 339.

49. "York Wills" volume of the Surtees Society, cited by Jusserand, ibid.

50. King, *Way of St. James*, I, pp. 1–3.

51. J. Toulmin Smith, *English Guilds* (London: Trübner, 1870), pp. 157, 177, 182, 231.

52. "*O quam beati illi, qui talem habent apud Deum intercessorem, talemque remissorem*" (*Codex Calixtinus*, I, xvii, Whitehill transcription, p. 150).

53. This miracle is the second recorded in the *Book of Miracles* and must go back three centuries since Theodomir, a ninth-century bishop of Iria in Galicia, is said to be the man who, guided by a holy hermit Pelagio, discovered the tomb of Santiago. The *Miracula sancti Iacobi* are also contained in the *Acta sanctorum* (1729), VI (July), pp. 47–59.

54. Fr. Pierre David in his *Etudes sur le livre de saint Jacques attribué au pape Calixte II*, p. 49, draws attention to the similarity of this Jacobite narrative to a miracle attributed to Saint Gilles—whose tomb was on the southernmost route to Compostela—for the benefit of Charlemagne, whose note confessing his worst sin was also found erased.

55. The meaning of the event for modern playgoers has been imaginatively conveyed in T. S. Eliot's *Murder in the Cathedral*.

56. Used here is the vivid reconstruction of the event based on records of the time by Heath, *Pilgrim Life*, p. 192.

57. Sumption, *Pilgrimage*, p. 99, lists all these examples with their sources.

58. Ibid.

59. Ibid.

60. F. L. Cross, ed., *The Oxford Dictionary of the Christian Church* (London: Oxford University Press, 1963), p. 185b.

61. Sumption, *Pilgrimage*, p. 100. In fact, he fulfilled none of the proposed penances because the pope was in no position to enforce them against the will of the French king.

62. On the entire subject, see the well-documented essay by Cyril Vogel, "Le pèlerinage penitentiel" in *Pellegrinàggi e culto dei santi in Europa fino alla Iª Crociata* (Todi: Centro di Studi sulla Spiritualita Medievale, 1963), pp. 37–94. The penitential pilgrims were *nudi homines, nudis pedibus*, "naked men with bare feet" (p. 62).

63. Sumption, *Pilgrimage*, p. 100.

64. So important did the concept of *satisfactio* become that Saint Anselm formulated an original theory of the atonement of Christ entirely based upon it. This was contained in his famous *Cur Deus homo?* of 1097.

65. Apart from the dominical "counsels of perfection," which are, of course, central to monasticism, the images of the warrior and the athlete were to be found in the Pauline Epistles, For the warrior see, inter alia, Romans 8:37 and especially Ephesians 6:10–17; for the athlete, a concept important in the first part of the *Regula* of Saint Benedict (*The Rule of Saint Benedict in Latin and English*, trans. and ed. Justin McCann [London: Burns, Oates, 1952]), see also I Corinthians 9:24–25, and note that the next two verses use the warrior metaphor.

66. For this summary of the development of indulgences we are indebted to Sigal, *Les marcheurs de Dieu*, pp. 12–14.

67. Our prosaic poet asserts that there are 4,000 bodies of martyrs in Saint Prudence, 1,300 at Saint Prassede, and 7,000 at saints Vitus and Modestus, all churches in Rome (Jusserand, *English Wayfaring Life*, pp. 381 ff., relying on F. J. Furnivall, ed., *The Stacions of Rome and the Pilgrim's Sea Voyage* [London: Early English Text Society, 1867]).

68. "Kateryne" refers to the famous monastery of Saint Catherine, which was situated on the lower slopes of Mount Sinai, a place sacred to both Jews and Christians.

69. Jusserand, *English Wayfaring Life*. This particular indulgence was granted to pilgrims visiting the vernicle, or holy sudary, in Rome, which bore the imprint of the Savior's face. If the pilgrim had come to Rome from another country overland he received an indulgence reducing his years in purgatory by 6,000. But if he was a local visitor it was further reduced by only 3,000 years.

70. Both in the catacombs of Rome and in, for one example, the Church of San Apollinare in Classe, near Ravenna. See André Grabar, *Early Christian Iconography* (Princeton, N.J.: Princeton University Press, Bollingen Series, 1968).

71. Erasmus rightly satirizes the crude view that one could get around Jesus by approaching his Mother to twist his arm in these words he attributes to her, as reported by Ogygiuss: "I have been plagued to death with the impertinent supplication of mortals. All things were demanded of me alone, as if my Son were always an infant, because he is represented and painted in my arms, and still hanging on his mother's breast; and as if he did not venture to deny any petition, for fear I should in turn refuse my nourishment to him" J. G. Nichols, trans. (*Peregrinatio religionis ergo*, in a compendium entitled *Pilgrimages to Saint Mary of Walsingham and Saint Thomas of Canterbury* [London: J. B. Nichols and Son, 1849], pp. 6–7).

72. This so-called restoration of the balance is a matter of some doubt. It might even be the invention of modern sentimentality that twists a complementary into an exaggeration. The view criticized here certainly neglects the fact that Christianity has almost always insisted on God as

holy love, hating the sin but loving the sinner, and expecting from human beings both reverence and love. This balanced view can, however, in popular religion, be upset by overstressing the reverence until it becomes intimidation, or by overstressing the love until it becomes sheer soft-heartedness. To use the definition made famous by Rudolf Otto in *Das Heilige*, religion is a *"mysterium tremendum et fascinans"* and thus holiness has two components, being both forbidding and fascinating at once. Furthermore, the stress on holiness is powerful even in the medieval Franciscan ideal, which emphasized compassion. In addition, as we shall argue later, Romanesque iconography gives considerable evidence of an awareness of the more consoling aspect of the life and teaching of Jesus.

73. John 7:53–8:11, which is omitted by most ancient authorities but was included in the Vulgate by Saint Jerome. This recounts Jesus' criticism of the hypocrites who stoned a woman caught in the act of adultery and tells of his compassion for her.

74. Erasmus ironically argues in a letter attributed to the Virgin that since the arrival of Luther the Queen of Heaven has lost her honors and profits, but has now an easier time of it: "Formerly, I was addressed as the Queen of Heaven, the Lady of the World: now I scarcely hear from a few a single 'Ave Maria'" (Nichols, *Peregrinatio*, p. 9). A few lines earlier (ibid., p. 8), the Virgin is purported to have said: "If I deny anything I am immediately cruel. If I refer them to my Son, I hear, He wills whatever thou wilt!" This was clearly the popular medieval expectation as late as the early sixteenth century.

75. 5:16b.

76. The point is also made by Stone, *Cult of Santiago*, p. 3.

77. As powerful as Christ, each apostle was regarded as an *alter Christus* and was believed to perform the same kind of miracles as those recorded of Christ in the Gospels—stilling storms, casting out demons, curing bodily ailments, and resurrecting the dead. Cf. *Liber miraculorum sancti Iacobi (Book of the Miracles of Saint James)* for attributions to Santiago of marvelous sea rescues (VII–X), miraculous cures (XII, XXI), and resurrections (III, XVII). It is also in *Codex Calixtinus*, Book II, and accessible in the Whitehill transcription, I, pp. 259–87.

78. John 14:12: "And greater works than these shall he do."

79. Not forgetting the marvelous gold or silver and begemmed reliquaries that attracted pilgrims or the *Book of Miracles* that, as mentioned earlier, advertised the efficacy of various saints, nor archbishops like Gelmirez of Compostela who traveled to Rome, Cluny, and Paris and extolled Santiago.

80. How base some requests for intercession could be is related by Erasmus (Nichols, *Peregrinatio*, pp. 7–8). These are, admittedly, exaggerations such as are appropriate for a satirist. We are told that some petitioners would make such requests to the Virgin "as no youth of modesty would venture to put to a bawd." Other requests to the Virgin were those made by a traveler asking for the protection of the virtue of his mistress, a nun preparing to flee her monastery asking for the safeguarding of her reputation, the godless soldier begging rich booty in battle, the gamester who treats the Virgin as if she were Lady Luck, and the speculator who asks for a large fortune. But these requests are those of unprincipled persons. While such were undoubtedly encountered among pilgrim bands, it is unlikely (unless they were confidence men or other professional beggars) that those who began with the basest religious motives—a crude *do ut des*—would survive more than a few days of a lengthy, fatiguing, and hazardous pilgrimage to a distant shrine. On this issue, it is worth comparing the contrasting views of two erudite scholars, E.-R. Labande in "Recherches sur les pèlerins dans l'Europe des XIe et XIIe siècles" in *Les cahiers de civilisation médiévale*, January–March 1959, who stresses the lower motivation, and Oursel, in *Pèlerins* , p. 29, who emphasizes the higher.

81. Ibid, p. 82.

82. Ibid.

83. John 11:17.

84. Oursel, *Pèlerins*, p. 36.

85. John 15:16b.

86. Acts 3:6b.

87. Victor W. Turner and Edith Turner, *Image and Pilgrimage in Christian Culture* (New York: Columbia University Press, 1978), p. 198.

88. See the letter of Margaret Paston, September 28, 1443, in James Gairdner, ed., *The Paston Letters* (London: Constable, 1872), I, p. 48.

89. Two famous *libri miraculorum* of the saints were those of Saint James of Compostela and of

Saint Gilles-du-Gard. The former is found in the *Codex Calixtinus*, II, and was republished in Acta sanctorum (1729), VI (July), pp. 47–59. The latter, known as the *Liber miraculorum sancti Aegidii*, was edited by P. Jaffé in the *Monumenta Germaniae historica scriptores*, XII (Hanover, 1861), pp. 316–23.

90. Originally *The Golden Legend* was titled *Legenda sanctorum* (Readings from the Saints) and was written between 1255 and 1266. It is the work of Jacobus de Voragine, a distinguished Dominican who became archbishop of Genoa. His work became immensely popular—there are over 500 ms. copies extant and over 150 different editions and translations of it appeared in the first century after its publication. It was intended as a layman's lectionary to be read as the feasts of the saints occurred during the Church year. All citations will be from *The Golden Legend of Jacobus de Voragine*, trans. from the Latin and adapted by Granger Ryan and Helmut Ripperger (New York: Arno Press, 1969).

91. Ibid., p. 668.

92. Ibid., p. 202.

93. Ibid., p. 517.

94. Ibid., p. 358.

95. See Michel Penicault, *Eglises de la Creuse* (Paris: Nouvelles éditions latines, 1977), p. 7. For this information we are indebted to Madame Geneviève Baudy of Paris.

96. Voragine, *Golden Legend*, p. 480.

97. Ibid., pp. 374–75.

98. Ibid., pp. 90–91.

99. Ibid., p. 199.

100. Ibid., p. 374.

101. Ibid., pp. 657–61. Richard Coeur de Lion is reported to have visited this shrine in 1197, and Bohemund, Norman prince of Christian Antioch, gave a set of silver chains commemorating his release. Saint Léonard also became a healing saint, and even today is reputed to ease difficult births and to cure barrenness. (See J. Maury M.–M. S. Gauthier, and J. Porcher, *Limousin roman* [Yonne: Zodiaque, 1960] p. 115).

102. *Pilgrimage Life*, pp. 40–41 makes much of this, possibly too much, in reaction from the hagiographers. It is difficult to keep the balance between the "sanctifiers" and the "debunkers" on any medieval topic.

103. William Langland, *The Vision of Piers the Plowman*, ed. W. W. Skeat (London: Oxford University Press 1873), Text C, I, lines 51–52.

104. "The Examination of Master William Thorpe, 1407" in E. Arber, ed. *English Garner*, 8 vols. (London: E. Arber, 1887–96), VI, pp. 84–85.

105. Ibid.

106. *The Canterbury Tales*, Prologue, lines 773–74. See Chapter 7 about pilgrims' diversions.

107. King, *Way of Saint James*, I, p. 108.

108. During our first visit to Compostela in July 1973, we noted a bloodthirsty statue of Saint James with Muslim heads rolling at his feet, proving him indeed a *conquistador* or *Matamoros*. On asking one of the guides in the cathedral whether this statue did not offend visiting Arabs or Africans, we were told that on the occasion of official visits the heads were smothered in flowers. See the Marqués de Loyola's article, "De Santiago peregrino a Santiago matamoros," *Cuadernos Hispanoamericanos*, 238–40 (1969), pp. 399, 405.

109. "The Center Out There: Pilgrims' Goal," *History of Religions* 12 (1973): 191–230. See also his *Image and Pilgrimage in Christian Culture*.

110. Ibid., p. 307.

111. Cited in Jusserand, *English Wayfaring Life*, p. 389.

112. Heath, *Pilgrim Life*, p. 25.

113. Jusserand, *English Wayfaring Life*, p. 369.

114. The Council of Oviedo of 1115 ruled that for certain serious ecclesiastical offenses, the criminal must become a Benedictine monk, an anchorite, a church serf, or a perpetual pilgrim. It is interesting to note that the Capitularies of Charlemagne had forbidden this last punishment as it was thought that it ruined the man for life. See King, *Way of Saint James*, I, p. 119. See also Sumption, *Pilgrimage*, p. 298.

115. Langland, *Piers the Plowman* (Skeat), Text C, passage 1, lines 47 ff.

116. King, *Way of Saint James*, I, p. 123.

117. Sumption, *Pilgrimage*, p. 175, points out that the Roman pilgrimage declined in the tenth

and thirteenth centuries due to the chaotic state of central Italy, while the Hundred Years' War ruined the abbey of Saint Gilles-du-Gard in Provence and even reduced the flow of pilgrims to Santiago.

118. See King, *Way of Saint James*, I, pp. 118–21; Jusserand, *English Wayfaring Life*, pp. 341–42; and Sumption, *Pilgrimage*, pp. 104–5.

119. King, *Way of Saint James*, I, p. 117.

120. *Acta sanctorum*, X (October), pp. 847–48. For penal pilgrimages see U. Berlière, "Les pèlerinages judiciaires au moyen âge," *Revue Bénédictine* 7 (1899): 525, where it is indicated that all such pilgrims had to travel on foot. In this type of pilgrimage, prayers, fasting, and alms were strictly enjoined. See also note 62 of this chapter.

121. Sumption, *Pilgrimage*, pp. 105–6.

122. Joan Evans, *Life in Medieval France* (London: Phaidon, 1957), p. 76.

123. See Eutychius, *The Book of the Demonstration* [Kitāb-al-Burhān], trans. W. M. Watt, ed. P. Cachia, in *Corpus scriptorum Christianorum orientalium, scriptores Arabici*, 2 vols. (Louvain, 1960–61), cited by Wilkinson, *Jerusalem Pilgrims*, p. 43.

—— 2 ——
The Allure of Compostela

ON the face of it, there was no reason at all to go to Compostela. No one outside Galicia had even heard of it before the eighth century, and, far from being an important shrine at that time, it was not even the center of a diocese. The bishopric was at Irun, itself of little significance. Compostela could hardly have been located at a more out-of-the-way place, for it was near the limit of the ancient and Mediterranean world, close to Finisterre, literally "land's end."[1]

Perhaps Compostela's most attractive feature was its name, Compostela, or "the field of the star"—from *campus stellae*—because this recalled the star-led discovery by hermits of the place where the sarcophagus of Saint James the Greater lay, thus mirroring the discovery of the humble birthplace of the infant Messiah by the star-led Wise Men. But as its fame grew, Compostela's name suggested to would-be pilgrims that the Milky Way in the heavens was also the direction to Santiago de Compostela.[2] Its less romantic but likelier derivation is from *compostum*, suggesting a cemetery.

Even so, allowing for the celestial advertising of its benefits, Compostela did not have the historical associations, or the succession of saints, or the religious resonance of names such as Jerusalem or Rome, its greatest competitors for pilgrims. Was not Jerusalem a holy city for three religions—Judaism, Christianity, and Islam—all united by the ethical demands of the monotheistic God in the Ten Commandments? Until A.D. 70 here stood the Temple, the supreme and historical center of Judaism. Here the founder of Christianity had come to pay his homage to God; here he had been found questioning the elders and showing the precocity of his wisdom. Here he would return in wrath, overturning the money changers' tables and telling them they had turned his Father's house into a den of thieves. Jerusalem was where the Lord of the Christians had prayed until his sweat was like drops of blood in the Garden of Gethsemane that the chalice of suffering might be taken away, only to accept it as the divine will. Here Jesus was

49

betrayed, crucified, died, buried, and here he rose from the dead. Hence he ascended into heaven, and thence sent his Holy Spirit to the waiting disciples. Jerusalem became the very symbol of heaven itself. How could any other city in the world compete with Jerusalem for the Western soul's allegiance?

As for Rome, it, too, had considerable claims on the allegiance of the Christian faithful. It was important long before the time of Christ. Indeed, as Saint Augustine well knew, the pagans claimed that it was the worship of the Nazarene Jesus that led to its downfall, and the historical theologian had written the *De civitate Dei* to refute that very charge. Rome was the headquarters of the largest and most just empire that the ancient world had known. Along its famed roadways, aided by the *pax Romana* that guarded them, Saint Paul had carried the Gospel of Christ, which conquered sin, suffering, and death, to his Jewish and Gentile converts. At Rome this former Pharisee who so proudly claimed Roman citizenship had been beheaded, a privilege of which his wholly Jewish associate, Saint Peter, the first bishop of Rome, could not avail himself, but insisted, so goes a powerful tradition, that he be crucified upside down as a final act of contrition and humility. Here lay the bodies of Saint Peter and Saint Paul. Rome was not only in name but also in fact the "mother of the saints." Christian Rome would always remain the most powerful center of Western Christianity, outliving the successive invasions of fifth-century Goths and Vandals, the eighth-century invasion of the Muslims who penetrated as far as Tours in France, and the eleventh-century invasion of the Normans who left their impact as far south as Sicily, and even surviving the Babylonian Captivity of the papacy at Avignon of the fourteenth century. Christian Rome did more than survive. It regenerated the Church in the West through its approval of successive monastic reforms, Cluniac and Cistercian, and its recognition of the Franciscan and Dominican friars, and through a whole group of new orders, whose disciplined spirituality and corporal works of mercy, together with their contribution to the intellectual life, provided streams in the desert and light in the Dark Ages and afterward. Rome was a name that might evoke corruption for some who, like Wycliffe or Hus, had experienced the bureaucratic chicanery, financial extortion, and postponements of the curial machinery, but for most of the time it was the protector of the Church and of its teaching, healing, charitable, and, above all, sacramental ministry.

It seems strange that a time would come when Compostela would attract more pilgrims than Rome. One reason for Rome's poorer showing as a pilgrimage center was that until the eighth century the popes had forbidden the translation of the bones of the saints. However, just before the widespread profanations caused by the war at the end of the eighth century, the popes changed their policy and recommended that the relics of the saints be transferred to churches in the center of Rome. In the following century the disappearance of the bones of the martyrs from the catacombs led to a lessening of interest in the Roman pilgrimage. Rome did not recover its significance as a pilgrimage center until 1300. Then Pope Boniface VIII's granting of jubilee indulgences brought new multitudes to the Holy City.[3]

Moreover, surely anyone who has undertaken the pilgrimage must confess that as the *camino francés* proceeds through northern Spain after Pamplona (forgetting the oases of Burgos and León), it seems not only metaphorically a "return to the desert" but literally such. Those long, arid stretches and rocky defiles (where the most aptly named town is Carrion) mean that beyond France the way to Saint James is no tourists' attraction. This also causes one to wonder at the medieval importance of Compostela.

How, indeed, could little, far-off, historically unheard-of, insignificant Compostela compete with renowned historical shrines hallowed with associations of glory, with architectural monuments of splendor, and with the sanctified blood of the martyrs? "Can anything good come out of Nazareth?" was the question posed by critics of the ministry of Jesus. "Can anything good come out of Compostela?" might well have been the jealous questioning of the Spanish bishops of Oviedo and of neighboring Lugo and Orense when the shrine was first established.

To answer this question it will be necessary to delve not only into history but also into the slippery subterranean caves of legend. But it is worth remembering as the Bollandists remind us in considering legend that behind the legend lies the deep will of the people for whom this leap of the imagination is a psychic necessity.

The most convincing explanation for the rapid rise of Compostela from obscurity to fame is that the shrine of Saint James the Greater arose from a Spanish need to find a Christian equivalent to the Muslim Kaaba, or shrine, of Mecca. In the terminology of Américo Castro, we see in the northwest corner of Spain a *mythomachia,* a struggle of myths, the fight of Cross against Crescent, of Christians against Moors, a Christian *jihad,* or holy war, waged beneath the banner of Great Saint James against the armies of the Prophet, Great Mohammed. Christians indeed came to believe with Mohammed that "Paradise is in the shadow of the swords."

We have argued that the Spaniards needed a Christian shrine equal in importance to the Kaaba as a national religious focus. In the tenth century Christians also felt a sense of cultural inferiority. The whole of Europe was impressed by the achievements of the Islamic civilization in

Spain in the areas of mathematics, philosophy, medicine, poetry, architecture, wrought iron, enamel work, and carpets. Who could not fail to be impressed by the lovely cities of Sevilla, Almeria, and Cordova?

By the end of the thirteenth century Dante, commenting on the twenty-third sonnet in Chapter XI of the *Vita nuova* (1294), informs us that while any man leaving his birthplace may be called a pilgrim, yet in the narrower and more accurate sense, he only is a pilgrim who goes to or from the house of Saint James. There are, he writes, "three separate and suitable names for those who journey to the glory of God. They are called palmers [*palmieri*] who go beyond the seas eastward whence often they bring back palm-branches." Those are, of course, the Palestine pilgrims. Dante also mentions a third sort of pilgrim, those who go to Rome [*Romie*]. But he reserves the name of "pilgrims" [*peregrini*] for those "who go to the house of Galicia; seeing that no other apostle was buried so far from his birthplace as was the blessed Saint James" (*in quanto vanno a la casa di Galizia però che la sepultura di sa'Jacopo for più lontana de la sua patria, che d'alcuna altro apostolo*).

The importance of Santiago was not only due to the fact that Saint James was the first apostle to be martyred, or even that he was supposedly buried in the westernmost part of Europe and farthest from Palestine, but even more because Saint James the Great was confused with Saint James the Less, first bishop of Jerusalem, and more importantly, the brother of Jesus himself. It is not too much to say that the cathedral authorities did not discourage this confusion, since they obviously approved of Maestro Matteo's Portico de la Gloria, in which the likeness is accentuated. But the association of Compostela was far from being the only cause of its fame.

Compostela shared with Jerusalem one considerable medieval advantage over Rome: both were in countries overrun with Saracen infidels, and in times when the routes to Jerusalem were closed, the routes to Compostela were still open but with sufficient danger to add spice to the journey. A pilgrimage to Compostela was, in short, the peaceful equivalent of a Crusade, as much a *reconquista* as a Crusade, for it was recovering Christian kingdoms and holy places from the infidel Moors. In fact, the Crusade went westward to Compostela and eastward to Jerusalem and thus the roads on which the pilgrims marched were defended by crusading warriors.[4]

Compostela had one advantage over Jerusalem only in this respect: the Spanish Muslims were more tolerant than those of the eastern Mediterranean. They were willing to trade and even to intermarry with Christians.

Then, again, the route to Compostela, once well secured, was more convenient than the long land and sea route to the Holy Land. It was cheaper, too, and was provided with more frequent hospices. Yet it also offered in due course the same advantages in terms of indulgences. Furthermore, it offered the chance to travel through strange lands, where foreign tongues were spoken (the *Codex Calixtinus* views the Basques as if they were as barbaric as the remote Scots with their unintelligible tongue), and where landscape, flora, and fauna differed from the homeland. And if one were seeking difficulty, there was enough sand, dust, and heat, and sufficient precipitous ascents and rocky defiles to satisfy the most ardent ascetical or guilt-ridden traveler.

The pilgrimage to Compostela offered what the true pilgrim would consider a major advantage, and the dubious pilgrim a disadvantage. It was distant, but not *too* distant, like Jerusalem when the route was open, which often it was not. It was dangerous, whereas the route from France to Rome through either the Saint Bernard pass or over Mount Cenis was safe. The early Cluniac admirers of Saint Mayeul, their abbot, had made the itinerary appear dangerous with stories of a miraculous escape from Saracens, which they told at his shrine in Souvigny, but it never became more than a local shrine. Besides, it was difficult to regard the journey to Rome as heroic since every bishop was supposed to undertake it shortly after his consecration. The pilgrimage to Compostela was a valiant alternative to crusading. Its very difficulty constituted a challenge only the daring and devoted pilgrim would take up since it might mean death or imprisonment at the hand of the Moors. In comparison, the local pilgrimages in France, from Mont-Saint-Michel in the northwest to Saint-Gilles-du-Gard in Provence, were lighthearted affairs. Compostela was distant, dangerous, and difficult. These were not its least attractions.

A very important factor in popularizing the pilgrimage to Compostela—and the Crusade to win back both Christian Spain and the Holy Land from the Saracens—was the link forged between France and Spain through Cluniac popes and abbots, Spanish kings, and French princes and nobles.

It has been calculated that the chivalry of France mounted thirty-four expeditions through the Pyrenees for the Christian reconquest of Spain from the eleventh to the thirteenth centuries, led by barons and men of Burgundy in 1078 and 1089, of Gascony (about 1020), or Aquitaine (in 1064), and of Normandy, Poitou, and Angoulême. While the barons recruited their pilgrim-soldiers at the instigation of Rome, it was the leaders of the great Benedictine monastery of Cluny, which at its peak had over three hundred dependencies and an abbey church vaster than Saint Peter's in Rome, that fueled the fire of *reconquista*. Cluny was the chain that linked these separate regional enterprises and provided the spiritual ferment that kept enthusiasm high for Crusade and pilgrimage. This was the period when the Cluniac abbeys placed the symbolical cockleshell of Saint James on their coats of arms.

Yet Cluny was called to this task by the initiative of the Spanish sovereigns. About 1032 Sancho the Great of Navarre sent the hermit Paterno to Cluny to seek the aid of the Benedictine monks. Paterno returned to reform, according to the Cluniac rule, the two abbeys of Saint Juan de la Peña and of Leyre, both near the beginning of the *camino francés* of Spain. Later his three sons, although hostile to one another, retained their links with Cluny. Alfonso VI of Castile sent the monk Robert to France to arrange for the reform of Sahagún and proved extremely generous to Cluny. He sent them the proceeds of an annual tax—a single munificent donation of ten thousand talents for the construction of their vast abbey church. In return, to fasten ever more firmly the temporal and the spiritual links between Cluny and northern Spain, the great abbot of Cluny, Saint Hugh, sent his niece, Constance, who was also the daughter of the duke of Burgundy, to marry Alfonso VI of Castile, as his second wife. From this marriage was born Urraca who married Raymond, a prince of Burgundy.

In this period, it should be recalled, Cluny was able to boast that three of its monks wore the triple tiara of the papacy: Urban II, Pascal II, and Calixtus II; while the primate of Spain and archbishop of Toledo, Bernard of Sédirac, was also a monk from Cluny.[5] Cluny and Christian Spain thus remained intimately linked to the joint advantage of pilgrimage and Crusade.

A powerful fusion of French religion and patriotism emerged so that the interlinked forces were almost inseparable. One astounding example was the association between the *Chanson de Roland* (which recounts the epic fight of Charlemagne's rearguard under earl Roland, with the assistance of the warrior-bishop Turpin), and the westernmost route through France to Compostela, where the relics of the heroes at Blaye, Belin, Bordeaux, and Roncevaux were venerated as if they had been saints. The brilliant though now disputed thesis of Joseph Bédier in *Légendes épiques* illuminated the intertwining of sacred and secular motives, for he argued that the various cantos of the *Song of Roland* were sung by minstrels to pilgrims en route to Compostela at the places where the events had occurred, thus increasing their patriotic and religious ardor simultaneously. Though unhistorical in basis (for it was Basques not Saracens who defeated Roland), the legend linking Charlemagne and the Jacobite pilgrimage was reinforced by iconography and relics.

This combination of French religion and patriotism continued to assist both pilgrims and Crusaders. When the Crusades were necessitated by the blocking of the pilgrimage routes to Jerusalem, the alternative pilgrimage through Muslim lands to Compostela became popular.[6] Jerusalem's disadvantage became Compostela's great gain. It was precisely when the Seljukian Turks closed the route to Jerusalem and the First Crusade was rendered necessary that Compostela began to flourish. Furthermore, it is significant as evidence of the impact of Cluny that it was a great speech by a former prior of Cluny, Pope Urban II, at Clermont in France at the council of that name, that fired France for the Crusade in 1095. The leaders of that Crusade were predominantly French, including Raymond of Toulouse, Bohemund of Otranto and his nephew Tancred, Godfrey of Bouillon, and Robert of Normandy. The Second Crusade also shows the French Benedictine impact, for it was preached by Saint Bernard of Clairvaux, the Cistercian reformer, at the Benedictine shrine of Vézelay in 1147, where the relics of Saint Mary Magdalene were venerated, and from which the second major route through France to Compostela started. Also, this Second Crusade was backed by Bernard's former pupil, Pope Eugenius III.

The Cistercian white monks followed the black monks in erecting churches in Spain that were the daughter houses of Grandselve, Bonnefort, and L'Escale-de-Dieu, paralleling in Spain the daughter houses of Cîteaux and Clairvaux in France. But, as far as the Crusades were concerned, the influence of the most famous of all Cistercians, Saint Bernard, ultimately failed to stop the thrust of the Saracens. The sacred sites of Palestine remained inaccessible to Christians.

It was during these two centuries that Compostela reached its apogee of fame, and this was used to the full by the ambitious and enterprising prince-archbishop of Compostela, Diego Gelmirez.[7] In 1120 he was given authority over Merida, the ancient metropolitan see of Lusitania, and thereafter until 1399 the archbishop of Compostela held authority over all the dioceses of Portugal. It was Pope Calixtus II, crowned at Cluny, who gave these privileges to Compostela, and in 1122 he extended to the cathedral church the most valuable indulgence of the Holy Year, a notable attraction for pilgrims. He also made Gelmirez the papal legate, allowed him to make seven of his canons cardinals and allowed them to wear jeweled miters. Gelmirez naturally received pilgrims to Compostela *apostolico more*, as if he were the pope himself.[8] Little wonder that the *Codex* that glorified the shrine of Compostela, advertised the power of the Apostle James's miracles, and provided the guide for pilgrims to that shrine was attributed to Calixtinus, and is now named the *Codex Calixtinus*, although the attribution is spurious. In the first quarter of the twelfth century "the *camino* [*francés*] was probably the busiest trunk road in Christendom."[9]

However important all these factors were in accounting for the immense popularity of far-off Compostela as a shrine of pilgrimage, it was its legendary link with the Apostle Saint James, publicized by ambitious bishops, that lifted it out of its obscurity. And it is to this set of improbable legends that we now turn.

We have deliberately used the term *improbable* because until the seventh century there is no surviving document, or record of any kind, claiming that the Apostle Santiago had preached in Spain, far less that his tomb was to be found there.

There is enough evidence in the New Testament to establish Saint James as one of the greatest of the apostles. The elder brother of Saint John, the "Beloved Disciple," Saint James, together with Saint Peter and Saint John, belonged to the inner circle of disciples who were present at those climactic, revelatory events in the life of Christ, the Transfiguration and the Agony in the Garden of Gethsemane.[10] The overly ardent zeal of saints John and James caused them to be named *Boanerges* (that is, "sons of thunder"), since they wished to bring thunder from heaven down against the Samaritans who, seeing that Jesus was determined to go to the rival city of Jerusalem, refused to invite him to Samaria to stay.[11] It is definitely known that Saint James was the first of the twelve apostles to suffer martyrdom, since he was beheaded at the command of Herod Agrippa I in A.D. 44.[12] The seventh-century legend that he preached in Spain is contradicted by the tradition of the early Church that the apostles did not leave Jerusalem until after his death, as well as the testimony of the Epistle to the Romans 15:20–24. It is not too much to say that there is no shred of evidence either from the New Testament or from the early Church that points to Saint James's ever having visited Spain. A fortiori, there is no evidence that his body was entombed in Spain; the very most one can say is that it is possible that his remains might have reached Compostela, in the way that so many relics of saints moved in the Middle Ages, as they were either purchased by personages from Constantinople or Jerusalem and brought back by crusading kings or nobles, or they were translated for fear of the invading Arabs, Vikings, or Magyars, or stolen by monks from another monastery for their own.[13]

But whether legends have a historical basis or none, they can have a very powerful impact on those who believe, especially when the legend is liturgically reiterated on festivals. What, then, were the legends that linked Saint James with Compostela? There are, in fact, two major legends. One asserts that Saint James preached the Gospel in Spain, and the other asserts that his body was brought to Spain by his followers and buried in Galicia, where it was found almost eight centuries later. Each of these will be examined in turn.

The first reference to Saint James preaching in Spain appears in a seventh-century Latin version of a Greek original of an apocryphal document, *The Catalogue of the Apostles* (or *Breviarium Apostolorum*), but the Greek versions of the fifth and sixth centuries are entirely unaware of it.[14] Even as late as the second half of the tenth century, while it was generally admitted that the relics of Santiago were in Spain, there was still a division of opinion as to whether he had visited Spain during his lifetime or not.[15]

The various versions of the Byzantine *Catalogue of the Apostles* disagree on the location of the tomb of Saint James. Some place it in Jerusalem, others in Caesarea in Palestine, and yet others have him buried in a town or on a point of the Marmaric, which through many transpositions of copyists becomes *Arcis marmoricis,* a name used in Galicia since the ninth century.[16] The most anciently attested name of this place in Galicia is between the rivers Sur and Tambre in the district of Amaia in the diocese of Iria, where the relics of Saint James are venerated. It is called *Sanctus Jacobus in Arcis* or *in arcis marmoricis.* Moreover, authentic (not invented) charters show that the church of Saint James about 880 was served by a monastic community dependent on the bishop of Iria. By 915 this town was important enough to have the right to free all slaves who stayed for forty days near the tomb of the Apostle James without being reclaimed by their masters.[17] The association of the body of Saint James with Galicia is said to have begun before the death of Charlemagne in 814, but the beginning of the Spanish Jacobean tradition cannot be fixed with any certainty before A.D. 825–30 at the earliest. And this date is determined by a reference in a Latin manuscript of *The Martyrology of Adon* (Ms. lat. 3879 of the Bibliothèque Nationale of Paris), which was composed at Lyons before 859. It characterizes the Galician cult as *celeberrime veneratione,* already most renowned, and asserts that "the bones of this most blessed apostle were brought to Spain to its very end, that is, over against the British sea."[18] A conservative date would allow some thirty years in which the cult could develop, that is, between 825 and 830.

There is no contemporary relation of the finding of the body of Saint James. The account that survives comes from the end of the eleventh or the beginning of the twelfth century. It is found on a document that is alleged to be an agreement between the bishop Diego Peláez and the abbot of a monastery annexed to the basilica, and it is dated 1077; but its authenticity is doubtful. This, however, is the account of the finding of Saint James's tomb and body.

It is related that a hermit called Pelagius, Pelagio, or Pelayo was warned in a vision that God was about to reveal the tomb of his Apostle James. At approximately the same time reliable inhabitants of neighboring villages noticed lights shining above a little wood, and angels appeared there. The bishop Theodomir was informed and, after preparing for the event by a fast of three days, he penetrated through the thicket and discovered among the bushes a little house covering a marble sarcophagus. King Alfonso II hurried to construct a church on the site of the tomb.[19] This is the very simplest form of the legend.

Later elaborations of the legend of the finding of the body of Saint

James, which need not detain us, recount that shepherds joined the angels in pointing out the tomb to the holiest of the hermits, and that there was a cave inside which was found an altar beneath an arch supported by pillars (an obvious reference to *in arcis marmoricis*), and underneath the altar was a sarcophagus covered with a stone slab. This when lifted revealed the body and severed head of Saint James. Fortunately (or rather, providentially), a letter was observed lying near the body that read: "Here lies Santiago, Son of Zebedee and Salome, brother of S. John, whom Herod beheaded in Jerusalem: he came by sea borne by his disciples to Iria Flavia of Galicia, and from thence on a car drawn by the oxen of the Lady Lupa, owner of these states whose oxen would not pass on any further."[20]

The most significant later development of the legend of Saint James is that he becomes a *Matamoros,* a slayer of infidel Moors, and the patron of the *reconquista*. There is an advance indication of this possiblity in the New Testament naming him and John (later to be known as the "Beloved Disciple," which excluded the original designation) the *Boanerges,* or "sons of thunder." This, however, was a nickname, ironically given by Christ in rebuke. This is, therefore, literally a transformation with a vengeance! It occurred when the Christian forces under King Ramiro of the Asturias were hard pressed by the Moors at the battle of Clavijo in 844 in the Rioja near Najera. During the night, before the dawn when his soldiers would confront an overwhelming army of Moors who would inflict certain defeat on them, the king fell into a deep sleep. In a vision Saint James appeared promising him victory. The king told his followers of the celestial vision. They, cheered by this supernatural promise, joined together in prayer, and then rushed on the enemy, crying, *Santiago! y cierra, España!* ("Saint James! and close up, Spain!") This was only the beginning of the Christian reconquest of Spain from the infidels for in the sky at the head of the Christian legions and leading them on appeared the Apostle James, shining in his armor, mounted on a white horse, holding in one hand a flashing sword and in the other a pure white banner on which was emblazoned a blood red cross. In the slaughter that ensued Saint James himself is said to have killed 60,000 Moors single-handed. Mariana's *Historiae de rebus Hispaniae* affirms that the victorious army, grateful for the divine aid, vowed to Santiago, the battle leader, that all Spain should pay tribute to the church of Compostela, and that every acre of plowed and vine land should annually pay a bushel of corn or wine to that church.[21]

Yet the battle of Clavijo was unheard of until the end of the twelfth century, so one supposes that this legend was fabricated to account for the tributary tax exacted by the cathedral of Compostela and to provide a romantic foundation for the Order of Saint James of the Sword, which was organized both for the winning back of Spain from the Moors and for the defense of pilgrims to Santiago's shrine. It was confirmed as an order by Pope Alexander III in 1175.[22] Here again we see that pilgrimage and Crusade are complementary.[23] We are not surprised to learn that the Spanish order that was modeled on that of the Knights Templar had as its bloodthirsty motto, *Rubet ensis sanguine Arabum* ("The sword is scarlet with the blood of Arabs").

The son of thunder continued to thunder for Spain since the fisherman of Galilee had become the Jove of Galicia. As we shall see, in our examination in a later chapter of the liturgical celebrations of the feasts of Saint James in Compostela, most of the elements of the tradition, excluding some details, are taken into the worship and James is celebrated as an *alter Christus*. As the first of the apostles (since he entered heaven first) he even displaces Saint Peter, whether as guardian of heaven's gate or as the most important apostle. This shows that Compostela, with its canons named cardinals at the middle of the thirteenth century, saw itself as another Rome.[24]

The extraordinary veneration of pilgrims of Saint James is also reflected in the French version of the great hymn of Saint James sung by pilgrims, which includes the lines:

> Qu'en Paradis nous puissions voir,
> Dieu et Monsieur Saint-Jacques.

The thirteenth-century Spanish *Poema de Fernán González* exults:

> Fuerte m[i]ent quiso Dios a España honrrar,
> quand al santo apostol quiso y enbyar,
> d'Inglatierra e Françia quiso la mejorar,
> sabet non yaz apostol ed tod aquel logar.[25]

J. S. Stone rightly observes that the James who returned to Spain, as the legend insists, was "no mere fisherman of Galilee, plain, uncultured, and poorly bred, but a prince and a knight—a prince nobler than Turpin and a knight more dauntless and valiant than Roland."[26] Indeed, it is alleged that one night Charlemagne had a vision in which a handsome knight appeared and when asked his name and mission, replied in the French of that day, "I am James the Apostle, Christ's servant, Zebedee's son, John Evangelist's brother, elect by God's grace to preach his law, whom Herod slew; observe, my body is in Galicia but no man knows where, and the Saracens oppress the land. Therefore God sends you to retake the road that leads to my tomb and the land in which I rest. The starry way that you saw in the sky signifies that you shall go into Galicia at the head of a great army; and after you all nations shall come in pilgrimage, right to the end of time. Go, then, I will be your helper, and as a reward for your journeying I will get from God a heavenly crown for you, and your name shall remain in the memory of mankind until the day of judgment."[27] Here we suspect the hand of Cluny, which is also evident in the entire *Codex Calixtinus*. It is worth remarking, perhaps, that before the discovery of the tomb of the apostle-martyr, Spain had no relic to equal that of Mohammed at Cordova, and Charlemagne's confidant Archbishop Turpin may have influenced him in this regard. But this is sheer conjecture. What is sober truth, however, is that the fisherman James became not merely the guardian of net makers but the patron saint of Christian Spain, *Padrón y Capitán General de las Españas,* and his very name the war cry of Spain, fighting infidelity in temporal as well as spiritual battles.

The victory of Saint James as the protector of pilgrims was not won without a struggle. The devotees of other saints in France and Spain, notably Saint Martin of Tours and Saint Isidore of León, also staked their claims and won considerable support. Another competitor appeared in 1010 when Alcuin, abbot of Saint Jean d'Angély, on the most popular route to Santiago, announced the discovery of the head of John the Baptist. He also called several princes together to make the discovery credible and public. However, it created only a local cult, although the *Guide* indicates that a choir of a hundred monks venerated it day and night.[28]

The major competitors, saints Martin and Isidore, also had their tombs located at strategic points on the pilgrimage way to Compostela: Tours at the very start of the westernmost of the four routes through France and León on the central route westward through northern Spain. But once again and in a different kind of battle Saint James proved himself most invincible, gloriously *invictissime!*

It was asserted that the great soldier of the Roman emperor who became Christ's soldier and a dramatic exemplar of charity, Saint Martin of Tours, was no whit inferior to the apostles. The visit to his tomb was the major pilgrimage of the French people at an early period, in fact, the essential *Gallicana peregrinatio.* Eminent personages came to pay their respects at his shrine. These included such notabilities as King Clovis and Queen Clothilde, Saint Geneviève of Paris and Saint Columban in Merovingian times, and after them the Carolingians, including King Pepin the Short, Charlemagne himself, Louis the Pious, with most of the Capetian kings following them. Thus the holy bishop of Tours led a long line of confessors and penitents who through him won many favors from God.[29]

The attempt to gain apostolic status for Saint Isidore of León was equally unsuccessful but not for want of guile on the part of his royal promoters.[30] The attempt to contrive either a double of Saint James or, better, a colleague, successor, and even substitute for him was made by King Alfonso VII of León. Apparently he could not bear to see the growing crowds of pilgrims as they passed westward through León to Compostela with their best gifts and money kept for offerings to Saint James. Just prior to 1149 when the king and his army were encamped before Baeza and had learned that the Moors were coming to relieve the besieged city, he claimed to have had a heartening dream, suspiciously like that of King Ramiro before the battle of Clavijo almost three centuries before. Saint Isidore, it was alleged, had appeared in the vision and promised to be his helper the next day in the fight against the Moors. The archbishop of León, Don Rodrigo, perforce acknowledged the miracle and established the church of Saint Isidore in León with canons regular to serve it.[31] Luke of Tuy, who compiled the *Book of the Miracles of San Isidore* for Queen Berenguela, embroidered the legend: "When Saint Isidore appeared, as a venerable Pontiff, shining like the sun, near him could be seen a shimmering right hand with a fiery sword. To the King's question, Who are you? he replied, I am Isidore, Doctor of Spain and successor by grace and preaching of the Apostle, Saint James, whose is the right hand going with me for your defense." In the battle before Baeza it was reported that San Isidoro was seen on a white horse, holding a sword in one hand and a cross in the other, and above him was the right hand of Saint James with a sword.[32]

The intention behind the legend is clearly to create a new Spanish "pontiff"—to superannuate Saint James with his blessing for his successor, Saint Isidore. Meanwhile, the church of San Isidoro in León was elegantly rebuilt, befitting the royal pantheon of sacred tombs, and richly redecorated by King Alfonso VII and his sister Sancha—the present splendid south door dates from about 1150. It became a gloriously convenient center of pilgrimage. Thus building, relics, and legend all conspired to make a more popular attraction for pilgrims through a combined political and commercial ploy.[33] Saint James, however, refused to be upstaged by an unapostolic and unmartyred newcomer, unknown to the sacred pages of the New Testament. It mattered little that this holy upstart was erudite or that he was both a Spaniard and a distinguished member of the hierarchy of the Spanish Church. He never ousted Saint James from the hearts of the pilgrims who still made Compostela their ultimate destination, only staying briefly at the impressive way station of León.

Our first chapter, attempting to cover the vast complex of motives both sacred and secular that accounted for the great medieval streams of pilgrims, was a general answer to the question addressed in this chapter. In this second chapter we have tried to account for the popularity of Compostela itself as a pilgrimage center, despite its apparent and real disadvantages compared with Jerusalem and Rome, even allowing for other saints whose supporters tried to wrest pilgrim affections away from Saint James. We now ask: were there any other special advantages this pilgrimage had to offer, apart from the complementarity of pilgrimage and *reconquista* in Saracen-infested Spain? Admittedly, this was a signal advantage when, as we have seen, the route to the Holy Land was blocked by the infidels. Nor are we, for the present, concerned to stress another great advantage—that the four routes through France to Santiago's shrine provided other important sanctoral relics and therefore pilgrimage centers, thus offering greater merit for religious pilgrims and increased insurance and protection by the saints.[34]

We now have to consider what may be called the medieval equivalent of modern billboards for Santiago de Compostela, that is, the advertising of the powers of Saint James in the *Book of Miracles (Liber miraculorum)* in the *Codex Calixtinus*, Book II. This will show us exactly how in the first half of the twelfth century, when the Compostela pilgrimage was at its apex, Saint James was to be viewed as a phenomenally successful plenipotentiary of the court of heaven and a worker of miracles of many different kinds who was entirely deserving of the trust of thousands upon thousands of pilgrims from many lands.

It should be noted that while books of miracles were one successful way of advertising the powers of a saint in his shrine, they were not the only way.[35] News of cures would be quickly passed on by returning pilgrims, eager to share their knowledge. During and after the thirteenth century certain friars were paid to advertise the shrines of saints. Finally, the monks of the Cluniac and Cistercian Benedictine reforms also had a special interest in recommending the shrines for which they were responsible, as were the Augustinian canons. French monks who became Spanish bishops would feel a particular responsibility to recommend pilgrims to the shrines of their native regions. Books of miracles, especially those of Saint Gilles, Saint Foi of Conques, and Saint James, were successful forms of advertisement and kept the stream of pilgrims flowing in hope that they might be helped by the saint in the way he or she had helped others.

The Compostela *Book of Miracles*[36] is a collection of twenty-two chapters of miracles and constitutes the most widely known and most frequently cited book of the entire collection of documents making up the *Codex Calixtinus*.[37]

Our examination of it will consist chiefly in the summary of its stories, their classification, and their implications.[38] The primary purpose of these miracle stories is to present Saint James as a superlative protector of pilgrims, who outshines all competitors even on the route to Compostela. He is, for example, as good a deliverer of prisoners as the famed Saint Léonard of Noblat whose shrine, near Limoges, is filled with ex-voto chains and fetters. Hence we are told several stories of liberation from prison.

Saint James frees a group of prisoners, including a priest, from a dungeon at Saragossa,[39] and one of them returns to Compostela, which he reaches on December 30, a Jacobite festival occasion. A miracle of the same type is recorded in which an Italian, Bernardus,[40] is imprisoned in a high tower from which James enables him to escape by jumping sixty cubits safely to the ground. He thereupon goes to Compostela to thank the saint who had answered his prayer.

Another liberation story narrates how the count of Forcaiquier in upper Provence had a feud with his vassal William.[41] The latter is taken prisoner by the count and ordered to be decapitated. William cries to Saint James, with the result that three otherwise mortal cuts of the rapier leave him unscathed, as also when the executioner tries to cut his throat. When the exasperated count has him imprisoned, it is of no avail because Saint James in person frees him from the castle prison the next morning. The clear implication is that Saint Léonard of Noblat must look to his laurels.

Saint James is able to accomplish the difficult task of obtaining absolution for a heinous crime confessed at his shrine, in exactly the same way as Saint Gilles-du-Gard is reported to have done.[42] An Italian penitent committed so serious a crime that his bishop did not dare to give him absolution and advised him to go on pilgrimage to Compostela and there to place on the altar of Saint James a paper recording the infamous sin.[43] This was done. As Bishop Theodomir came to the altar to celebrate Mass he found the paper, but the name of the sin had been erased—miraculous proof that Saint James had absolved his distant pilgrim, as completely as Saint Gilles had absolved Charlemagne.

Saint James is also like Saint Gilles in being able to grant heirs to those who need them. A French pilgrim is promised a son, the wish is gratified, but at fifteen the boy dies while on pilgrimage to Santiago on the Castilian hills of Oca.[44] He is resuscitated by Saint James, and a happy family reaches Compostela to give him double thanks.

Saint James is as effective a promoter of charity as Saint Martin of Tours, another competitor for pilgrims en route to Compostela. That, at least, is the implication of one miracle story. It tells how three horsemen from Donzy (where an admirable Romanesque church is extant) near Lyons who were on the way to Compostela met a poor woman.[45] She was on foot carrying all her necessities in a sack, and she asked them if they would carry her sack for her on the back of one of their horses. One horseman agreed to do this. But while they were still twelve days' journey from their destination, the woman and the horseman encountered a sick pilgrim. The horseman put the sick man on his horse and walked the rest of the way. Finally, in an exhausted state, he reached Compostela. His companions advised him to prepare for death. For three days he remained speechless, but on regaining his voice said that when he was assaulted by a horde of demons, Saint James appeared holding the sack of the poor woman in one hand and the staff of the sick man he had succored in the other hand. Saint James had put the demons to flight. The sick man then told his companions to fetch a priest for the last rites. This might seem a poor reward for one who had played the role of Good Samaritan so sincerely, but it was the guarantee that he was ready for heaven sponsored by so strong an advocate as Santiago. He died in the odor of sanctity, and, it is assumed, went to heaven.

Saint James is a valiant protector of his pilgrims on land as well as on sea. Indeed, in respect to saving seagoing pilgrims he is as effective as Saint Nicholas of Bari, whose altar was also to be found in the cathedral of Compostela in the twelfth century at the end of the north transept. Thirty cavaliers set out from Lorraine on pilgrimage[46] and all except one vowed never to leave one another in distress—a wise vow in view of the dangers and difficulties on the road and the shorter span of medieval life. But when one cavalier fell ill, it was the horseman who had not taken the vow who alone remained with him to nurse him and eventually to bury him at Col de Cise. Saint James appeared as a cavalier, carrying the dead man on his horse, and asking the man's protector to mount behind him, carried them both the twelve days' journey remaining in a single night, leaving them at dawn on Mountjoy in sight of Compostela below.

Another land rescue by Saint James and an exorcism of his are recounted in a further miracle story. A pious French furrier[47] who had lived chastely with his mother had, since his maturity, gone each year on pilgrimage to Compostela. On the eve of the next pilgrimage, however, he had a carnal lapse before setting out for the Galician shrine. As a consequence he was assaulted by Satan who, in the name of Saint James, reproved him for his sin and tried to dissuade him from continuing the pilgrimage. The second night the devil, who can turn himself into angel of light, appeared in the guise of Saint James and told the furrier that the only way to save his soul was to mutilate his body and commit suicide. The desperate man took his own life, and his bloody corpse was being conveyed to the place of burial when he sat up in his coffin and told how Saint James had implored the Blessed Virgin to unite his soul with his body when the demons were carrying his soul to hell.

Saint James also protects his seaborne pilgrims. Another miracle story recounts how Frison,[48] a ship's master carrying pilgrims to Jerusalem, was attacked by a Saracen pirate, fell in the water, and cried for help to Saint James. The apostle of Spain thereupon lifted him above the waves, and he went immediately on pilgrimage to Compostela to give thanks to his protector at his own shrine and to tell his story. The implication of this story is, of course, that the pilgrimage to Compostela is as efficacious as that to the Holy Land.

Another sea miracle narrative recounts how a bishop,[49] reading his psalter, and his companions were returning from the Holy Land when a wave pushed them into the water, and Saint James, as another Christ, walked across the waves and rescued them.

A third ocean miracle reports how a man was upheld three days in the sea and enabled to swim behind the ship he had originally embarked upon and follow it into harbor.[50] He reported that Saint James held him up with his own hand and kept his head above water. The moral of this story is that Saint James is so good a protector that you can safely trust him however far your sea voyage is from Compostela, and that the apostle is certainly not inferior to Saint Nicholas of Bari.[51]

Yet another sea miracle story exhibits Saint James in a threefold capacity, as *Matamoros* against the infidel Turks, as thaumaturge, and as savior from the sea. A French nobleman fighting the Moslems in the Holy Land vowed to visit Saint James's tomb if the apostle would grant him victory in all his encounters with the Turks.[52] When the prayer was granted and the nobleman forgot his vow, he was punished by an illness that was almost mortal. Saint James appeared to the nobleman's squire, telling him to assure his master that if he kept his vow he would be cured. The sick man then asked the priests to give him the emblems of pilgrimage (the staff and scrip), and soon he was aboard a ship that would take him partway to Santiago. A fierce tempest battered the ship. The passengers invoked Saint James, and promised either to go to Compostela on pilgrimage or to give money for the building of the basilica dedicated to Saint James. The saint appeared, stilled the storm, and the twice-saved nobleman brought the group's donations to Compostela. Saint James hereby also showed what a practical man he was, and so the word went round that one could send money if he could not or would not go to Compostela.

There must have been some doubts in the minds of persons who compared the simple fisherman of the Gospel with the claims of the *Matamoros*. One miracle story is intended to dispel such distrust and to repristinate the reputation of Saint James as a genuine knight *sans peur et sans reproche*.[53] The point is made very effectively, while also observing that Compostela was such a holy place that a Greek bishop gave up his diocese to live as a hermit in a cell close to the tomb of Saint James. One day the new hermit heard some peasants who were pilgrims invoking Saint James thus: "Blessed James, good knight, preserve us from present and future ills!" The hermit then informed them that according to the Gospel, Saint James was a fisherman not a knight. The following evening, however, the Apostle appeared dressed in white, covered with shining armor, bearing two keys in his hand. He then addressed the hermit: "Stephen, servant of God, you do not want people to call me knight. I reveal myself to you thus, armed, so that you may know that I march at the head of Christians in their battle against Saracens, and I bring them victories." He asked the hermit to observe the two keys he carried and said that they were the keys of the city of Coimbra in Portugal. It was being besieged by King Ferdinand, and the city would be in the hands of the king at nine in the morning of the next day. This was supposed to convince Stephen of the truth of Saint James's appearance as the knight of Spain. Stephen told the leading clergy of his vision, and next day Ferdinand's envoys brought the news of victory that had been gained the very hour promised by Saint James. The *Matamoros* strikes again!

Saint James not only rid the insane of their demons, but he was also a physician in general practice with astounding success. A Burgundian noble,[54] Guibert, paralyzed since he was fourteen, was carried to Compostela. After a vigil of two nights in the cathedral of Compostela, he was cured during the third night.

Saint James also rectified injustice, especially if the victims were pilgrims, no matter how far their starting point may have been from Compostela. One miracle narrative illustrates this. A man and his son, as part of a company of Germans en route to Galicia, stayed at an inn at Toulouse.[55] There the avaricious host hid a silver vase in the son's baggage, pretending that the latter had stolen it so that in recompense he could claim all the goods of the father. As a result the boy was condemned as a thief and hanged. The wretched father continued his journey and on the way back again reached Toulouse to find his son's body still hanging on the gibbet. But by the power of Saint James the lad was resuscitated and returned to his joyful father.

The saint's protective power was also seen in the case of a father, mother, and two small children who left Poitiers because of the plague.[56] They reached Pamplona on their pilgrim way where the wife died, and the father's goods and horse were stolen by an innkeeper. As the father pursued the journey afoot, an anonymous benefactor lent him an ass, and at Compostela the benefactor revealed himself to be Saint James. The same saintly rescuer informed the father that on his return to Pamplona he would find the nefarious innkeeper dead, damned like all those whose deeds resemble his. A similar blunt warning to innkeepers who exploited pilgrims was sounded loud and clear in the famous pseudo-Calixtine sermon, *Veneranda dies.*[57]

Saint James honors the nobility who venerate him, but he is no snob. The count of Toulouse, Ponce de Saint Gilles,[58] his brother, and their retinue reached the basilica at Compostela after sundown. Despite their pleading the sacristan refused to open the gates leading to the apostle's tomb until the next morning. The count and his friends implored Saint James to grant their request. A great clanging noise was heard as the gates opened and the pilgrims were immediately able to begin their vigil, with the blessing of Saint James.

Another miracle story attests that Saint James respects the peasant pilgrim as well as the nobility. Rambert,[59] a peasant, was on the way to Compostela when he was punched in the face by a brutal horseman. He cried out, "God and Saint James help me!" Immediately the horseman's arm fell inert at his side; he begged the peasant to intercede with Saint James for him, and he finally rose from the ground healed.

Saint James is powerful even in the domain of Saint Peter, that is, in Italy. During a feud between two Italian cities, a horseman of the defeated army invoked the aid of Saint James in defending him from his pursuers. He then fulfilled his vow to go to Compostela with his war-horse to venerate his protector.[60]

Appropriately we end this consideration of miracle stories with one emphasizing that Saint James protects pilgrims who fall into the hands of Saracens no matter how far from Christendom they may be forcibly removed because the saint's power is universal on the sea, on the land, and repeatedly. All Saint James expects in return is that pilgrims come to his shrine in Compostela to express their gratitude. A citizen of Barcelona[61] beseeched Saint James to deliver him if ever he should fall into the hands of his enemies. When on the sea he was overtaken by Saracens, then sold as a slave, but no sooner were his chains put on than they were shattered. Thirteen times he was compelled to go on slave marches—in Slavonia, Turkey, Persia, India, Ethiopia, Egypt, and Barbary. Finally, he escaped only to run aground at Almeria where a Saracen put him in double fetters. Once again he invoked Saint James, and his bonds broke apart. Holding in his hand a piece of chain, he then started on the way to Compostela through lands held by the Saracens but escaped all the dangers. Finally he was encountered by the narrator of the story between Estella and Logroño. This and all the Jacobite miracle stories end with the refrain from Psalms 118:23, *A Domino factum est istud et est mirabile in oculis nostris.*[62]

One has to acknowledge how very persuasive this set of advertisements was for recruiting pilgrims to Compostela. Saint James was shown to be greater than his saintly rivals en route, whether Saint Léonard, Saint Gilles, Saint Martin, or Saint Nicholas. His powers were effective thousands of miles away from Compostela, but he expected their grateful recipients to acknowledge them at his shrine. If their vows were not kept, they would be bereft of his supernatural aid or even punished by him. Pilgrims came to him from all over France and, of course, Spain, but also from Germany, Italy, and Greece. They were always protected by their patron saint, however fearsome the dangers, as soon as they invoked the name of Saint James. He conquered Saracens as *Matamoros*. He healed the seriously ill, whether of body or of mind. He restored the dead to life. He brought life to barren wombs. He vindicated pilgrims exploited by scoundrels of innkeepers. He inspired richer to help poorer pilgrims and the young and strong to help the old and weak. He sustained pilgrims on land and on sea, and was as ready to help the peasant as the noble. Saint James even anticipated the objection that he appeared to have changed character from being a fisherman to being a Moor slayer by insisting that he was a thoroughly up-to-date medieval knight. But, above all, he was an effective intercessor. Once he acted with power delegated by the Virgin and often with power delegated by Christ. But in Saint James's claim of the right to absolve the most heinous of sins, in his walking on the water in a storm, in his resurrecting the dead, and in his driving out demons, he seemed to have replaced Christ as *alter Christus*. Altogether he was represented as invincible over Saracens, demons, all kinds of suffering, and even over mankind's two worst enemies—the devil and death.

With such a protector no wonder the pilgrimage to his shrine prospered. The legendary Saint James is himself the ultimate answer to our question about why one should go to Compostela. Moreover, there is a sense in which Saint James could be said to be a truer pilgrim than many of the saints: his tomb was situated far from his homeland, for he was buried as a wanderer, and that is what a pilgrim is. He was both an exile from his native land and an exile from his celestial home. He is thus the preeminent pilgrim-saint.

NOTES

1. Américo Castro, in *The Structure of Spanish History*, tr. Edmund L. King (Princeton, N.J.: Princeton University Press, 1954), pp. 130–31, says that "in spite of all that has been written about Santiago of Compostela, we continue to wonder how such an event was possible, because Galicia was completely lacking in importance, and because the miracle of the finding of the body of Santiago in Galicia would seem to have only a local authority and be rejected as illegitimate when it came to be known outside Spain." Yet this did not happen in actual fact. Castro believed that the legend took hold because popular opinion confused James the Greater with James the brother of Jesus (the likeness is clearly to be seen in the reliefs of Christ and Saint James the Greater on the Portico del Gloria in the cathedral of Compostela), and identified Jesus and his brother with the earlier sky deities, Castor and Pollux, one of whom descended to earth to help humanity. These confusions may well have formed part of folklore, but the identification of the pagan deities with Christ and his brother James seems improbable to us because we know of no claims that Jesus and James were heavenly *twins*, like Castor and Pollux. Also, although James becomes a "thunderer" from being merely a *Boanerges* in the Gospel, it hardly makes him a Jove. More convincing, with documentary proofs, is Castro's contention that pontifical claims on the part of the bishops of Compostela from A.D. 954 onward are correlated with imperial claims on the parts of the kings of Galicia, the Asturias, and León. See also A. López Ferreiro, *Historia de la iglesia de Santiago de*

Compostela 11 vols. (Compostela: Imp. del Seminario conciliar central, 1898–1909), II, pp. 482–83.

2. In his *Convivio* Dante refers to the galaxy thus: "that is, the white circle which the common people call the way of Saint James." Behind this, however, was the legend of Charlemagne's dream in which Saint James himself is supposed to have directed the emperor to the importance of Galicia, and to the Milky Way as the future path of multitudes of pilgrims menaced by the Muslims. This dream is commemorated in the royal chapel of Aachen (Aix-la-Chapelle), Charlemagne's capital, in a vivid Romanesque relief reproduced in Vera and Hellmut Hell, *The Great Pilgrimage of the Middle Ages* (German original, Tübingen: Wasmuth, 1964; English tr., London: Barrie & Rockliff, 1966).

3. L. Vázquez de Parga, J. M. Lacarra, J. U. Riú, *Las peregrinaciónes a Santiago de Compostela*, 3 vols. (Madrid: Escuela de Estudios Medievales, 1948–49), I, pp. 20–21. It is worth noting, however, that the three major Western Christian pilgrimage centers were popular at different times. According to the erudite E.-R. Labande in *Spiritualité et vie littéraire des XIe et XIIe siècles* (London: Variorum Reprints, 1974), p. 167, Rome predominated in the tenth, Jerusalem in the eleventh, and Compostela in the twelfth century. He adds, however, that this is an impression rather than a certitude.

4. Joan Evans, in *Life in Medieval France* (London: Phaidon, 1957), pp. 74–75, wrote: "The shrine of St. James of Compostela became the goal of a pilgrimage under arms. . . . Pilgrim and crusader were one and the same, the one defended himself, the other attacked his enemies in order to reach the goal." She adds that they had the same rallying cry, *Sus eja! Ultreja!*, and that the Crusaders set out on the first stage of the journey unarmed and in pilgrim's garb.

It should also be recalled that in the chronicles of the period the Crusaders were called pilgrims, for the cross they bore on their shoulder was the sign of a solemn vow they had made. Their contemporaries made almost no distinction between armed and pacific pilgrimages. See J. Madaule, B. Luc, G. Gaillard, and Abbé Branthomme, *Pèlerins comme nos pères: retour à Saint Jacques* (Saint-Mandé: La Tourelle, 1950), p. 16.

5. Several French Benedictine monks came to Spain or Portugal to support the Compostela pilgrimage and the *reconquista;* some are referred to in our chapter 6. See Jean Secret, *Saint Jacques et les chemins de Compostelle* (Paris: Horizons de France, 1957) for an excellent correlation of the links between the small kingdoms of Spain and the Cluniac and Cistercian houses, as also those of the Augustinian canons. The list is impressive. The daughter abbeys of Cluny on the way to Compostela included Moissac, Vézelay, Saintes, Saint Jean d'Angély, La Sauve-Majeure, Conques, Saint Pons-de-Thomières, Saint Gilles, Saint Victoire de Marseilles, and Saint Pé-de-Bigorre. Also the following abbeys and priories of the Benedictine rule were founded in Aragon, Navarre, and Castille: Leyre, Hirache, Silos, Burgos, Fromista, Carrion, and Sahagún.

Credit for the fame of the pilgrimage is not to be attributed solely to the efforts of Cluniac monks and Augustinian canons, or of the later Cistercians and Premonstratensians from France. Spain made its own considerable contributions through Visigothic monasteries that antedated the Cluniac impact, the bridge-building hermits, and the royal supporters of the *reconquista*, as well as through the orders of chivalry both from Spain from and beyond the Pyrenees.

6. The competing pilgrimage to Rome (where could be found the relics of Saint Peter in Saint Peter's, Saint Paul in Saint Paul-outside-the-Walls, and at various times the relics of the apostolic saints, Bartholomew, James the Less, Simon, Jude, Andrew, and Matthias) was seriously threatened by Saracens in the Alpine passes in the tenth century. This was to Compostela's advantage, as Saint Mayeul, abbot of Cluny, learned to his cost in returning from Rome in 972. As Rome's popularity diminished, the vogue for Jerusalem and Compostela grew. See Raymond Oursel, *Les pèlerins du moyen âge: les hommes, les chemins, les sanctuaires* (Paris: A. Fayard, 1963), pp. 29–30.

7. The only modern biography based on the *Historia Compostellana* commanded by Diego Gelmirez and reproduced in *España sagrada*, Vol. 20 (Madrid: Rodriguez, 1775), is that of Anselm G. Biggs, *Diego Gelmirez, the First Archbishop of Compostela*, (Washington, D.C.: Catholic University of America Press, 1949). The brilliance, organizing gifts, and ambition of Gelmirez, as a bishop and then archbishop, are evident.

8. Biggs, *Diego Gelmirez*, p. 156; Castro, *Structure of Spanish History*, p. 134; J. S. Stone, *The Cult of Santiago* (New York: Longmans, 1927), p. 208; Marilyn Stokstad, *Santiago de Compostela in the Age of the Great Pilgrimages* (Norman: University of Oklahoma Press, 1978), p. 100.

9. Jonathan Sumption, *Pilgrimage: Image of Medieval Religion* (London: Faber & Faber, 1975), p. 109.

10. The Transfiguration is related in Matthew 17:1–13, Mark 9:2–13, and Luke 9:28–36; and the Agony in Matthew 26:36–46.

11. Mark 3:17.

12. As reported in the Acts of the Apostles 12:2.

13. One of the most notable cases of theft is that of the relics of Saint Foi now at Conques in Rouergue. Her body was stolen in 866 from the neighboring Benedictine monastery of Agen by a monk named Arisviscus who had been delegated for that purpose. See G. Gaillard, M.-M. S. Gauthier, L. Balsan, A. Surchamp, *Rouergue roman* (Yonne: Zodiaque, 1963), pp. 87–88. The euphemism by which the theft was disguised was a "furtive translation." The occurrence was not uncommon. See Patrick Geary, *Furta Sacra: Thefts of Relics in the Central Middle Ages* (Princeton, N.J.: Princeton University Press, 1978).

14. Pierre David, *Etudes sur de livre de saint Jacques attribué au pape Calixte II*, 4 vols. (Lisbon: Institut français des études portugaises 1945–49), I, pp. 2–3; and L. Duchesne, "Saint Jacques en Galice," in *Annales du Midi*, April 1900. See also García Villada, *Historia eclesiástica de España*, 3 vols. in 4 (Madrid: Compañía Ibero-Americana de Publicaciones, 1929), I, pp. 26–79.

15. Caesar, abbot of Montserrat, in the latter tenth century, considered having himself nominated as the metropolitan of Tarragon by the bishop of Santiago because this church was also an apostolic see founded by James the Greater, but the bishops of the province of Tarragon replied that Saint James had never come to Spain while living.

16. It appears in the charters of King Alfonso III (866–910), according to David, *Etudes sur le livre de saint Jacques*, p. 9.

17. Torquato de Sousa Soares, "Les bourgs dans le nord-ouest de la péninsule ibérique" in *Bulletin des études portugaises* IX (1943), cited ibid., p. 12. See Ferreiro, *Historia de la iglesia*, II, pp. 32–33.

18. The key passage in Latin is: "*VIIIº Kalendas augusti. Natale beati apostoli fratris Johannis evangeliste qui decollatus est ab Herode rege Hierosolymis ut liber Actium Apostolorum docet. Hujus beatissimi apostoli ossa ad Hispaniam translata et in ultimis earum finibus, videlicet contra mare Britannicum, condita celeberrima illarum gentium veneratione excoluntur.*"

19. This legend is printed in Lopez Ferreiro, *Historia de la iglesia*, III, Appendix III.

20. This is the elaborate version of the legend included in Stone's *Cult of Santiago*, p. 149, which is here summarized.

21. In the narration of this legend we have summarized the vivid account in Stone, ibid., pp. 172–73. The early accounts can be found in Rodrigo Jiménez de Rada, *De rebus Hispaniae*, in *Opera*, ed. M. D. Pecanes Pecourt (Valencia: Textes Medievales, 1968); and R. Menéndez Pidal, ed., *Primera crónica general de España*, 2 vols. (Madrid: Nueva Biblioteca de Autores Españoles, 1955) II, pp. 360–61.

22. Stone, *Cult of Santiago*, p. 181.

23. Secret in *Saint Jacques et les chemins*, p. 5, insists on this point, with documentation to support it: "*C'est que le culte des reliques jacobites ne doit point être séparé de l'idée de la croisade. C'est que Santiago symbolisa la reconquista de l' Espagne sur les Maures: croix contre croissant, Christ contre Mohamet.*"

24. As an anticipation of our liturgical analysis, it is worth noting that the *Codex Calixtinus* includes in Book I for the first vespers of the Feast of Saint James an antiphon (folio III vo. in ms., p. 193 in Whitehill's transcription) beginning: *Apostole Christi Iacobe, eterni regis miles invictimissime, qui in preclara apostolorum curia ut sol micans inter astra refulges in gloria* . . . which can be literally translated, "O James, apostle of Christ, most victorious soldier of the eternal king, in the distinguished court of the apostles, you shine as the sun amid the stars brilliant in glory." Since in the medieval heaven the sun shone with greater splendor than all other heavenly bodies, the metaphor implies the primacy of Saint James, the first martyr among the apostles. The *invictimissime* is at least a hint of the *Matamoros*. Another response at vespers of the vigil of the feast addresses Saint James as *O lux et decus Hyspanie, sanctissime Iacobe, qui inter apostolos primatum tenes, primus eorum martirio laureatus* . . . where the claim to primacy is explicit *(C.C.,* Whitehill transcription, pp. 211–12).

25.   God wished to honor Spain highly
                 when he sent the holy apostle there;
                 he gave Spain preference over England and France;

for you must know that no apostle is buried in all those lands.
A. Zamora Vicente, ed. (Madrid: Gredos, 1946) p.47, v.153

26. *Cult of Santiago*, p.146.

27. James was uncommonly loquacious in this vision; usually he is a "doer" of the word, not a talker, as recommended by his namesake who wrote the Epistle of James. Here we use Stone's translation of the speech but divested of the chivalric archaisms of his diction (ibid., p. 145).

28. Castro, *Structure of Spanish History*, pp. 159–60.

29. For a list of royal and saintly visitors, see Oursel, *Pèlerins*, pp. 35–36.

30. Saint Isidore (ca. 560–636) was archbishop of Seville, where he was born. Remarkable for his asceticism, his charity, and his encyclopedic learning, he was, in fact, only given the formal title of "Doctor of the Church" in 1722 but had virtually earned it much earlier, since the Eighth Council of Toledo named him *nostri saeculi egregius doctor*. His exhaustive works are found in *Patrologia Latina*, ed. J. P. Migne (Paris: Garnier, 1844–64), volumes 31–84. As compared with Saint James he had unquestionable Spanish connections and was a learned theologian.

31. In the eagerness of historians to do justice to the French Benedictines of Cluny and to acknowledge their contributions to both the *reconquista* and the Compostela pilgrimage, less justice has been done to contributions of the Augustinian canons and their imitators, who often staffed the cathedrals, while monks served the abbeys and priories. Augustinian canons maintained important stages on the way to Compostela, at Tours, Poitiers, Bordeaux, Toulouse, Blaye, Saint Léonard, Périgueux, Somport, Roncesvalles, and León. Moreover, they also provided hospitals and chapels attached to their churches for pilgrims (cf. Elie Lambert, *Etudes médiévales*, 4 vols. [Toulouse: Privat, 1956–57], I, p. 135). Further Giles Constable, in "The Study of Monastic History Today" in V. Mudroch and G. S. Couse, *Essays on the Reconstruction of Medieval History* (Montreal and London: McGill–Queen's University Press, 1974), p. 33, draws attention to the importance of early reformers among the Augustinian canons of Tours in their impact on monastic renewal, including the Blessed Hervé, an example of the "compenetration of strict canonical and monastic ideals."

32. Georgiana Goddard King, *The Way of Saint James*, 3 vols. (New York: Putnam, 1920), II, pp. 193–94, translates the account of Luke of Tuy, which we have summarized above. It is based upon J. M. Quadralo's *Asturias y León* (Barcelona: D. Cortezo, 1885), pp. 403–4.

33. See King, *Way of Saint James*, II, pp. 221–24; and Quadralo, *Asturias y León*, pp. 494–95. Sancha's epitaph is interesting. It reads: *Hic requiescit regina domina Sancia soror imperatoris Adefonsi filia Urrace regine et Raymundi. Hec statuit ordinem regularium canonicorum in ecclesia ista; et quia dicebat beatum Isidorum sponsum suum, virgo obiit era MCILIX pridie Kal Martii* (ibid., p. 494, cited by King, *Way of Saint James*, II, p. 193). The correlation of Isidore as "pontiff" with Alfonso as emperor *(imperator)* is worth observing: dynastic and ecclesiastical ambitions marched together.

34. This is reserved for fuller treatment in chapter 4.

35. Other notable "advertising" collections of miracles were those of Saint Gilles-du-Gard and Saint Foi of Conques, two very important shrines en route to Compostela.
The Guidebook itself (Book V of the *Book of Saint James* in the *Codex Calixtinus*) was another medium of advertisement and was by no means unique in the medieval world. Guidebooks to the Holy Land include the *Brevarius* (or, *Short Account of Jerusalem*) and *The Topography of the Holy Land* of Theodosius at the beginning of the sixth century; and the earliest version of the *Account of the Holy City*, by Epiphanius the Monk, was probably written early in the seventh century (cf. John Wilkinson, *Jerusalem Pilgrims before the Crusades* [Warminster: Aris & Phillips, 1978], pp. 1, 5, 7, 20, 79, 81).

36. Apart from the Whitehill transcription (I, pp. 250–87), it can be found as *Miracula sancti Iacobi* in *Acta sanctorum* (Paris, 1868), VI (July), pp. 47–58.

37. It is the only work attributed to Pope Calixtinus II both by Trithemius in his *De scriptoribus ecclesiasticis* and by Vincent of Beauvais in his *Speculum historiae*. It is significant that Armand du Mont, a monk of Ripoll, who made an extract from the *Codex* in 1173, chose to transcribe only the miracles section and that in its entirety and integrity. Medieval interest lay chiefly there, whereas modern interest lies in the Baedeker volume of how to get to Compostela, in what to see on the way, and to a lesser degree in the *Veneranda dies* and other sermons that shed light on the aims and difficulties of the pilgrimage. (See David, *Etudes sur le livre de saint Jacques*, II, pp. 47–48.)

38. For their derivation from other collections and provenance, see ibid., passim.

39. C.C. II, i, Whitehill, pp. 261–62.
40. C.C. II, xi, Whitehill, pp. 273–74.
41. C.C. II, xx, Whitehill, pp. 285–86.
42. In the case of the miracle attributed to Saint Gilles, the sinner was no less than Charlemagne. Cf. David, *Etudes sur le livre de saint Jacques*, p. 49. See also *The Golden Legend*, entry for September 1, for details of the story of Saint Gilles and the visit of Charlemagne as recorded by Jacobus de Voragine a century later than the *Codex Calixtinus*.
43. C.C. II, ii, Whitehill, pp. 262–63.
44. C.C. II, iii, Whitehill, pp. 268–69.
45. C.C. II, xvi, Whitehill, pp. 276–78.
46. C.C. II, iv, Whitehill, pp. 265–66.
47. C.C. II, xvii, Whitehill, pp. 278–82.
48. C.C. II, vii, Whitehill, p. 270.
49. C.C. II, viii, Whitehill, pp. 270–71.
50. C.C. II, x, Whitehill, pp. 272–73.
51. Saint Nicholas's connection with western Europe was as slight as that of the terrestrial Saint James with Spain. But when his bones were translated to Bari in Italy in 1087 he became an immensely popular saint of the sea and of voyaging pilgrims.
52. C.C. II, ix, Whitehill, pp. 271–72.
53. C.C. II, xix, Whitehill, pp. 283–85.
54. C.C. II, xxi, Whitehill, p. 286.
55. C.C. II, v, Whitehill, pp. 267–68.
56. C.C. II, vi, Whitehill, pp. 268–69.
57. C.C. I, xvii, Whitehill, p. 161.
58. C.C. II, xviii, Whitehill, pp. 282–83.
59. C.C. II, xiii, Whitehill, p. 274.
60. C.C. II, xv, Whitehill, pp. 275–76.
61. C.C. II, xxii, Whitehill, pp. 286–87.
62. "This is the Lord's doing and it is marvelous in our eyes."

——— 3 ———

Preparation for the Pilgrimage

LET us imagine that the would-be pilgrims, singly or in company, inspired by religious and secular motives, have heard of the protection and the miraculous powers of Saint James. They would also be lured by the splendor of his sanctuary at Compostela through the advertisement of some cleric who had read the *Book of Miracles* or by the excited reports of those who had returned with joy and gratitude from the saint's shrine. At this point they would prepare for the journey that would be a blend of holy days and holidays.

What form did that preparation take? If one was a member of a party led by a bishop (as was often the case in earlier days when Godescalc,[1] bishop of Le Puy, in 951 led his flock to Compostela and is today often the case of pilgrimages to Lourdes), or if it was a prince with his retinue, or a judicial pilgrimage under duress and supervision, then the entire responsibility would be undertaken by the leader. But if one went as a member of a family or as an individual, or even as one of a small group of friends, then preparation was necessary in five ways.

It was first of all essential for a layman in the feudal system to get permission of his liege lord to leave the neighborhood, to secure his wife's position and, if necessary, to nominate his heir. If one were a priest or a monk, permission would be required from one's bishop or abbot or prior, and similarly in the case of a nun, from her ecclesiastical superiors, though women pilgrims were discouraged.[2]

In earlier days intending pilgrims would go to a monastery to confess their sins, make their wills, deposit their valuables, and receive as a gift from the monastery the staff and wallet blessed by the abbot. The wealthy abbey of La Grande Sauve in Gascony even supplied a horse or a donkey to pilgrims.[3]

Second, when the permissions had been granted, most pilgrims from the eleventh century onward went to their village church, or to a neighboring abbey, or to the cathedral if part of a diocesan group where they brought the staff, wallet, and tunic of pilgrims. These were then blessed (see frontispiece), and the pilgrims themselves were commended to God's protection in a prayer for their safe return.

Third, some financial arrangements had to be made, unless one could count on begging one's way to Compostela, and this only became possible at the end of the tenth century and during the eleventh and subsequent centuries when travelers on the roads were fairly secure from the molestation by Saracens and robbers and travelers on the seas were secure from pirates. Then there were commanderies or fortresses, and the roads were patrolled by Hospitalers, Templars, and Knights of Saint James of the Sword. Strong bridges had been built across the rivers, and one could count on a chain of hospices for free lodging and board as well as on crowds of fairly affluent pilgrims from whom to beg for charity. The financial arrangements would depend on one's status: patrimony and savings if an individual, the support of a feudal overlord, one's membership in a corporation (as in a religious order or guild), or later in a confraternity, and circumstances of other kinds varying in each individual case.

The importance of making sound financial preparations was insisted upon by the Compostela guide: "If I rapidly recapitulate the previously mentioned towns and stages, it is so that the pilgrims leaving for St. James, being thus informed, can foresee the expenses in which their travels will involve them."[4] Sometimes the charges of the poor were paid from an impulse of genuine charity, though it could also include a degree of ostentation. Charity was probably the reason that Richard, the abbot of Saint-Vannes, brought along seven hundred in his train.[5] Ostentation played a considerable part in the magnificent retinue that marked the progress of the pilgrimage of two German bishops, Lambert de Hersfeld and Günther of Bamberg, through central Europe in 1065.[6] On the other hand, some persons of rank had to mortgage their lands to provide the expenses for pilgrimage. For example, Johan Sunason, a knight from Denmark, borrowed two hundred marks of silver from the abbey of Sorö before setting out for Jerusalem in 1197 and promised the monks land that would accrue to them should he die on the way, which in fact happened.[7] The pilgrim was expected to give generously of alms at the outset, to continue to give alms throughout the pilgrimage, and to make a generous gift at the center of pilgrimage. Otherwise there would be little point in the expectation that the *peregrinus* and the *pauper* might be equivalent terms.[8]

Fourth, the route would have to be planned with great care. This, again, would depend on one's starting point and whether one wished to go directly by the shortest route, or to divagate, taking in as many pilgrimage shrines as possible on the way; whether one wished to go all the way by road, or partly by sea and partly overland. The time and money available and how urgent was one's need of the aid of Saint James were also to be taken into account.

Information on the financing of the pilgrimage is difficult to obtain, partly because of the various contingencies involved, partly because of the change in circumstances of the pilgrimage through the centuries, and partly because of the paucity of the evidence available. Some masons, carpenters, painters, sculptors, artists, and artisans worked their way along the pilgrimage roads, creating what Kingsley Porter called "the pilgrimage style."[9] Tradesmen were often helped by members of their guild. Merchants were tempted to return from the pilgrimage with silks and spices and other costly commodities bought en route. We can be sure, however, that the poorer pilgrims had to rough it since they were entirely dependent upon alms and offers of free hospitality.

It was fortunate for the poor pilgrims that the Church encouraged the affluent to be generous to them. The godly poor as well as serious pilgrims were regarded as the most deserving cases of charity.[10] Charity was a highly valued medieval virtue, and the Christian society took with the utmost seriousness Saint Paul's eulogy of *caritas* as more valuable than either faith or hope.[11] The necessity for charity was stressed in sermons, in devotional literature (including hagiography and books of miracles), as well as in iconography on the churches of the routes to Compostela. The briefest sampling will make the point vividly.

Charity was frequently recommended in the celebrated sermon attributed to Pope Calixtus II that was to be read on the feast of the election of Saint James and the "invention," or finding, of his body in Spain (which was celebrated at Compostela but rarely elsewhere on December 30), known as the *Veneranda dies [gaudeamus]*. The congregation was reminded forcefully that Christ admonished the wealthy man who wished to be perfect in this way: "Go and sell all you have and give it to the poor and follow me,"[12] that the true pilgrim is one who dispenses generosity to the needy,[13] and just as all good things are born of charity so do all vices spring from greed.[14] In our last chapter we mentioned how central in the life of Saint Martin of Tours was his extraordinary charity. This was, we recall, the saint who though neither an apostle nor a martyr but a confessor was *the* patron saint of France in the fifth and succeeding two centuries. Even as late as the end of the thirteenth century, his generosity was celebrated in the passage in *The Golden Legend* of Jacobus de Voragine,[15] and the division of his cloak and sharing of it with a beggar was narrated on his feast day on November 11 each year. This symbolic event is depicted on the famous capitals of the cloister of Moissac erected in 1100, perhaps the leading daughter house of Cluny on the route to Compostela.[16] On the right side of the famous portal of Moissac, depicting the elders of the Apocalypse adoring Christ in glory, is a persuasive reminder of the consequences of charity and miserliness. On the upper register this masterly sculpture depicts in the left panel Lazarus the poor man resting happily in Abraham's bosom in heaven, while in the right panel he is seen languishing, as he did on earth, while the miserly rich man stuffs himself like a hog with viands. On the lower register in the right panel we see the rich man dying surrounded by demons and in the left panel tormented in hell.[17] It was a pointed reminder of the eschatological fate and state, as also of the Gospel's reversal of human estimation. It is also intriguing that among the pathetic ruins of the ancient basilica of Saint Martin of Tours there has recently been identified a mural of Saint George distributing alms to the paupers,[18] as if to imply that the patron Saint Martin was not the only saint to encourage charity. Many other examples of iconography inculcating charity on the way to Compostela might also be given. Suffice it to state that it was emphasized in sermons and on stones.

Wealthier persons could afford to pay their own way or in some cases even partly earn their way. This would be the case with tradesmen or entertainers who combined business with piety and pleasure. It is very likely also that certain artists as well as musicians and acrobats contributed their skills in carving or mural painting to shrines en route even though such work slowed down their progress toward their shrine of pilgrimage.

Persons who were seriously ill or infirm must have had acute difficulties in finding transportation, and they must in most cases have sought the nearest pilgrimage centers presided over by thaumaturgical saints. They would require a donkey or if desperately weak a litter, carriage, or cart, and these with the requisite horse could only be provided by a wealthy patron of a poor man or woman. In some cases a sick person would be carried on the back of a healthy man.

As we have reported, it is difficult to obtain information about the costs of pilgrimage until the very late Middle Ages. It is, however, easier to learn about the permissions required (including the passports necessary if one were leaving one's own country, as all French and English pilgrims to Compostela did). Such information is plentifully available especially after the pilgrimage to Spain became popular since laws regulating such matters and written accounts were kept.[19] But since it is more of a bothersome necessity than a delight to read about pilgrimage preparations, this chapter will concentrate on the two most important aspects of preparation.

These are, to our mind, the blessing of the Church on the pilgrims and their equipment, including the consideration of their symbolical meaning, and the decision about whether to take a sea route or to take one of the four major land routes to Compostela through France with a view to visiting the important shrines and hospices on the way. A formula for the blessing of pilgrims and an explanation of the symbolism of the apparel and equipment of pilgrims can be found in the famous *Veneranda dies* sermon in Book II of the *Codex Calixtinus* of Compostela and in various "uses" of the Roman rite that became standard in the West after 1080 and that offer slight but occasionally significant modifications. The information on the four major routes through France and the way through northwest Spain is described in some detail as it was seen by a mid-twelfth-century monk in Book V of the *Codex Calixtinus*, especially in the part titled *De viis sancti Jacobi*.[20] Apart from the absence of maps and of town plans and of the exact distances between stages, it is the medieval equivalent of a modern French *Guide Michelin*, an English AA or American AAA guide, or a German Baedeker.[21]

The author of the *Veneranda dies* sermon insists that each would-be pilgrim must be thoroughly prepared to be reconciled before departure. This involved making amends to all whom he had injured, and confession of (and where possible, reparation for) all activities of which his conscience accused him, as well as gaining the approval of his wife, his parish priest, and any other person to whom he was obligated. He must aim at sanctity in his pilgrimage, practicing generosity and other good works, so that he may begin with a good conscience.[22]

In the fifth place, one had to decide when to go. This was usually dictated by a combination of two factors: the natural and the liturgical seasons of the year. Winter was too cold and summer required work in the fields. Hence spring was the fittest season. The great religious festivals drew the faithful to the sanctuaries at Christmas, Easter, and Pentecost, as well as the feast day of the patron saint. Thus spring and Easter coalesced and were the most popular time. The *Historia Compostellana* tells how disturbed the clerical custodians of the sanctuary were when the number of pilgrims was only a trickle in winter and the offerings of wax so few that it was only with difficulty that the cathedral church would be illuminated. Indeed, this may be one of the reasons that at the end of the year the authorities devised a service for a feast of the "translation" or removal of the body of Saint James and the celebration of his being called by Jesus and of his evangelization of Spain—to give a reason for coming to Compostela in the cold months. If one were able to take in some of the feast days of the saints in pilgrimage centers en route to Compostela all the better, and the essential information was provided in the guide. If one were attending a local sanctuary, then it was preferable to go on the saint's day, for then the saint was greatly honored and likely to be propitious to the pilgrims. Also with a market and a fair it was an occasion of festivity.

The earliest surviving rite for blessing pilgrims is found in a pontifical of Germanic origin of the tenth century, namely that of the abbey of Saint Alban of Mayenne. This ceremony's importance was attested throughout the Middle Ages not only in liturgical texts, such as the Sarum Rite, but also in literary texts such as *chansons de geste*, chronicles, and romances. The blessings were simple ceremonies, usually taking place in a local parish church in which the pilgrims heard a Mass for their intention during which they confessed their sins and received absolution. They then knelt before the altar, prayers were chanted and psalms sung, and then the priest blessed and gave to each pilgrim the staff and the satchel, usually of leather, that was to be worn on the pilgrim's right shoulder.

The *Veneranda dies* sermon includes the formula with which the staff and wallet were blessed and handed over to the pilgrim. Handing over the *pera* (wallet, pouch, or satchel), the priest says, "In the name of our Lord Jesus Christ receive this wallet, the habit of your pilgrimage, so that being well chastened and amended you may deserve to reach the threshold of Saint James,[23] where you desire to go, and when your journey is finished you may return to us safe and with joy . . ." When the staff is handed to the pilgrim the formula of transmission is: "Receive this staff for the support of your journey and for the labor of your pilgrimage, so that you may be able to overcome all the hosts of the enemy and arrive safely at the threshold of Saint James, and when your journey is ended[24] you may return to us with joy . . ."[25]

The sermon continues by describing the different terms by which the *pera*, or wallet, is known in Italy, in Provence, and in other parts of France and then gives the symbolic significance of both wallet and staff.

The formulas of manducation are, however, only the bare bones of a significant rite of initiation. It is important to understand both the context of psalms and prayers as well as the ceremonial gestures in order to appreciate the full significance of the service of blessing the pilgrims. Some of the psalms and parts of the responses are taken from the venerable "Psalms of Ascent" that the ancient people of God, the Hebrews, sang as they climbed up the hills to Jerusalem as pilgrims to the Temple.[26] It is important to realize that the opening psalms and prayers are sung or said while the pilgrims in their distinctive habits lie prostrate before the altar of the parish church. This is therefore a most meaningful ceremony, reminiscent of that of the profession of a monk or nun or of the ordination to the priesthood or diaconate. The implication could not be plainer in the blessing, the distinctive uniform, and in the gesture of prolonged prostration that the pilgrim is entering into an order requiring a higher standard of obedience than hitherto. Nor should it be forgotten that in the earlier and austere days of pilgrimage, those going overseas and on the three long pilgrimages to Compostela, Rome, or

Jerusalem were given crosses that were sewn onto their garments, and that the tunic, wallet, and scrip all had holy water sprinkled on them. There was a definite sense of obeying Christ's demand that his true followers should take up their cross and follow him. Abnegation and even mortification were the intentions of the pilgrims and those who advised them to go.

The formulas are hardly changed in the Sarum "Use"[27] of England, except that obedience in the pilgrimage is stressed as a condition of blessing, and instead of the general and hallowed term for the destination, namely, "to the threshold of the saints" *(ad limina sanctorum)*, it reads "to the threshold of Saint James" in the pseudo-Calixtine sermon. The preliminary prayers of the rite clearly indicate the primary importance of salvation, which is walking in the ways of God, who is "the way, the truth, and the life."[28] One early manuscript of the Sarum Rite is called simply "a service for pilgrims" but another is entitled "an absolution for pilgrims," implying a clean start in life, almost a second baptism.[29] The prayers ask for the protection of God and for an escort of angels (thus presuming the existence of opposing demons, Satan's ministers, with whom they would do battle for the souls of pilgrims), and affirm the divine presence in the loneliest of places ("who are in no place far distant from them that serve thee");[30] while a closing prayer before the Mass that follows begs for the protection of the archangel Raphael.[31] This is again a reminder of the power of Satan and of the greater power of God's servants, for the book of Tobit records that the archangel Raphael bound Satan in the deserts of Egypt. Also, and this is appropriate for pilgrims, Tobit (12:12 and 15) affirms that Raphael hears the prayers of holy men and brings them before God. Such powerful intercessors as saints and archangels were needed for those undertaking so long and perilous a journey as the pilgrimage to Jerusalem, Rome, or Compostela.

Another significant ceremony in the rite of pilgrimage was one that emphasized humility and possibly also obedience through wearing the yoke of Christ symbolically accepted. This is the requirement that the kneeling pilgrim shall bend his or her neck so that the priest can place the strap from which the wallet is suspended around it. The rubric of manuscript A in the Sarum Rite reads: "Here place the wallet on the neck, saying . . ."[32] This central ceremony, shown in our frontispiece, is depicted in a French manuscript of the first half of the thirteenth century.[33] Four pilgrims are standing in a line and each carries a staff. The foremost pilgrim, a woman, has a hood on her head that falls down over her shoulders. She holds her staff in her left hand and bends her neck to receive the wallet, the band of which is held by the tonsured priest. Bent knees and bent neck perfectly illustrate the humility and obedience desired by and demanded of the true pilgrim. A male pilgrim in the background wears a broad-brimmed hat, a style that became fashion-able about this time, especially for pilgrims to Compostela. Significantly, a hand emerging from a cloud indicates the divine ratification in heaven of the terrestrial blessing. Unquestionably the entire service is an initiation into the order of pilgrimage—with distinctive tunic, staff, and wallet, and requiring a greater faith in God and deeper obedience to the demands of Christ in the hazards of the road, including the deceptive stratagems of demons.

An equally fascinating rite for the initiation of pilgrims is the *Liturgia de la peregrinación* in the Missal of Vich of the year 1038,[34] which is important because it antedates in Spain the imposition of the Roman liturgy. An admirable prayer immediately following the fraction in the Mass, begins, "O Eternal God, from whom to deviate is to die, and following whom to walk is to live," and continues to beseech God to lead the pilgrims in his way of truth, as the first pilgrims Abraham, Isaac, and Jacob were led, that by God's direction they may be fortified against all adversity, and proceed and return in integrity and joy, absolved from their sins.

The prayer for those going on a journey is reminiscent of the Roman rite in its plea to so order the journey for salvation that amid all the chances and changes of this life God's help will always protect. A later prayer for those journeying has a vivid account of the dangers and joys anticipated en route: "Be to them, O Lord, a defense in danger, a port in shipwreck, a diversion in the journey, a shade in the intense heat, a light in darkness, a staff in carnal temptation, rejoicing in bitterness, consolation in sadness, security in adversity, and a warning in prosperity."[35] After such prayers a rubric indicates that the pilgrims now rising from the ground *(surgentes autem a terra)*, presumably where they have been prostrated before the altar all this time, will receive the wallet and the staff from the bishop or presbyter.

The formula of handing over the wallet and staff is much the same in the Sant Cugat ritual as in the Mass of Vich, which is not surprising since Sant Cugat was a Benedictine monastery affiliated with Cluny. However, its prayer for the pilgrims, a long and tender one, seeks the intercession of the blessed Mother of God, Mary, the blessed Julian, confessor and bishop, with all the saints, that God will be their leader and companion, that "no adversity may harm, no difficulty stand in the way, that all things may be prosperous and all healthy beneath God's right hand, that whatever is sought in righteous petitions may speedily be effected."[36]

It should also be recalled that the juridical pilgrims or, properly, exiles like Cain (and many like him homicides) had their place in the liturgy of the church. Just as Cain pleaded with God, "I shall be fugitive and vagabond in the earth" and "everyone that findeth me shall slay me"

(Genesis 4:14) and was marked to prevent retribution, so was the penal pilgrim marked. The tau mark in Exodus, Ezekiel, and Revelation provided those bearing it with protection. Such signs were either branded on the pilgrim's skin or cut with the point of a sword upon the forehead or shoulder. Thus marked, and bearing chains into which were forged the weapons they had used to inflict injury or death, the penitential pilgrims appeared on Ash Wednesday before the bishop in his cathedral. There he put ashes on their foreheads and formally expelled them from the presence of the people of God. They were readmitted (unless they were perpetual exiles) only on Maundy Thursday after they had made their painful pilgrimage on foot to some distant shrine.

In the course of time the sheer utility of the pilgrim garb and equipment came to have a symbolic meaning often quite different from that of its origin in Genesis and Exodus. But at the beginning of Christian pilgrimage the staff, with its pointed metallic end, [37] was a useful crutch for the weary and sick, and a defense against the attacks of men or wild beasts. The wallet, usually made of soft leather, was also functional in origin, intended for carrying portable valuables as well as food and drink for the next stage of the pilgrim journey. The tunic was a coarse, strong, long, and easily washable garment of linen or sacking, with sleeves, over which a surcoat was worn. The hat, with its upturned broad brim, had in the mid–thirteenth century a long scarf attached to it that was wound round the body. This was a very effective guard against the searing sun of a Spanish summer or the piercing cold of the Pyrenees at all other seasons.

Piers the Plowman provides a vivid picture of a palmer, that is, a pilgrim who had been to the Holy Land (and, incidentally, as his scallop shell showed, to Compostela):

> Apparelled as a pagan, in pilgrim's guise
> He bare him a staff, with broad strip bound,
> That round it was twined like a woodbine's twist;
> A bowl and a bag he bare by his side;
> A hundred of vials was set on his hat,
> Signs from Sinai, Gallician shells;
> With crosses on his cloak, and the keys of Rome,
> And the Vernicle before, for that men should discern
> And see by his signs what shrines he had sought.
> Then fain would this folk know from whence he had come.
> "From Sinai," he said, "and the Sepulchre Holy,
> Bethlehem and Babylon, I've been in them both,
> Armenia, Alexandria, and other like places.
> Ye may see by the signs that sit here or my hat

> I have walked full widely, in wet and in dry,
> And sought out good saints for the health of my soul."[38]

Echoes of Compostela still resonate in the Elizabethan age. They are heard in Sir Walter Raleigh's famous poem:

> Give me my scallop shell of quiet;
> My staff of faith to walk upon;
> My scrip of joy, immortal diet;
> My bottle of salvation;
> My gown of glory (hope's true gage)
> And then I'll take my pilgrimage.[39]

They also resound in Shakespeare's *Hamlet:*

> How should I your true love know
> From another one?
> By his cockle hat and staff
> And his sandal shoon.[40]

The wallet and staff were, of course, the standard equipment of ancient pilgrims, including the Hebrews. It is most significant, however, that Jesus forbade the first twelve disciples and the later seventy or seventy-two whom he sent forth as representatives of the Kingdom of God to take staff, wallet, or money with them on their travels.[41] Evidently the closest followers of Jesus were to depend upon God to provide their hospitality. Also the immediacy with which they followed Christ, without making delaying excuses, indicated that they had severed worldly entanglements and proved the sincerity of their radical response to the Messiah.[42] Most important of all, such a trust in the sovereign power of a beneficent God was an imitation of Jesus who said that "the foxes have holes and the birds of the air have nests, but the Son of Man has nowhere to lay his head."[43] Jesus was the supreme pilgrim because he had neither house nor home and was always in transit and always directly dependent upon the providence of God to which he responded in complete trust. It is strikingly clear from the *logia* of Jesus that, however much they might hope to imitate Christ as pilgrims and live at a higher religious level than usual, most medieval pilgrims were, in actual fact, lowering the austere, otherworldly standards of pilgrimage Jesus had set for his supporters.

Our question is: did this not present a problem for the medieval Church? One attempt at a solution among many in the history of Western Catholicism was the founding of the orders of mendicant friars in the thirteenth century, thus providing one way of taking the radical and perfectionist demands of the Gospels with the utmost seriousness. But the ordinary folk with their family ties and duties could not live like the Franciscans and Dominicans by begging for alms. In any case, most of the friars mitigated the rules of their founders and followed the monks in refusing personal but using corporate possessions. In any case, it was not practical to demand such conditions for pilgrims who were going on long journeys through relatively uninhabited regions.

The writer of the *Veneranda dies* sermon is, however, most anxious to remind his hearers that Jesus was the supreme pilgrim. "Our Lord Jesus Christ himself," he declares, "after he rose from the dead appeared first as a pilgrim returning to Jerusalem."[44] The sermon reminds the hearers that Christ was only recognized as Lord when he broke bread, and this is applied to the pilgrim to mean that "while a happy pilgrim feeds the poor he is recognized by the Lord."[45]

The sermon also provides an allegorical meaning for the wallet (or pouch) and the staff. The pouch is the emblem of pilgrimage because, being made from the hide of a dead animal, it signifies that the pilgrim must mortify his flesh. It is also the emblem of almsgiving because it has no firm fastening and so symbolizes the ready giving or receiving of alms, as pilgrims all depend upon charity whether as givers or recipients. The staff of the pilgrim is used for driving off wolves and dogs, representing the snares of the devil. It is also the third leg of the pilgrim, symbolizing the Holy Trinity and therefore, in consequence, stands for the combat of the Triune God against the hosts of evil.[46]

We must conclude that the developing allegorical interpretation of the equipment of pilgrimage, the wearing of a distinctive uniform, the solemn rite of initiation with its gestures of humility and obedience resembling the profession of a monk or nun or the ordination of a priest, all signified entering upon a new status for the pilgrims and a higher type of religious duty and moral behavior. It is almost as much as to say that pilgrimage offered, as hitherto only martyrdom had, a second baptism, another chance to enter heaven. One significant indication of the high estimation in which pilgrimage was held as a secure path to salvation is that on the half drum carved over the west door of the cathedral of Autun by Gislebertus, which depicts the Last Judgment and the weighing of souls, the only three figures who are not naked (and do not need to be weighed) are two pilgrims, who have died on pilgrimage, and a monk. The pilgrims still have their wallets, the one bearing the cross of Jerusalem and the other the scallop shell given to those who have reached the shrine of Saint James. Even if one could not count on immediate entry to heaven after death, yet as a pilgrim to a distant shrine such as Jerusalem, Rome, or Compostela, one had increased one's fire insurance immeasurably.

When pilgrimage became popularized, routinized and commercialized, so that the holiday was more important than the holy day, this was, of course, no longer true. But whether the pilgrim received his or her blessing privately from the parish priest, or from a holy monk or hermit, or in a group led by the bishop in a cathedral, or, more commonly, in his parish church, anxious for the company of his family and friends in this new experience of liminality,[47] it was a solemn and soul-searching occasion.

It is likely that the provision of phrase books for travelers (and pilgrims) going through different nations and speaking various tongues, as on the pilgrimage to Compostela, was a late development,[48] although the pilgrim's guide (Book V, Chapter VII of the *Codex Calixtinus*) gives a list of fifteen Basque words with their Latin equivalents. But the planning of the route (or routes, if one were to return by another way) must have been undertaken in the earliest Christian pilgrimages.[49]

The fifth book of the *Codex Calixtinus* is a remarkably detailed guide for pilgrims to Compostela.[50] It was not compiled as every traveler's *vade mecum*, for the cost of having such a manuscript for one's personal use, to say nothing of its bulkiness, would have been quite prohibitive. Copies of it were in various monasteries (such as the one at Ripoll in Catalonia), and because of its augmentation by Aimery Picaud, the Poitevin monk whose admiration of his native countrymen was so pronounced, Cluny probably had a copy,[51] as did several of its dependencies. After all, it was at Cluny in Burgundy that Guido of Burgundy was elected pope and took the title of Calixtus II, reigning from 1119 to 1124, and to him the authorship of the entire *Codex* is attributed. Cluny's influence was profoundest in the mid–twelfth century when it had 314 dependent houses. Its church was then the largest in Europe.[52] It was, as we saw earlier, the Benedictines of the Cluniac reform who blazed the trail on the road to Santiago both in France and Spain, and almost wherever they were encountered in the medieval world, one or two of their dependencies are churches dedicated to Saint James, even including Saint James of the Butchery (Saint Jacques de la Boucherie) in Paris.

The pilgrim's guide, consisting of some thirteen thousand words, is devoted to the pilgrim's body and soul. It is physically a guide to the main routes, regions, and their customs, towns, potable or poisonous rivers, hostels, food, and drink. It is also a spiritual guide recommending the best sanctoral shrines that the pilgrims should visit on the four major roads through France and on the two major routes through northern and northwestern Spain. To elicit and sustain the interest of the pilgrim or his adviser (a *literatus*, which most pilgrims were not), he is informed about the life and heroic death of each saint whose bones lie beneath the altar of the church dedicated to the apostle, martyr, or confessor, as the case may be, in descending order of importance. He is told of the relics in each church, occasionally of the magnificent reliquaries in which they are contained, and of the effectiveness of each saint in curing ills, removing barrenness, or arranging for prisoners to be freed. Also, of almost equal importance (corresponding to a modern railroad or bus timetable), he is informed of sacred time—that is, when the feast day of each particular important saint en route is celebrated and thus when he or she is likely to be most propitious to those invoking the saint's aid. Also, there would almost certainly be a fair held on that day, so that sacred and secular motivations were appealed to simultaneously.

This combination of physical and spiritual, secular and sacred, is one of the outstanding qualities of the guide. The writer clearly is interested in good food and good wine, comfortable lodgings for both those who come on horseback and those who come on foot. He equally wishes to warn pilgrims against dangers on the way. He wants them to be prepared to make the eight-mile ascent of the Pass of Cize, to be on their guard not to wander off the road on the three-day trip through the Landes, below Bordeaux, where they might quickly find themselves up to their knees in the marshes, and to be careful of impassable rivers such as that at Sorde where pilgrims have been drowned, and to avoid lethal rivers such as that at Lorca where men and their horses have sickened and died. The spiritual and aesthetic values of the guide are found in the detailed descriptions of the splendid churches on the way to Compostela, their locations, size, monuments, relics, and history. The lengthy concluding section describes the destination, the basilica of Santiago de Compostela, with its solid silver and gilt offertory table in front of the high altar, its marvelous doors, altars, lamps, and impressive carvings of marble and stone. He insists upon the assurance that all pilgrims, poor and rich, will be welcomed for the love and glory of Saint James. The guide concludes: "Wherefore it must be known that the pilgrims of St. James, whether poor or rich, have the right to be received and looked after."[53]

Before describing the routes and the shrines on them, some account should be given of the biases of the writer or redactor of the guide. The primary religious aim of the pilgrim was prominent. Pilgrimage was clearly to be undertaken as a following in the footsteps of the most faithful followers of Christ and his Virgin Mother in order to reach heaven at the last. There was also a profound belief in the efficacy of the intercession of those saints who were honored by visits to their shrines, with benefits in the here and now as well as in the hereafter. The Benedictines on the four ways and the eighty-two canons of the rule of Saint Isidore were honored by the redactor for their generous hospitality. There was considerable French chauvinism evident and within France a proud provincialism about his native region of Poitou. This

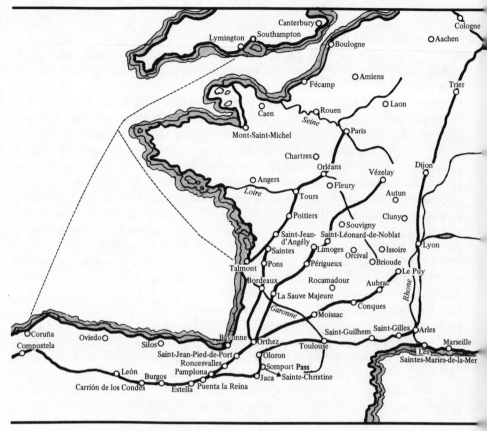

The Routes through France to Compostela.

was evident in the choice of routes (little or nothing is said of routes from Italy or the Low Countries or Britain, except a scathing reference to the Scots being as bad as the Basques). It was also evident in the treatment of Charlemagne's peers as saints and in the redactor's intense dislike of the barbarous Basques, with their vile tongue and vicious habits, and his denigration of the Gascons.[54] But the outstanding characteristic of the guide was its double appeal, religious and secular. So first, one senses that a pilgrimage encourages better stamina and health, good and varied food and wine, and social travel, and indulges curiosity about history and monumental art and architecture. But second, it also increases spirituality through devotion to the saints by attending Mass at their shrines, by learning hagiography without tears, by hearing sermons and miracle stories, and by singing psalms and hymns as well as cheering songs on the road. Nor should one forget the entertainment provided by acrobats, jugglers, troubadours, showmen, and dancers.[55] All this and heaven too! Fasting may be admired in a specialist like Saint Eutropius of Saintes, but it is the equivalent of "caviare to the general."

In its opening chapter the guide states that there are four ways that lead to the shrine of Saint James, all of which meet at Puenta la Reina. (Here the map should be consulted.) The first begins at Saint-Gilles-du-Gard in Provence and proceeds via Montpellier and Toulouse to the port of Aspe. The second goes from Saint Mary of Le Puy through Saint Foi of Conques and Saint Peter of Moissac. The third begins at Saint Mary Magdalene of Vézelay and goes by way of Saint Léonard of Noblat and the city of Périgueux. The fourth way starts at Saint Martin of Tours and continues through Saint Hilary of Poitiers, Saint Jean d'Angély, Saint Eutropius of Saintes, and the city of Bordeaux. The roads through Conques, Saint Léonard, and Saint Martin all join at Ostabat and having crossed the port of Cize link up with the road that has come through the port of Aspe.

In the course of time these routes would begin even further away. The Saint-Gilles road would begin at Arles by the shrine of Saint Trophime, with a link to Les Saintes Maries and Marseilles. The monks from Cluny could go either by way of Le Puy or via its pilgrimage shrine at Souvigny that joins the route from Vézelay. Vézelay itself was at the crossroads of routes from the German states and the way to Rome. Furthermore, the westernmost starting point, given by the guide as Tours, would link up with Orléans, the great Marian pilgrimage shrine of Chartres, and Saint-Denis near Paris, not to mention the pilgrimage center of Mont-Saint-Michel further to the northwest.

Pilgrims did not start only, as the guide might imply, from the sanctuaries of Saint-Gilles, Le Puy, Vézelay, and Tours. These were the assembly points of common departures. Even before the pilgrims reached these assembly points they would have found hospitals, churches, and confraternities of Saint James. Many pilgrims came from the north of France and from Flanders, as well as from Holland, Hungary, Germany, Sweden, Switzerland, and Italy. Among the most notable were Nicolas, bishop of Cambrai in 1153; in 1170 the Countess Sophia of Holland; in 1192 the archbishop of Liège; Henry and Leon the dukes of Saxony in 1190; and Princess Ingrid of Sweden in 1270.[56]

One third of the pilgrim's guide is devoted to chapter VIII entitled "the bodies of the saints resting on the way to St. James which are to be visited by his pilgrims."[57] While it was the main aim of the pilgrims to reach the shrine of Saint James, the first apostle of Christ to be martyred, it was obviously important to take in as many shrines of saints en route as possible, for they were intercessors and had great influence in the court of the King of Kings in heaven. In our chapter 4 we shall discuss the astonishing popularity of the veneration of the relics of the saints and the different styles and history of relics, their invention (in both the technical and commonsense meanings of that word) and translation, and their role in the life of the faithful. Here we need only consider which of the saints the pilgrim to Saint James was expected to visit and why.

First the pilgrim would visit the shrine of Saint Trophime of Arles on the Saint-Gilles route. He was thought to be the Gentile disciple of Saint Paul and traditionally the first bishop of Arles, but he is only mentioned for the first time in an epistle of Pope Zosimus to Bishop Patroclus of Arles in 417 as an early preacher of the Gospel sent from Rome to Gaul.[58] Highly revered in the Middle Ages, the saint was confused with the companion of Saint Paul, and his church still has a Romanesque cloister worthy of comparison with that of Saint Peter of Moissac. Thereafter on the same route saints Caesarius and Honoratus were to be venerated, both former archbishops of Arles, and the latter the founder of a great monastery of Lérins in which Saint Patrick, the apostle of Ireland, was trained. They are buried with Saint Genesius in a vast cemetery, the Alyscamps, with a thousand others. Saint Gilles was deserving of the highest honor in his own sanctuary, for, after the prophets and the apostles none of the saints was as worthy, more glorious, holier, or quicker to aid the pilgrim invoking him. He hastened to help the poverty-stricken and the suffering who cried to him. Immediately in the guide there follows a summary of his miracles including his ability to heal those bitten by serpents and even to calm a raging sea. The guide then points out, contrary to the claims of other monasteries or churches to have parts or the whole of the bodies of some of the saints, that there are only four saints on all of the routes to Saint James whose bodies have never been moved from their resting places. This is part of their greatness, for the relics of other saints were moved about to secure them from falling into the hands of Muslim infidels or pagan

Norsemen. These four great immovable saints are Saint Gilles-du-Gard, Saint Martin of Tours, Saint Léonard of Noblat near Limoges, and Saint James of Compostela. Those who continue on their way through Toulouse must visit the tombs of Saint William, one of the counts of Charlemagne, who fought against the Saracens and then became a hermit, and those of three martyrs in the Diocletian persecution—saints Tiberius, Modestus, and Florentia. In the same town could be found the body of Saint Saturninus, bishop and martyr, and over his tomb a vast church had been built which was served by Augustinian canons.

Pilgrims coming from Burgundy and Germany by the way of Le Puy must visit the most holy body of the blessed Saint Foi of Conques, virgin and martyr, which was guarded by Benedictines in her church. She helped many who were sick.

Then on the way to Compostela via Saint Léonard, the body of the most worthy Mary Magdalene at Vézelay must justly be venerated by pilgrims.[59] Her basilica is described as most beautiful *(pulcherrima)*, but there is no description of the splendid carving of Christ sending the Holy Spirit to the apostles at Pentecost, which is the glory of the church, while we get full details of the iconography of the tombs and altars at Saint-Gilles and Compostela. The writer of the guide seems to have been much more impressed with precious metals and jewels than with carvings in mere stone. Through Mary Magdalene's love, we are told, serious sins are forgiven, and the blind, the lame, and the deaf are cured.

Next the basilica of Saint Léonard at Noblat is to be visited on this route. Though of noble birth he gave up the delights of the court for the life of a hermit with its vigils, cold, nakedness, unending works, and fasts. His power to free captives is proven by the thousands of chains the liberated ones have left in his church. Then the pilgrim must proceed to Périgueux to visit the body of Saint Front, bishop and confessor. His, like Christ's, is a round sepulcher. Then on the way from Tours, reverting to Orléans, the pilgrims must not miss the wood of the True Cross and the chalice of Saint Evurcus, bishop and confessor, in the church of the Holy Cross. In the same town in the church of Saint Samson there is the genuine paten of the Last Supper.

At Tours there is the magnificent sarcophagus of Saint Martin, bishop and confessor, in his basilica. It is made of silver and gold and illustrates his miracles. The basilica is like that of Saint James at Compostela. Here according to the guide all types of sicknesses of body or mind are healed.

Next at Poitiers the most sacred body of Hilary, bishop and confessor, and defender of orthodoxy against the Arian heretics, is to be honored. Many miracles take place here at his sepulcher, which is radiant with precious metals and gems.

Then the venerable head of Saint John the Baptist at Angély is to be visited, where a choir of a hundred monks honors this relic with praises by day and by night. According to the guide it is proved to be the true head of the precursor of Christ by the fact that it escaped many perils on the sea when carried by holy men from Jerusalem, and it restored dead persons to life in its translation to land.

Next the body of Saint Eutropius, bishop and martyr, at Saintes is worthy of a visit by pilgrims, and the guide gives a summary of his *passio*. In addition to performing the usual thaumaturgical miracles, he can placate the divine judge at the Last Assize of history and lead us to the supernal kingdoms of the skies. Then at Blaye on the coast in the basilica of Saint Romanus there lies the body of blessed Roland, the martyr, who was slain at Roncevaux after entering Spain twelve times to fight the infidels. His ivory horn is kept at the church of Saint Severinus at Bordeaux. Saint Severinus was a bishop and confessor, and his body should also be visited. Then in the area known as the Landes the town of Bélin should be visited because there lie the bodies of the holy martyrs Oliver and the Christian kings who were his allies in the epic fight against the Muslims.

In Spain Dominic de la Calzada's body, in his town beyond Najera, should be visited for he was a confessor; also Saints Facundus and Primitivus, martyrs, whose basilica was erected at Sahagún by Charlemagne.[60] At León the body of Saint Isidore must be venerated, for he was a bishop, confessor, and learned doctor whose erudition instructed Spain and whose writings were an ornament of the whole Church.

The chapter ends, after insisting that the body of Saint James is worthy of the most enthusiastic veneration in the city of Compostela, with the pious wish that the previously mentioned saints, together with all the other saints of God may help us by their merits and their prayers, which are presented to Jesus Christ who, with the Father and the Holy Spirit, lives and reigns as God forever.

After a lengthy and detailed description of all the glories of the basilica of Saint James, the final chapter stresses that both poor and rich pilgrims are to be received and treated with eagerness and charity. It was an assurance to pilgrims and a timely reminder to their hosts and hostesses.

While some pilgrims would avoid both the high passes and the marshy Landes area below Bordeaux by taking ship thence to northwest Spain, and others might avoid the Alps by sailing from Italy to Marseilles, neither of the alternatives is mentioned in Book V of the *Codex*. Yet the relative frequency of marine miracles in the *Book of Miracles* suggests that these sea journeys were undertaken, often interrupted by great storms or the depredations of Saracen pirates.

From England, however, it was essential to cross the ocean, either going from Calais to Boulogne and taking the land route via Tours for the rest of the way, or as later became more convenient by embarking from a southern English port, for example, Plymouth, and disembarking at Coruña. William Way, a fellow of Exeter College, Oxford, and later a fellow of the new royal Eton College in Windsor, left a valuable manuscript of his pilgrimages to both the Holy Land and Compostela, which he visited in 1456.[61] He left Eton on March 27 and reached Plymouth on April 30. He waited for a ship until May 17 and the voyage took five days, reaching Coruña Friday, May 21, in the afternoon. A day later he had traversed the forty miles to arrive on the evening of Saturday, May 22, the eve of the feast. It is rare to receive such specific traveling information, but, unfortunately, it is a late, fifteenth-century account. It does, however, give evidence of the popularity of the Compostela pilgrimage at that time, because it says there were eighty ships, of which thirty-two were English, and the voyagers included English, Welsh, Irish, Normans, French, Bretons, and others.[62]

Travelers were crammed into the many ships going from England to Saint James, and there might have been from thirty to a hundred travelers in each. The discomfort, including seasickness in the Bay of Biscay, provided all the penance they needed. An amusing account of the sea trip in the fifteenth century is provided by one who is a versifier rather than a poet, but who enables us to share all the inconveniences of the voyage. He warns us that any seagoing pilgrim traveling by this route will have *mal de mer*, will be treated as obstacles in their way by the sailors, and will find shipboard odors unpleasant.

> Men may leve alle gamys
> That saylen to Seynt Jamys!
> Ffor many a man it gramys [annoys]
>   When they begin to sayle.
>
> Ffor when they have take the see,
> At Sandwych or at Wynchylsee,
> At Bristow, or where that thi bee,
>   Theyr hertes begyn to fayle.

The pilgrims had little desire to eat, and this the captain expected:

> Some are lyke to cough and grone
> Or hit be full mydnyght;

He then gives orders:

> "Hale the bowelyne! now, vere the shete!
> Cooke, make redy anon our mete,
> Our pylgryms have no lust to ete,
> I pray God yeve hem rest!"

As the ship was crowded and the voyage monotonous, some attempted to read, but unhappily:

> Som layde theyr bookys on theyr kne,
> And rad so long they myght nat se;—
> "Allas! myne hede wolle cleve on thre!" [split in three]

A sarcastic sailor would then make a wisecrack:

> Then cometh oone and seyth, "Be mery;
> Ye shall have a storme or a pery." [squall]

And for most of the voyage

> Thys mene whyle the pylgryms ly
> And have theyr bowlys [basins, not bowels] fast theym by,
> And cry after hot malvesy.[63]

It is not in the least surprising that the shorter local pilgrimages by land were preferred. One has only to compare this sea voyage with the happy-go-lucky jaunt of the Canterbury pilgrims leaving the Tabard Inn at Southwark "the holy blisfull martyr for to seke."

Nevertheless, an essential part of the preparation for a long and tough pilgrimage was negative, monitory, and dissuasive. Compostela was a penance, while Canterbury (or any other local pilgrimage) might be only a pantomime.[64]

NOTES

1. See Georgiana Goddard King, *The Way of Saint James*, 3 vols. (New York: Putnam, 1920), I, p. 98; Elie Lambert, *Etudes médiévales*, 4 vols. (Toulouse: Privat, 1956–57), I, p. 127; Jean Secret, *Saint Jacques et les chemins de Compostelle* (Paris: Horizons de France, 1957), p. 30; and L. Vázquez de Parga, J. M. Lacarra, J. U. Riú, *Las peregrinaciónes a Santiago de Compostela*, 3 vols. (Madrid: Escuela de Estudios Medievales, 1948–49), I, pp. 39, 41–42.

2. So much was this the case that the determined woman would sometimes dress as a man. Saint Hildegonde reached Jerusalem in 1188 disguised in menswear (P. A. Sigal, *Les marcheurs de Dieu* [Paris: Colin, 1974], p. 44; see also chapter 7, note 17).

3. King, *Way of Saint James*, I, pp. 91–92. Whether a pious or a technically penitential pilgrim, each was required to make his will before departure, as one who was dead to this world. Margery

Kempe, Guillaume de Deguileville, Sir Richard Guylforde, and many others did so. Then exempt from taxes and tolls, except those that might be exacted from Byzantine or Muslim authorities, they were also freed from feudal obligations. The pilgrims now owed only to God and his saints.

4. *Idcirco has villas et praefatas dietas perscriptione restrinxi ut peregrini ad Sanctum Jacobum profiscentes expensas itineri suo necessarias sibi, haec audientes, premeditari, studeant* (Codex Calixtinus, final paragraph of Book V, chapter III, in the Fita-Vinson transcript, p. 7).

5. *Acta Sanctorum*, III (June), p. 469.

6. *Monumenta Germaniae historica*, S.S., V, 168; L. de Herfeld, *Annales*. Bishop Gunther of Bamburg is said to have left with 7,000 to 12,000 pilgrims in his train in 1064 (Sigal, *Les marcheurs de Dieu*, p. 50).

7. Paul Riant, *Expéditions et pèlerinages des scandinaves en Terre Sainte* (Paris: Lainé & Havard, 1865), pp. 299–300. This and the previous three references are listed by E.-R. Labande in *Spiritualité et vie littéraire des XIe et XIIe siècles*, Article XIV (London: Variorum Reprints, 1974), pp. 167–69.

8. Furthermore, it should be remembered that before the advent of capitalism, avarice was considered a capital sin in the Middle Ages, and poverty was the virtue of those emancipated from worldliness rather than a cause for shame. Those who preached poverty, such as the followers of Saint Francis of Assisi, himself a pilgrim to Compostela, followed to the very letter the teaching of Christ that "it is easier for a camel to go through the eye of a needle than for a rich man to enter the kingdom of heaven." The tenth- and eleventh-century "poor" pilgrims were distinguished from the Crusaders of the same period not only by their peaceableness but by their indifference to personal gain. The Crusaders were not averse to combining adventure and plunder with holy ferocity (see E. B. Mullins, *The Pilgrimage to Santiago* [London: Taplinger, 1974], pp. 53–54).

9. A. K. Porter, *Romanesque Sculpture of the Pilgrimage Roads*, 10 vols. (Boston: Marshall Jones, 1923). This contention is now controverted, on the grounds of the variety of pilgrimage styles and their provenance. Also, while Porter argued for the priority of Spanish influence, many French art and architectural historians argue for the priority of French influences on the iconography and shape of ecclesiastical buildings on the pilgrimage roads. One suspects in these evaluations the unconscious impact of national one-upmanship!

10. See Jonathan Sumption, *Pilgrimage: An Image of Mediaeval Religion* (London: Faber & Faber, 1975), p. 207.

11. I Corinthians 13:1–13, especially 13:13.

12. *Si vis perfectus esse, vade et vende omnia que habes et da pauperibus et sequere me* (Codex Calixtinus [henceforth, C.C.] I, xvii, Whitehill transcription, p. 156).

13. *Sed quem dispergit egenis largitas diligit* (C.C. I, Whitehill, p. 152).

14. *Sicut ex caritate omnia bona nascuntur, sic ex cupiditate cuncta vicia oriuntur* (ibid., p. 169).

15. Translated and adapted by Granger Ryan and Helmut Ripperger (New York: Arno Press, 1969), p. 664.

16. According to Emile Mâle, in his *L'art religieux du XIe siècle en France* (Paris: Colin, 1924), p. 4, one of the greatest monuments of medieval France.

17. M. Vidal, J. Maury, and J. Porcher, *Quercy roman*, 2d ed. (Yonne: Zodiaque, 1969), plate 22, provides a photograph of the low relief.

18. Charles Lelong, *Touraine romane*, 3d ed. (Yonne: Zodiaque, 1977), p. 65, and plate 7.

19. For English permissions see J. J. Jusserand, *English Wayfaring Life in the Middle Ages*, rev. ed. (London: Unwin, 1925), pp. 369–70. Special "leave of the king" or "licences" were necessary and could only be obtained at certain ports.

20. The transcription of the Latin of the Book V of the *Codex Calixtinus* we are using is that of F.-J. Fita and J. Vinson, *Le codex de saint Jacques de Compostelle* (Paris, 1888), pp. 2–63.

21. Although the guide does not provide exact distances, it gives some rough idea by indicating for northern Spain and the approaches how far pilgrims may be expected to travel for a stage between two towns. Chapter II lists the stages and chapter III the cities for overnight stops. If one approaches from Somport, then overnight stops can be made at Jaca, Monreal, and Puenta la Reina. If one approaches from the pass of Cize, the stages are Viscarret, Pamplona, and Estella, where one joins the previous route. The remaining stages to Compostela are Najera, Burgos, Fromista, Sahagún, León, Rabanal del Camino, Villafranca, Triacastela, Palas de Rey, and, finally, Compostela. Hence from the Pyrenees passes there are thirteen stages. We know that some travelers from Liège made the journey to Compostela and back in thirty-six days in 1056 beginning on April 7 and reaching home on May 13 (Sigal, *Les marcheurs*, p. 65). But the intervals between stops in Spain were shortened with the guide, probably to encourage would-be pilgrims.

22. *C.C.* I, Whitehill, p. 157.

23. The Sarum Rite reads instead, more generally, *"ad limina sanctorum"* ("to the threshold of the saints"). The same change is made in the second formula for handing over the *baculum,* or staff.

24. Significantly, the Sarum "Use" adds the adverb *obediencie* or "obediently" since some pilgrims were presumably mere wanderers or worse, outlaws.

25. *C.C.* I, Whitehill, p. 152. The Latin of this important passage reads: *In nomine domini nostri Ihesu Christi, accipe hanc peram habitum peregrationis tue, ut bene castigatus et emendatus pervenire mearis ad limina sancti Iacobi quo pergere cupis, et peracto itinere tuo ad nos incolumnis cum gaudio revertaris, ipso prestante qui vivit et regnat Deus per omnia secula seculorum. Amen. Item cum baculum ei damus, sic dicimus: Accipe hunc baculum sustentacionem itineris ac laboris ad viam peregracionis tue, ut devincere valeas omnes catervas inimici, et pervenire securus ad limina sancti Iacobi, et peracto cursu tuo ad nos revertaris cum gaudio, ipso annuente qui vivit et regnat Deus per omnia secula seculorum. Amen.*

26. The "Psalms of Ascent" are nos. 120–34. The term applied to them may refer to the "lifting up of the heart" or to the "going up" of the Jews to Jerusalem from Babylon after the Exile, or to the "going up" of pilgrims to Jerusalem for annual festivals, or to the fifteen ascents, or steps, from the Women's Court to that of the Men in the Temple area. Middoth 2:5 describes these steps as "corresponding to the fifteen songs of ascents in the Psalms," implying that one was sung on each step (see F. L. Cross, ed., *The Oxford Dictionary of the Christian Church,* corrected imprint [London: Oxford University Press, 1863], s. v. "Gradual Psalms, The"; see also C. C. Keet, *A Study of the Psalms of Ascent* [London: Mitre, 1969]).

27. For a critical edition, see *The Sarum Missal Edited from Three Early Manuscripts,* J. Wickham Legg, (Oxford: Clarendon Press, 1916). A fairly literal translation, with modernized rubrics, is provided in *The Sarum Missal in English* (London: De La More Press, 1911), and the "Order for Pilgrims" is found on pp. 166–73. The Sarum Rite is possibly founded in part on the offices compiled by Saint Osmund, bishop of Salisbury (1017–99), but more probably on the revision undertaken by Richard Poore, dean and bishop of Salisbury (1198–1228), under whose direction the diocesan headquarters was moved from (Old) Sarum to Salisbury. A further revision took place in the fourteenth century. The "Use" of Sarum, or Salisbury, is the local medieval modification of the Roman rite used in the cathedral church of Salisbury. It was the "Use" of most other dioceses in England and in 1457 was said to be the "Use" for almost the whole of England, Wales, and Ireland.

28. John 14:6.

29. Legg, *Sarum Missal,* p. 451: *absolucio peregrinorum* in the B. Ms.

30. Ibid., p. 452: *Et a servientibus tibi nulla est regione longinquus.*

31. Ibid., p. 453.

32. *Hic impone peram collo ita dicens.* Manuscript B reads: *Hic impone singulis collo peram dicendo.* Both rubrics will be found ibid., p. 452.

33. Ms. Lat. 11560 of the Bibliothèque Nationale, Paris. The illustration enclosed in a medallion appears on folio 97 verso, and has been reproduced in *La bible moralisée,* A. Laborde, ed. (Paris: Société des bibliophiles français, 1912), II, plate 32 (reproduced in this volume).

34. This is Codex XLVIII (or in modern enumeration, ms. 66), fols. 56–58v. in the chapter library of Vich. It was printed in Vázquez de Parga, Lacarra, and Riú, *Peregrinaciónes,* III, pp. 145–47. It should also be compared with the *Ordo ad sportas dandas his qui peregrinandi sunt* of the *Rituale monasticum* of San Cugat del Vallès, now in the Royal Archives of Aragon, as ms. 72, fols. 23–24, which is printed in ibid., p. 148.

35. Fol. 57 verso in the original reads: *Esto eis, domine, in procincta deffensio, in naufragio portus, in itinere diversorium, in estu umbraculum, in tenebris lux, in lubrico baculus, in merore gaudium, in tristicia consolacio, in adversitate securitas, in prosperitate cautela.*

36. . . . *nichil nobis adversitatis noceat, nihil difficultatis obstat, cuncta sint prospera cuncte nobis salubria et sub ope dextere tue quicquid iusto petierimus desiderio celeri consequamur affectu* (ibid.). It should be observed that special Masses for pilgrims, such as those of the Three Royal Wise Men and the Mass of Saint Raphael are late medieval developments.

37. Its end was like a climber's alpenstock, while the top was occasionally crook shaped like a shepherd's, but more often ball shaped and sometimes metal with a device such as one found at Hitchen in England with the inscription, *Haec in tute dirigat iter* ("*May this safely guide the way*"). Jusserand, *English Wayfaring Life,* p. 368, describes such staffs, and p. 369 provides an illustration taken from British Museum ms. 17 cxxxviii. Occasionally staffs bore crosses at the top.

38. William Langland, *The Vision of Piers the Plowman,* ed. W. W. Skeat (London: Oxford University Press, 1922), Passus V, lines 523–39.

39. *The Passionate Man's Pilgrimage.*

40. Act 4, sc. 5, lines 23–26.

41. In Luke 9:1–6, Jesus tells the disciples who are commissioned to heal and to preach, "Take nothing for your journey, neither staff nor wallet nor bread, nor money, neither have two coats." In Luke 10:1–10, Jesus sends the seventy (some ancient mss. read seventy-two) in twos, as lambs among wolves, with the following prohibitions: "Carry no purse, no wallet, no shoes, and salute no man on the way, and into whatsoever house ye shall enter, first say, Peace to this house, and in that same house remain, eating and drinking such things as they give: for the laborer is worthy of his hire." Even though Jesus forbade his disciples to carry scrip, staff, or shoes, there was a biblical authority for doing so. It came from the days of the Exodus of Israel from Egypt when a paschal lamb was slain and eaten and its blood marked the doorposts with a tau mark to protect the Israelites from the tenth plague sent to the Egyptians, the death of their firstborn. At that time God commanded the Israelites: ". . . thus shall ye eat it; with your loins girded, your shoes on your feet, and your staff in your hand: and ye shall eat it in haste for it is the Lord's Passover" (Exodus 12:11). The pilgrim scrip was used for carrying the bread for the journey and written documents, such as the license of the bishop to go on pilgrimage. Pilgrims, it will be recalled, were the letter carriers of the Middle Ages.

42. Such natural reasons for delay included the need to bury a father, bidding farewell to the household, and a marriage recently contracted. These, however, were unacceptable to Jesus on the grounds that "no man, having put his hand to the plough, and looking back, is fit for the kingdom of heaven" (Luke 9:62).

43. Luke 9:58.

44. *Ipse dominus noster Ihesus Christus postquam suscitavit a mortuis a Iherosolimis rediens primus peregrinus extitit* (C.C. I, Whitehill, p.–155).

45. *Sic dum peregrinus felix pauperes pascitur a domino cognoscitur* (ibid.).

46. Ibid., pp. 152–53.

47. This term implying a crossing from the secure boundaries of conventional domestic life toward strangeness, danger, and uncertainty in search of the sacred is a concept usefully employed by the social anthropologist Victor Turner in "The Center Out There: The Pilgrims' Goal," in *History of Religions* 12 (1973): 191–230. He also stresses that the transition involves a difference of status and outlook from the usual.

48. About 1483 William Caxton published a phrase book entitled *Dialogues in French and English,* which was based upon an early fourteenth-century work compiled in Bruges. Caxton's book was republished by the Early English Text Society in 1900. It gives revealing glimpses of travelers and the life at inns.

49. As early as A.D. 333 a pilgrim from Bordeaux went to Jerusalem via Constantinople and wrote an account of all the stages on the way. This was only seven years after the Empress Helena had visited Jerusalem and found the True Cross, and it would not be long before Saint Jerome visited there and ultimately settled in Bethlehem. The most important early account of the Palestinian pilgrimage is known as *The Pilgrimage of Etheria,* a report by an intelligent Galician nun and careful observer who visited Egypt, the Holy Land, Edessa, Asia Minor, and Constantinople at the end of the fourth century. This narrative treatise was an invaluable guide for others. Originally discovered by J. F. Gamurrini and published by him in 1887, it was reedited for the *Corpus scriptorum ecclesiasticorum latinorum* (Vienna, 1898) by P. Geyer. See also *Egeria's Travels,* translated into English and annotated by J. Wilkinson (London: S.P.C.K., 1971).

50. The *Pilgrim's Guide* was the Book V of the *Codex Calixtinus* according to Arnaud Dumont, monk of Ripoll, who described it in 1173 (the copy of which ms. remains in the archives of Compostela today). It was first transcribed and printed by F.-J. Fita and J. Vinson and published in Paris in 1888 under the title *Le codex de saint Jacques de Compostelle.* This refers to the *Pilgrim's Guide* as Book IV, but we are using this transcription in this chapter because it identifies the various places en route with useful footnotes. A more recent scholarly edition is Jeanne Vielliard, *Le guide du pèlerin de saint Jacques de Compostelle* (Mâcon: Protat frères, 1950; reprint, 1963), which we have consulted. It is a translation from Latin into French, admirably done with the Latin text facing the French rendering.

51. Pierre David in his analysis of the first book of the *Codex Calixtinus* points out that it was originally a liturgical volume intended not for canons living according to the Augustinian rule or an adaptation of it but for monks of the Cluniac rule. The prefatory letter was addressed to the "very holy community of Cluny" and the colophon (folio 184) that indicated the collection of sermons and other readings was to be found principally in the same abbey (*Etudes sur le livre de saint*

Jacques attribué au pape Calixte II, 4 vols. [Lisbon: Institut français des études portugaises, 1947], II, pp. 44–45).

52. Its length was 555 feet. Its importance is partly indicated by the fact that in 1095 Paschal II himself consecrated the high altar, and Innocent II the entire church, the narthex excepted, in 1131–32 (Cross, *Oxford Dictionary of the Christian Church*, s.v. "Cluny, Order of"). The great reforming pope, Gregory VII, was a former monk of Cluny.

53. *Quapropter sciendum, quod sancti Jacobi peregrini, sive pauperes sive divites, jure sunt recipiendi, et diligenter procurandi* (Fita and Vinson transcription, chapter XI, p.–63).

54. This information can be found in Chapter VII: *De nominibus terrarum et qualitatibus gentium, quae in itinere sancti Jacobi habentur.* The Gascons are said to be impulsive, verbose, fond of ridicule, libidinous, drunken, trenchermen, badly dressed, and wastrels who sit around a fire and do not eat at a table. They freely use one drinking cup, and a husband and wife and their children all sleep together without any privacy. The Basques are terrible, as are the inhabitants of Navarre: foul, impious, fierce, and oppressors of pilgrims.

55. It should be made clear that secular entertainment is not mentioned in the pilgrim's guide, but no one attending the feast days of the saints would be unaware of the fairs and the accompanying jollification that went on with circus acts. There was also the presentation of early liturgical interludes and the later miracle and morality plays in which humorous additions were made to the biblical and sanctoral episodes reenacted. The dangers and delights of the road are considered in our chapter 7.

56. The list of personages from afar who were Compostela pilgrims is that of Secret, *Saint Jacques et les chemins*, p. 13, who also points out that the *Jacoksbrüder* both German and Swiss left from the famous Benedictine monastery of Einsiedeln in Switzerland. This travelers' organization preferred to go by the route of Arles, passing through Lucerne, Berne, Lausanne, and Geneva where there was a hospice and a chapel of Saint James. Like the English, Vikings came via Coruña, for it was at this port Sigurd, later to be king of Norway, came circa 1110. The local inhabitants were never sure whether Norsemen came for piety or piracy (see Marilyn Stokstad, *Santiago de Compostela in the Age of the Great Pilgrimages* [Norman: University of Oklahoma Press, 1978], p. 18).

57. *De corporibus sanctorum, quae in itinere sancti Jacobi requiescunt, quae peregrinis ejus sunt visitanda.*

58. The earliest Trophimus is mentioned in Acts 20:4 and 21:29 and in 2 Timothy 4:20 as a companion on Saint Paul's third missionary journey.

59. The guide, in common medieval fashion, identifies her with the anonymous woman who anointed Christ's feet with oil and wiped them with her hair, and also with Mary, the sister of Lazarus and Martha, who also anointed him. But Luke 7:37 and John 12:3, which report both incidents, do not make such an identification.

60. This is a legend without historical basis.

61. He gives a vivid, detailed picture of Compostela and the splendor of its processions and worship in a year of jubilee with thousands of strangers present to gain the additional indulgences. On the day after his arrival, the feast of the Holy Trinity was being celebrated, and he saw the golden crown, which had been donated by Henry IV of Castile and León in gratitude for success against the Moors, and which was placed on the head of the statue of the Apostle over the high altar (See [William Way], *The Itineraries of William Way, fellow of Eton College, to Jerusalem, A.D. 1458 and A.D. 1462; and to Saint James of Compostela, A.D. 1456* [London: Roxburghe Club, 1857]).

62. Ibid., p. 154. These details may be interesting: "*LXXX^{ta} naves cum topcastellis et quatuor sine topcastellis.*"

63. F. J. Furnivall, ed., *The Stacions of Rome and the Pilgrim's Sea Voyage* (London: Early English Text Society, 1867), pp. 47–48.

64. In case this might be thought a harsh judgment about local pilgrimage, some corroboration other than Chaucer can be found in Joan Evans, *Life in Medieval France* (London: Phaidon, 1957), pp. 77–78. She relies on the *Roman de Mont-Saint-Michel*, written between 1154 and 1186, wherein is described the felicity of the young pilgrims and the old, with the minstrels playing their viols and accompanying songs, and even the palfreys and packhorses neighing for sheer joy, and round the mount the victuallers have set up their tents. It was a picnic as well as a pilgrimage, but more of a holiday than a holy day, though there was every reason for it to be both.

PART II
En Route

4

Resplendent Shrines and Relics

ONCE the pilgrims prepared themselves, decided their route for the long journey to Compostela, received the spiritual blessings of the Church, and had been sent off by their friends and neighbors—with some going the first few miles of pilgrimage with them—what did they look forward to most? Surely it was to visiting the resplendent shrines where the relics of the greatest friends of God, the saints, were kept in the bejeweled caskets displayed in the mysterious crypts or placed on the saints' feast days on the high altars of the great churches built in their honor. They also anticipated receiving the indulgences that the Church provided for such zealous honoring of the saints. Otherwise we cannot explain the vast crowds that filled the ambulatories of the huge pilgrimage churches of the tenth to the twelfth centuries.

Only respect for the saints accounts for the wealth of art that decorated the tympana on the doors and the capitals of the pillars that enrich Romanesque churches and retell the stories of the divine saga for each successive group of pilgrims. It is belief in the intercessory power of Christ's chief followers and friends that causes the clutter of ex-votos surrounding the shrine of each saint acknowledging the miraculous help that devotees have received and the creation and later embellishment of the gorgeous reliquaries themselves. They were clothed in gold, silver, or copper plate, were sometimes enameled, and often studded with gems. These were the gifts of kings, nobles, or their consorts. Humbler folk offered gold and jewels from their wedding rings.

In these circumstances it is no wonder that the author of the guide book in the *Codex Calixtinus* assumed that pilgrims would take in as many famous shrines as possible as they journeyed through France and Spain to Santiago's, the most splendid shrine of all. Nor are we to be surprised that he devoted little space to the routes themselves. Rather, he concentrated on describing the splendors of the great pilgrimage churches, of their reliquaries, and of the rich decoration of the altars beneath which saints' bones reposed.

This apparently morbid concern for the corpses and bones of the saints—with its associations of death, gloom, graveyards, sepulchers, and moldering crypts—this praying for the intercession of the saints that seems to turn a monotheistic faith into polytheism, seems a long way from the radiant faith in the life everlasting of the New Testament. It is also different from the more celebrative understanding of God today. How, then did it happen that resplendent shrines were inconceivable apart from the relics and reliquaries that attracted crowds of pilgrims as magnets attract iron filings?

The story is a long one. It is so long, in fact, that its origins precede the Christian era. The origin of medieval relics may well go back to the story of Exodus and the spoils of the Egyptians with which the Israelites adorned the Golden Calf, and, in atonement for their idolatry, offered for the decoration of the Ark of the Tabernacle. Within this richly adorned Tabernacle and its Ark were placed important relics: the tablets of stone inscribed by God with the Decalogue, Aaron's rod, and the manna of the wilderness. Medieval shrines adorned with gold, silver, and jewels recognized their biblical ancestry in their terminology as *arcae sanctae* (holy arks).

Before we tell this long story as concisely as we can, two facts should be remembered. The first is that from the ninth to the twelfth century God was conceived as a distant, severe, august Potentate, living with his faithful vassals, the saints, in the glory of the remote heavens. This view would not change until Christians in the twelfth century became deeply interested in the humanity of Christ. The second fact is that if one lived during the ninth to twelfth centuries and could not count on receiving justice from an earthly king or his representatives, if one were hungry or ill and had no powerful lord as a protector, to whom could one turn except to the intermediaries of the King of Kings and Lord of Lords?[1]

The saint, it should be remembered, is a spiritual protector of a city, an abbey, a prince, a kingdom, or of all Christians. The Church strongly encouraged the devotion to the saints as eminent imitators of God. The clergy wrote the lives and accounts of the miracles performed by the saints, and these texts were, in fact, read in churches on the vigils of feasts and of pilgrimages. Especially when they found few living saints in their midst, the faithful turned toward the martyrs of the first Christian centuries with great fervor and affection, and particularly toward the saints who had brought the faith to their own region.[2]

The tradition that associates a church with the repository of one body or bones of a saint is a very ancient one. Veneration of the relics, especially of deceased heroes, is referred to in the Old Testament[3] but was a matter of respect rather than a cult because of the Jewish fear of idolatry. The early Christians retained the Jewish respect for the dead[4] and the Book of Revelation recommends that the faithful dead and the deceased martyrs be left in peace.[5] Despite this negative view of the relics of martyrs, new converts in the time of Saint Paul revered objects that had belonged to the apostles and even acknowledged that clothing that had been touched by them had miraculous powers.[6] Thus the way remained open for the later development of the idea that the relics of martyrs were capable of producing miracles.

By the middle of the second century A.D. there is incontrovertible proof of the veneration of the relics of a martyr. On the death of Saint Polycarp, circa 156, the citizens of Smyrna declared their devotion to the relics of their saintly bishop and begged the magistrates to surrender the body of the saint who was accounted disloyal to the Roman Empire through his refusal to offer sacrifice to the emperor. The magistrates thought it unsuitable to allow Christians to "create a new Christ" and so refused permission at first. The Christians of Smyrna finally persuaded them to hand over the body and justified their action by declaring that the veneration offered to the martyrs was subordinate to that offered to Christ since Polycarp was "a disciple and imitator of Christ."[7] Each year on the anniversary of his martyrdom the faithful honored his memory in the place where he was buried.

A century later Saint Cyprian of Carthage justified the veneration of the instruments of the martyrs' suffering by asserting in his thirteenth epistle that the bodies of prisoners for Christ's sake hallowed their chains. The period of the persecutions led to the greater popularity of the veneration of the relics of martyrs. On the arrival of the peace of Constantine, it became common for churches to be built over the graves of martyrs, the most eminent examples being Rome itself where Saint Peter's was erected on the Vatican Hill and Saint Paul's on the Via Ostia. The justification for the cult of the relics of the saints is developed in the theologies of Saint Basil and Saint John Chrysostom in the East and of Saint Ambrose and Saint Augustine in the West.

The Church Fathers, in fact, provide four different justifications for the veneration of relics. It is argued, first, that the faithful see the saints in the relics they venerate. So affirmed Saint Ephrem the Syrian, Theodoret of Cyr, and Maximus of Turin. It is contended that since the martyrs were saints on earth, so their bodies were similarly sanctified. The second justification is that the blood of the martyrs and the record of their sufferings are powerful stimuli to the courage of the faithful and thus the relics are reminders of the saints who serve as models. This was the view of saints John Chrysostom and Basil of Caesarea. The third view justifies relics because of the miracles wrought through their instrumentality. Although glory is to be given to God alone, yet as his power is manifested in relics, they can be venerated. This was the conviction of Saint Gregory of Nazianzus, Saint Augustine, Paulinus of Nola, and Pope Leo I.[8]

Correlated with these justifications were two further, often opposed, developments in hagiography. Saints' legends were produced with the primary purpose of edifying the faithful. But there was also propagated the view that the more extraordinary the miracles, the more holy were the relics and the more efficacious the saints' intercessions with God.

Perhaps the most cogent argument for the veneration of relics is the human one employed by both Saint Augustine and Saint Gregory of Nyssa that relics are the remains of saints who as saints are close to God. Saint Jerome argued in a famous passage that "we do not worship their relics any more than we do the sun or the moon, the angels, archangels or seraphim. We honor them in honor of Him whose faith they witnessed. We honor the Master by means of the servants."[9]

In the East it became common practice to exhume, dismember and transport the bodies of the saints from place to place, surrounding these actions with significant ceremonies. Dismemberment was justified by the belief that the soul was totally present everywhere in every part of the body, and that every part of the body had enjoyed the vital force. On this account the great eastern cities of Constantinople, Alexandria, and Antioch gathered great agglomerations of the bones of saints translated from lesser sanctuaries.

In the West the Theodosian Code enjoined that severe penalties be applied to the spoliation of graves, a view supported by the popes. This attitude was relaxed under popes Paul I (757–76) and Paschal I (817–24) and led to the quick dispersal and dismemberment of the bodies of saints throughout Italy. Outside Italy, however, where martyrdoms had been relatively few, there was a cult of *brandea,* or substitute relics, and in the Carolingian era the cult of confessors or nonmartyrs grew rapidly. Furthermore, it was the requirement that bishops consecrate churches with relics in the altar or be deprived of their office, insisted on by the Second Council of Nicaea in 787, which led to the universal demand for relics, and to the greater appreciation of the relics of the apostles, deemed to be closest to Christ and therefore most effective. These factors increased the popularity of pilgrimages.

In the eighth and ninth centuries guidebooks for pilgrims in Rome advised them to go to the catacombs, where either their own pious fancy or the persuasiveness of charlatans led them to believe that they stood amid great collections of the bodies of the saints. From then on, bones became almost common coinage. The bodies of supposed martyrs were given by popes to visiting princes. Monastic founders sought sanctoral bones to provide sanctity and solidity for their monasteries. New nations were won from paganism by the encouragement of the cult of relics, as in the case of the Saxons. Especially because no church could be dedicated without the necessary relics of a saint in the altar, dismemberments continued apace. Inevitably, new sources of relics, most ex-

ceedingly dubious, had to be discovered. One unworthily named Deus-
dedit became a very successful entrepreneur of dubious relics from the
third cemeterial region of Rome, which he administered in the ninth
century. He sold these "relics" on his first venture through Germany to
such clients as Einhard and Rabanus Maurus.

Not only were the Roman cemeteries ransacked for relics, but the
commerce in relics reached its peak in 1204 with the taking of the city of
Constantinople by the Crusaders, when a vast store of relics was seized.
In turn Antioch, Jerusalem, and Edessa were also sacked and their relics
were sent back to enrich the churches and cathedrals of medieval
Europe.

Of course, the earliest and greatest of tomb-shrines was that of the
Lord himself, the Holy Sepulcher in Jerusalem, but this tomb was
empty in consonance with the central belief in the Resurrection of
Christ. After the location of the Savior's Resurrection, Constantine
ordered the bishop of Jerusalem, Macarius, to arrange for the construction of a magnificent basilica in order "to render the blessed locality of
our Savior's resurrection an object of attraction and veneration to all."[10]
But, apart from a few visitors and the generality of successful Crusaders, the Holy Sepulcher was in a distant and unattainable land. The
majority of Christians had to be satisfied with visiting the tomb-shrines
of saints, often renowned at great distances for their miracles. These
could be reached and offered the pilgrim a sense of closeness to the
saints in everlasting light who were themselves near to God. Here was a
sure way to gain merit.

The most famous of all saints' tombs was, of course, that of Peter in
Rome, and twentieth-century excavations carried out beneath the great
cathedral church enable us to reconstruct the evolution of the tomb-
shrine of that preeminent apostle. It appears that about the year 200 a
memorial shrine to Saint Peter called a *tropaion*, or trophy, existed on
the Vatican Hill and was a much-revered object to Christians. This has
recently been identified by archaeologists with the remains of the
Aedicula, a small, niched shrine that is adorned with colonettes. This
may have covered the grave of Saint Peter, or marked the place of his
martyrdom, though the former is the likelier probability. On the adjacent wall are numerous graffiti which testify to the devotion of visiting
Christians who there recorded their prayers for the welfare of their
loved ones, living or dead. This shrine remained in its original setting in
a pagan cemetery until Emperor Constantine enclosed it in the vast
basilica that became the old Saint Peter's, where it was the focal point of
the church and its worship. Writing in A.D. 406, Saint Jerome refers to
the bishop of Rome as "offering sacrifice to God on the tombs of St.
Peter and St. Paul which rank as altars of Christ (*Christi arbitratur
altaria*)."[11] The popular belief in the efficacy of Saint Peter's relics is

indicated by the account given by Gregory of Tours in about 590 of how it was usual for a petitioner, seeking a particular request from Saint Peter, to pass a piece of cloth into the shrine for weighing, and if the weight increased, it was taken as a token of the saint's assent.[12]

So powerful was the medieval cult of the tomb-shrine that, in the words of S. G. F. Brandon, the eminent historian of religions, "it could even cause the presence of a saint's remains to be located in an inherently impossible place."[13] The reference is to the tomb of Santiago, or Saint James, being located at Iria on the northwest coast of Spain. It may be recalled that in 813 Bishop Theodomir claimed he had located it there through the guidance of supernatural lights. Its presence was explained as due to a miracle: the stone coffin in which the body of the saint had been placed by his disciples in Judea was supposed to have sailed miraculously to Iria Flavia. Legend was piled upon legend to give credence, so that it seemed a marvelous confirmation of Theodomir's discovery when the Christian army at Clavijo was given the victory over a much vaster army of Moors in 844 through the visionary presence of Saint James the *Matamoros*.[14]

It is exceedingly difficult for us moderns to imagine what the splendor of a medieval shrine would be like, and this is the case for two reasons. The first is that so many abbeys and cathedrals that survive from the middle ages have lost a great deal of their former glory: their treasures have been stolen by invaders or secularizers, their gray walls would never lead one to suspect that the sculptures on half drums and capitals and even the length of the columns were brilliantly colored, nor that the wooden doors were a brilliant crimson with all bosses of gold. And we have lost the fervent belief and wonder that made every sanctuary a Jacob's ladder with angels ascending to and descending from heaven and every saint the proven loyal friend of God who dwelt in a paradise of coruscating light that was only just above the rooftop of the church or cathedral. For us the heavens have grown distant and become astronomical. Unless we recover their rapture, we shall never feel along the pulse the celestial and terrestrial joys of pilgrimage, where in the presence of the saint both aspiration and curiosity are elicited and satisfied.

A deviation from the route to Compostela can be justified if it enables us to experience the excitement and wonder with which our ancestors visited medieval shrines. In this special case the locale is the tomb-shrine of Saint Thomas à Becket, the murdered archbishop of Canterbury. The vivid description of it is provided, in part, by the researches of Dean Stanley and, in part, by the eyewitness account of Erasmus who visited Canterbury in 1510. Dean Stanley wrote:

The lower part of the shrine was of stone, supported on arches; and between these arches the sick and lame pilgrims were allowed to ensconce themselves, rubbing their rheumatic backs or diseased legs against the marble which brought them into the nearest contact with the wonder-working body within. The Shrine, properly so-called, rested on these arches, and was at first invisible. It was concealed by a wooden canopy, probably painted outside with sacred pictures, suspended from the roof; at a given signal this canopy was drawn up by ropes, and the Shrine then appeared blazing with gold and jewels. . . . As soon as this magnificent sight was disclosed, everyone dropped on his knees, and probably the tinkling of the silver bells attached to the canopy would indicate the moment to call the hundreds of pilgrims in whatever part of the cathedral they might be. The body of the saint in the inner iron chest was not to be seen except by mounting a ladder, which would be but rarely allowed.[15]

Erasmus confirms the accuracy of Stanley's reconstruction, but adds details:

A coffin of wood, which covered a coffin of gold, was drawn up by ropes and pulleys, and discovered the invaluable treasure. Gold was the meanest thing to be seen there; all shone and glittered with the rarest and most precious jewels of an extraordinary bigness; some were larger than the egg of a goose.[16]

Beyond the chapel of the Holy Ghost was to be seen "the whole face of the blessed martyr, set in gold and adorned with many jewels." Erasmus adds that when this was exposed to view, the prior, using a white wand, touched every jewel, describing its value and its donor since many were the gifts of great monarchs and nobles. Louis VII of France, for example, sent the precious jewel named the "Regale of France" as well as a cup of gold, while Edward I offered the golden crown of conquered Scotland. Finally, the relics of the martyr were displayed. This is how Erasmus describes them:

On the north door of the choir the guides opened several doors, and the pilgrim beheld an immense collection of bones of all kinds—skull bones, jawbones, teeth, hands, fingers, etc., which they kissed as they were severally taken out. In doing honour to the relics of Becket, they kissed the rusty point of the sword that split his skull and the fissure of the skull itself, exposed for that purpose in a silver case, and near the saint's monument were hung his hair-shirt, his belt and clothes.[17]

These descriptions convey a sense of the mystery unveiled, of the splendor of the earthly tributes to a martyred saint paid by monarchs and minions alike, of the holy excitement at realizing that the second most powerful man in the kingdom (for as Chancellor Thomas had been the King Henry II's chief advisor) wore a hair shirt like the most self-denying of ascetics, and of the desperate hope of the sick that they might be cured. For both those who sought treasures in heaven and those whose mouths gaped at earthly treasures there was no lack of interest. We know that when Henry VIII dissolved the cathedral priory of Canterbury, twenty-six carts were filled with its precious metals and jewels, and in England the Reformation achieved what the Revolution did in France, the wholesale destruction of the most splendid reliquaries of the saints.

It is almost impossible for us today to imagine how dangerous the press of the crowds could be on the anniversary of a saint in a pilgrimage church of great popularity. Jonathan Sumption's translation recreates the atmosphere at Saint Denis, just outside Paris, as Abbot Suger recalls the almost suffocated crowds in the pre-Gothic abbey that he rebuilt:

> As the members of the faithful increased the crowds at St. Denis grew larger and larger until the old church began to burst at the seams. On feast-days it was always full to overflowing, and the mass of struggling pilgrims spilt out of every door. Not only were some pilgrims unable to get in, many of those who were already inside were forced out in front of them. As they fought their way towards the holy relics to kiss and worship them, they were so densely packed that none of them could so much as stir a foot. A man could only stand like a marble statue, paralysed, and free only to cry out aloud.[18]

In the meantime, the lot of the women was worse. Suger continues:

> The women in the crowd were in such intolerable pain, crushed between strong men as if in a wine-press, that death seemed to dance before their eyes. The blood was drained from their faces, and they screamed as if in the throes of childbirth. Some of them were trodden underfoot and had to be lifted above the heads of the crowd by kindly men, and passed to the back of the church and thence to the fresh air. In the cloister outside wounded pilgrims lay gasping their last breath. As for the monks who were in charge of the reliquaries, they were often obliged to escape with the relics through the windows. When first as a schoolboy, I heard of these things from my monastic teachers, I was saddened and conceived an earnest desire to improve matters.[19]

Several attempts have been made to explain the medieval fascination with relics, none of them entirely convincing though cumulatively they are impressive. Jonathan Sumption in his fine work *Pilgrimage* argues that "the cult of relics was the counterpart of the fear of evil. Just as men tended to associate evil with objects familiar to them, so they attempted to give a human quality to the forces of good."[20] This tendency is exemplified by reference to Victricius of Rouen of the fifth century, a Frankish collector of relics who envisioned the saints as an army of auxiliaries in the cosmic battle against evil, saying, "See, a great host comes to us. . . . Victory is certain when we fight alongside such allies with Christ as our general."[20] The vividness of the personification of the forces of good and evil is undeniable as a medieval phenomenon and all the more powerful at the end of the Dark Ages when Christianity had barely triumphed over paganism, as we see in the involved interlacings of the Irish illuminated Gospels, or in the strange zoomorphic forms that decorated some of the early Romanesque church capitals and doors. But it is quite another thing to assume the deliberate sophistication of translating abstract forces into personal dualistic warfare; neither Scripture nor medieval theology of which we are aware makes this equation.

Perhaps, as L. F. Salzman has suggested in his *English Life in the Middle Ages,* we may explain the fascination with the relics of the saints as due to the inexpungable human instinct for hero worship, which sends English patriots to Portsmouth to view where Nelson fell aboard the *Victory.* Salzman argues: "Genuine admiration of the lives of holy men and women led in the first place to the desire to possess, or at least to see, objects which had belonged to them—a comb, a pair of shoes, or a girdle, or better still, a tooth, or a bone from their bodies. Then grew up the belief that these objects had in some way inherited the virtues and powers of their saintly owners and that through them miracles were wrought."[21]

This explanation seems partly convincing, but it hardly accounts for the religious factor; that is, that the hero chosen was not merely a famous person but a notable imitator of God and a close friend of Christ, and above all, one who cold help the pilgrim to attain eternal life.

The point is that the longing for relics was an *obsession*—no less. One stunning example of the craze for relics involves the monks of the Parisian abbey of Saint Germain-des-Prés, who like most of their contemporaries were eagerly searching for new discoveries of tombs, or even for the bones of recent martyrs. In 858, disappointed at failing to find the relics of Saint Vincent in Spain and fearing to return home empty-handed, they learned that Christians had just been martyred by the Muslims in Cordova. Immediately they rushed to this city to get the relics of George and Aurelius.[22] Another striking example of the lust for relics, if the term will be pardoned since the anecdote will justify the language, is attributed to Saint Hugh of Lincoln. When he was a guest of the abbey of Fécamp, Saint Hugh was allowed to see the arm of Saint Mary Magdalene, which was tightly wrapped in cloth and silk bandages and which the monks had not dared to unwrap. Despite the furious objections of the monks, Saint Hugh cut off the wrappings with a knife and tried to break off a piece of the arm. Finding this too difficult, he then tried to bite off a finger with his teeth "first with his incisors, and finally with his molars" and thus he succeeded in breaking off two fragments that he handed for safe keeping to his biographer. Saint Hugh then turned to the abbot and offered the following justification of his action: "If a short time ago I handled the sacred body of my Lord with my fingers in spite of my unworthiness [a clear reference to the reception of the Host in the Mass], and partook of it with my lips and teeth, why should I not treat the bones of the saints in the same way . . . and without profanity acquire them whenever I can?"[23] When an inventory of Cluny's relics, jewels, and ornaments was taken in 1304 no less than 225 items were listed.[24]

When relics arrived at a local church, the excitement of the populace was apt to get out of hand. The Council of Avignon of 1209 had to forbid unsuitable rejoicing in the church that took the form of dancing, games of chance, and even coursing.[25] Such excitement can only be explained by the conviction of the people, to use Dom Jean Leclercq's phrase in translation, that "the cult of relics materialized the protection of the saints."[26]

It was not enough, however, for pilgrims to be near the relics of the saints; it was also essential for them to be *visualized*. This demand led to the partial enclosure of the relics in magnificent settings such as chests, but gradually, if the relics were more than mere fragments, it became usual to place them in a statue. These statue-relics originated in southern France in the tenth century. We know that Stephen, bishop of Clermont, itself an important pilgrimage center on the way to Compostela, ordered a statue of the Virgin in 946 to house some of her relics. He also happened to be the abbot of Conques in the Rouergue, whose monks had stolen the relics of Saint Foi from Agen. It is probable that he commissioned the famous statue known as the "majesty" of Conques, on display today as a rare survival in the treasury of the famous pilgrimage church. This statue, made of gold and encrusted with precious gems, shows Saint Foi seated on a throne stretching out her hand. It may have once held a model of the grid on which—like Saint Laurence—she had supposedly been martyred, or supported a golden glove in each hand, or possibly held doves as symbols of her purity. This is a memento of a great number of similar statues that were honored in the south of France and elsewhere.[27]

We also know that at the Synod of Rodez in 1013 Bernard of Anger, who had been educated at Chartres and was a stranger to the south, indignantly described how every church was represented by its clergy carrying the statue-reliquary of its patron saint beneath a splendid canopy. Before the opening of the Council, Saint Armand of Rodez, Saint Marius of Vabres, Saint Sernin of Toulouse, a golden statue of the Virgin, and Saint Foi herself were all carried round the walls of the city in a solemn procession. Bernard also saw the statue-reliquary of Saint Gerard at Aurillac. He expressed his disapproval in the words: "Hitherto I have always believed that the veneration of images and paintings of the saints was improper, and to raise statues to them would have struck me as absurd. But this is not the belief of the inhabitants of these parts, where every church contains a statue of its patron made of gold, silver, or base metal, depending on the wealth of the church. And inside it they place the head or some other important relic of the saint. . . . Jupiter or Mars might well have been venerated like this."[28]

The creation of precious reliquaries was in part due to the desire to honor those divine persons or saints to whom the relics belonged by the quality and brilliance of the materials making up the covering of the relic, whether that was an instrument of Christ's Passion (such as a part of the True Cross, or a holy nail), or a part of a saint's body. But the reliquary served a further purpose: to make known the presence of the holy person in the relic. This was accomplished either in displaying the relic, in which case it was a kind of saintly monstrance, or in evoking the shape of the relic. It became very popular to make the container look like the content. Hence it is rare for a relic of the True Cross not to be contained in a cross-shaped reliquary or a reliquary of the holy nail not in the form of a nail (as in the treasury of Trier).[29] It was this imitation that led to the production not only of reliquary heads and busts (the latter is admirably exemplified by Saint Foi and Saint Baudime) but also of a reliquary foot (like that of Saint Andrew also at Trier),[30] or of an arm (like that supposedly of Saint George in the Conques treasury). It is worth noting that Saint James of Compostela has links with both Trier and Conques. For while the foot of Saint Andrew is at Trier, there was a medieval altar in Compostela dedicated to the same saint, and while Trier claimed to have a substantial section of the True Cross found by Saint Helena in its possession, there was an altar in Santiago and shrine commemorating the "invention" of the True Cross. Similarly, there was the "majesty" of Saint Foi at Conques and an altar dedicated to her in medieval times at Compostela. Clearly, relics and pilgrimage are as closely interrelated as shoe and foot, glove and fingers.

There appear to be three definitely marked stages in the development of the receptacles of relics. First they were deposited in a sarcophagus or coffer, which easily became an altar. Next, from the ninth century onward, portable chests and reliquaries became common, largely because of the pagan invasions of the Normans and Hungarians and the need for mobility, either in moving them to safer places or for processional purposes.[31] Finally, during the tenth century, with the development of radiating chapels to allow the devout to get nearer the relics and the desire to make them either more splendid or more realistic, or both, the chests changed from gilded wood to golden imitations of the shape of the church or in the form of a limb, or as a bust of the saint.

As we have seen, the earlier form of reliquaries was as chests and not surprisingly in the similar form of tombs such as the reliquary of Pepin in the treasury of Conques, or that of Saint John the Baptist at León, or that of Saint Peter at Minden. Since the relics had been first placed in tombs, one might expect tomblike miniature chests to be invented for their keeping. Furthermore, the altar placed over the holy body of a saint was itself a kind of chest, so that the *paliotto* of Saint Ambrose of Milan is simultaneously an altar and a reliquary.

The provision of statue-reliquaries that were so popular fulfilled a double function. In the first place they enabled the worshiper to visualize the saint and therefore to venerate him or her with greater focus in the imagination and devotion. It also made the cult object more significant when carried about in solemn procession on the festivals of the saint. Today one can imagine the splendor of the ceremonies that took place in the great abbeys and cathedrals, in the middle of a setting with a resplendent decor of shining precious metals and gems, like that of Saint Ambrose of Milan with its *paliotto* and its ciborium, or that of Aix-la-Chapelle with the antependium of its altar, close to the ambo covered with gold, filigree work, ivory, and hard stone.

The faithful came to expect splendor and to visualize their saints honored by precious gifts and their relics covered with the most precious materials. So much was this the case that they were bitterly disappointed if there was no great show. The disgust of one lady pilgrim at a too plain reliquary is on record. She arrived in the middle of the ninth century at the monastery at Prüm with a wagon packed with food, drink, and precious objects, which she intended to offer to God and to the holy martyrs. But as the tomb of the saint did not glisten with gold or silver, she snorted her disapproval and bade her friends retrace their footsteps, declaring, "you won't find anything holy in that place."[32]

We also know that it was often the custom to improve the reliquaries or statues to make them a greater attraction for visitors. One of the frankest admissions of this motive concerns a realistic crucifix sculpted for the choir of the monastery chapel of Meaux, near Beverley in the north of England. Thomas of Burton, abbot, tells of this in his chronicle, which he wrote at the end of the fourteenth century. Abbot Hugh of Leven, a predecessor at the beginning of the century, ordered the new crucifix:

> And the artist never worked at any fine and important part except on Fridays, fasting on bread and water. And he had all the time a naked man under his eyes, and he laboured to give to this crucifix the beauty of the model. By

the means of this crucifix the Almighty worked open miracles continually. It was then thought that if the access to this crucifix were allowed to women the common devotion would be increased and great advantage would result from it for our monastery. Upon which, the abbot of Cîteaux, by our request, granted us leave to let men and honest women approach the said crucifix provided, however, that the women did not enter the cloister, the dormitory, and other parts of the monastery. . . . But profiting by this license, to our misfortune, women began to come in increasing numbers to this crucifix, while in them devotion is cool, and all they want is to see the church, and they increase our expenses by our having to receive them.[33]

Relics, especially when thought to be wonder-working, proved a great source of attraction to pilgrims and of wealth to monasteries. Relics also presented opportunities for goldsmiths and silversmiths to display their arts. Yet the multiplication of relics in the twelfth and later centuries led to very great misgivings on the part of thoughtful persons. These misgivings were caused by false relics, by the rival claims of different sanctuaries to have the same relics, and by the way that relics were stolen. Each of these sources of misgivings warrants consideration.

The claims of different churches to have the same relics was vehemently criticized by the author of the pilgrimage guide in the *Codex Calixtinus*. He excoriated all those who claimed to have the true body of Saint Gilles, which really lay in the church of Saint Gilles-du-Gard in Provence: "Let the Hungarians be ashamed who say they have his body and cursed be the monks of Chamalières who pretend to have it totally; the same, also, for the folk of St. Seine who claim to have his head, and to the Normans who actually exhibit a body purporting to be his. For it is quite impossible for a single part of the holy body ever to have left its sacred tomb."[34] Similarly, he is critical of the monks of Corbigny who also claim to have the relics of Saint Léonard de Noblat and who attribute all his miracles to their relics.[35] But he did not mention that the authenticity of the head of Saint John the Baptist at Saint Jean d'Angély near Poitiers was also disputed.[36]

It is also significant that several of the relics in the shrines of the greatest pilgrimage churches of the West were stolen.[37] This was true of the relics of Saint Benedict at Fleury and of Saint Foi at Conques, both on the way to Compostela, but also of the relics of Saint Mark in Venice and of Saint Nicholas at Bari. However pious the frauds with their rationalizations that a saint would not permit removal if he or she did not wish it and that if the guardians had been devoted the translation could not have taken place, they must have been dissuasives for men and women of faith.

But the greatest dissuasive of all, if only the facts had been generally known, was the number of fake relics that appeared with fearful regularity in the High Middle Ages. Some of these were ingenious if barefaced inventions, including the rod of Moses supposedly excavated at Sens in the beginning of the eleventh century, the prepuce of Christ supposedly kept among the relics at Conques, the mark on Cain's forehead, the tip of Lucifer's tail, feathers of the Holy Ghost, a phial containing Christ's breath, and another with the tears of Christ, not to mention fraudulent mechanical devices that simulated miracles, such as the famous Boxley Rood of Grace. This last was in the possession of the Cistercian abbey near Maidstone in England. According to Foxe's Book of Martyrs this image was capable of assuming every type of facial expression according to the value of the offerings it received. At the dissolution of the abbey by Henry VIII, the figure was found to be full of concealed wires. The commissioner chosen by Cromwell, the Vicar General, reported that "upon the defacing of the late monastery of Boxley and plucking down of the images of the same, I found in the Image of the Roode of Grace, the which heretofore hath been hadde in great veneration of people, certen ingynes and old wyer with olde roton styk in the back of the same that dyd cause the eyes of the same to move and stere in the hede thereof lyke unto a lyvelye thyng. And also the nether lippe in lykewise to move as thoughe it shulde speke. Which so founde was not a little strange to me and other that was present at the plucking downe of the same."[38]

Having considered the reasons for the fascination of pilgrims of the High Middle Ages with relics, and the various kinds of reliquaries made as containers of the bones of the saints or the mementoes of Christ and the Virgin Mary, it is high time to attempt to reconstruct the particular attractions pilgrims to Compostela would find on the shrines en route. It is, of course, not to be forgotten that many of these are no longer extant, stolen by the invasions of pagan Norsemen or Muslim Turks in the earlier Middle Ages, or stolen and secularized during the Reformation, or destroyed by Huguenot iconoclasts or by devotees of the religion of humanity during the French Revolution. Some historical reconstruction will inevitably be required, but the assistance of the pilgrim's guide to Compostela and of the "Nuit des Temps" guides to Romanesque France and Spain will be accepted. This will be supplemented by the present writers' visits to the major sanctuaries on all four routes to Compostela undertaken in 1973, 1974, and 1978. We shall follow the routes according to their order in the pilgrim's guide.[39]

The earliest pilgrim guide that we possess is that of the fourth-century *Itinerarium a Burdigala Jerusalem usque,* and it is intriguing to note that this pilgrim took the via Domitia from Toulouse to Arles, which the pilgrims to Compostela seven centuries later would take in reverse.

In Provence the pilgrim in search of the relics of the saints would first stop at Arles, formerly the primatial see for Gaul. There near the banks of the Rhone he would find a high column of marble supposed to have been reddened with the blood of the martyr Saint Genes. In Arles itself after 1152 he would find a church dedicated to Saint Trophime, whom Gregory of Tours counted one of the seven missionaries sent by Rome to evangelize Gaul, the others being Gatien of Tours, Paul of Narbonne, Saturnin of Toulouse, Denis of Paris, Austremoine of Issoire, and Martial of Limoges.[40]

The pilgrim's guide to Compostela says nothing about the magnificent western front of Saint Trophime nor of its superb cloister with double historiated columns, because they may well have been built two or three decades after the production of the guide. Nonetheless it urges that the tomb of Saint Trophime, a confessor—that is, one who suffered for the Christian faith but not to the extent of martyrdom—is to be visited and also that of Saint Caesarius, bishop and martyr and founder of a monastic rule, also buried in Arles. In an adjacent cemetery the tomb of Saint Honoratus, another archbishop of Arles and the founder of the distinguished monastery of Lérins, as well as a great defender of orthodoxy in doctrine, must be venerated. The pilgrim is advised to proceed to the vast cemetery amid the cypresses of the Alyscamps, also near Arles, where he will see the largest collection of marble tombs anywhere in the world, where there are over a thousand dead, and where there are seven churches in each of which a priest offers Mass for the dead or reads from the psalter. This is a specially holy place "because many bodies of the holy martyrs and confessors rest there, whose souls rejoice together in paradise."[41]

The Compostela guide next advises pilgrims to visit Saint-Gilles-du-Gard where the author was deeply impressed by the reliquary chest, or coffin, containing the relics of Saint Gilles. The fullest description is provided of the decoration of the sarcophagus, a huge golden chest behind the altar of the basilica. According to the author, on the left side of the first register there are images of six apostles and of the Virgin, while the second register displays the twelve signs of the zodiac with flowers between each sign. On the topmost register are twelve of the twenty-four elders of the Apocalypse. On the right side of the first register are seven images, six of them apostles and the seventh of a disciple of Christ. Above the heads of the apostles are the virtues that they incarnated, each represented as a woman, such as Generosity, Kindness, Faith, Hope, and Charity. In the third register twelve more elders of the Apocalypse appear with this inscription above them: "This admirable vessel ornamented with gold and jewels contains the remains of St. Gilles. Whoever breaks into it God will curse for ever, and Gilles equally with all the sacred order."[42]

The lid of the chest is ornamented with fish scales, and at its apex thirteen crystalline stones are inserted, some looking like scales, others like seeds. One huge crystal is shaped like a fish with an upright tail. Another is as large as a pot over which a precious golden cross is placed. In the center of the front of the chest is a golden circle where there is a representation of the Lord blessing people. In his right hand he is holding a book on which is written, "Seek peace and truth." On the footstool below his feet he has a golden star and about his arms an alpha and omega. Above his throne two invaluable precious stones coruscate. The four evangelists are about his throne, with their feet holding scrolls. As on the porch of Saint Trophime in the tympanum one can see the tetramorph. There are other images: of the Holy Trinity, of the confessor Saint Trophime himself, and of the Ascension with six apostles watching the Lord rise. Over their heads an inscription reads, "O men of Galilee, this Jesus who is assumed into heaven away from you, will return just as you have seen Him."[43] It is obvious that the author of the guide thought the pilgrims would be impressed equally by the size and splendor of the gold chest as by the images carved on it, telling their story of the life to come and its guarantor, Christ.

We can also be certain that the wonders of the popular Saint Gilles would lose nothing in the telling, for he was the patron of cripples, beggars, and blacksmiths. Moreover, according to a tenth-century biography, Saint Gilles fled from Greece and its adulation of him to the mouth of the Rhone where he built a hermitage and where he lived on herbs and the milk of a hind. Here, when Flavius Wamba, king of the Visigoths, was hunting, he chased the hind to the hermitage where it sought protection, and so Flavius discovered the saint. So impressed was he with the holiness of Saint Gilles that he built him a monastery. The *Liber miraculorum sancti Aegidii*,[44] which appeared in the early years of the twelfth century, disseminated the stories of the miracles of the saint widely and, combined with his church's location on the main route from Provence to Compostela, assured its great popularity as a pilgrimage center.[45]

A deviation to the south would enable the more zealous pilgrims to venerate at Saintes-Maries-de-la-Mer the Mary who was the sister of the Blessed Virgin, Mary Salome,who was the mother of Saint James the Great, and their servant Sara. This was in the wild Camargues country where thousands of today's gypsies still offer annual devotions to the dark-skinned images.

The pilgrim, after a steep climb into rocky wastes, would next visit the tomb of one of Charlemagne's successful generals at Saint Guilhem-du-Désert.[4] This William, count of Toulouse, on the death of his second wife, and with two sisters buried in this valley and many of his children dead, prepared for the religious life with the assistance of his friend Saint Benedict of Aniane, the great restorer of monastic life in the ninth century. William took monastic vows at the age of fifty, established a monastery in the small town now named after him, and gave it the precious relic of the True Cross, which along with the bones of Saint Guilhem were the pilgrim attractions. This relic of the Cross, given to Saint Guilhem by Charlemagne and brought to Saint Guilhem-du-Désert in A.D. 806, is extant and is placed in the center of a reliquary cross. It is difficult to think of any more significant Christian relic than this, with the possible exception of the crown of thorns for which Saint Louis created the Sainte Chapelle of Paris in which to enthrone it. Pilgrims not going to the Holy Land could hardly come closer to the Savior than through this relic.

Next the faithful pilgrim would stop at the great pilgrimage basilica of Saint Sernin (Saint Saturninus) of Toulouse, the largest basilica he would enter on this particular route to Compostela until he reached the shrine of Saint James itself. So brave a martyr and bishop, who was dragged by wild bulls from the Capitol to the spot where his body would later lie, in the basilica of his name, with the resulting tearing of his body and the effusion of his brains, is worthy of a great sanctuary.

The author of the Calixtine guide speaks of the "vast basilica" *(ingens basilica)* that was built in Saint Sernin's honor by the faithful. Its architecture is worth examining because it is one of the remarkable family of Romanesque pilgrimage churches that are the glory of France. The sheer vastness of the edifice of rose-colored bricks and its ability to accommodate large numbers of pilgrims on saints' days must have created a big impression on visitors.

Raymond Oursel thinks that the remote origins of the pilgrimage churches can be traced to the first great Christian monuments erected by the emperor Constantine: the Basilica of the Nativity at Bethlehem and the Basilica of the Holy Sepulcher in Jerusalem.[47] In each case the basilical plan popular in the West was united with the rotunda under a cupola familiar to the East. This synthetic form, so Oursel argues, combined harmoniously the two basic necessities of a pilgrimage sanctuary: a place large enough to gather crowds on festival days, and arrangements by which the crowds could circulate about the sacred place of the martyr's remains. Rotunda churches could be found in the West from Sens to Geneva, at Auxerre, Flavigny, and Dijon. The last church was erected by William of Volpiano for Saint Benignus and its abbey about the year 1000, and the church became a great pilgrimage center.

Despite their remote origin a striking group of pilgrimage churches emerged on the route to Compostela late in the eleventh or early in the twelfth century. These are the basilicas of Tours, Limoges, Conques, Compostela, and Toulouse. Their principal distinguishing characteristics are the presence in them of ambulatories, allowing for the free circulation of pilgrims between the radiating chapels of the apse, or chevet, and the choir, thus enabling them to see the reliquaries in the choir above or behind the altar. These basilicas also have a triforium, which gave pilgrims an admirable view of the ceremonies on festival days from the upper story of the transepts and the nave, besides providing additional altars—usually including one dedicated to Saint Michael. Furthermore, the ambulatory allowed the pilgrims to go to the particular chapel of their favorite saint when visiting a sanctuary, without slowing down their approach to the place of principal devotion—the tomb of the saint to whom the church was dedicated. These conveniences of architecture also made it possible for processions to be held in the central aisle of the church without the necessity of going outside. The gallery of the triforium above the naves, apart from affording a splendid view of spectacles taking place below, also allowed indirect, filtered light to illuminate the church mysteriously, stressing its numinosity. No wonder that the tribunes were also called "paradise." The *Codex Calixtinus* declares of the gallery of Saint James, which is unique in encircling the entire church, that whoever ascends to it "if he goes up sad, will recover lightness of heart and joy after having contemplated the extreme beauty of this church."[48] Several of the pilgrimage churches also had side aisles, even double side aisles, in the nave to ease processions and the flow of pilgrims.

It is now seriously disputed whether there ever was a "school of pilgrimage churches" presumably copying each other. Elie Lambert, the distinguished architectural historian of Romanesque churches, believes that each of the five churches was an important pilgrimage center in its own right and that it was only the functional necessity of getting crowds of pilgrims on festival days to the chapels and the tomb of the saint that made them appear alike.[49] Furthermore, easily the most important of those churches was Santiago, and instead of affiliation between it and the other pilgrimage churches, there was from time to time acute rivalry. It is known, for example, that Saint Sernin's rivalry took the form of claiming at one time to have possession of the true body of Saint James.[50] It has been argued that Saint Foi of Conques was the earliest of the great pilgrimage chapels, but Lambert has countered by insisting that the earlier church had seven parallel chapels and that only the later pilgrimage church had an ambulatory with radiating chapels. Saint Martin of Tours, according to both Emile Mâle[49] and Elie Lambert, was the prototype of pilgrimage churches. They base this view on the evidence of excavations of 1886, which exposed an ancient ambulatory with the shape and dimensions of those of Saint Sernin and of Saint James. Today, alas, little remains of the most important pilgrimage shrine (apart from Rome itself) in western Europe before the rise of Compostela, except for two towers, the impressive north tower, or tower of Charlemagne and the tower of the Treasury on the western facade. Recent reconstruction attempts show that the Romanesque basilica was about 100 meters in length, the nave 63 meters, and the transept over 54 meters with high towers at each end. The facade had two towers also. It had an ambulatory between the choir and the five radiating chapels.[52]

Saint Martial of Limoges, an abbey church of pilgrimage, no longer exists, but its remains have been most carefully studied by Charles de Lasteyrie.[53] His conclusions are that the church consecrated by Urban II on his attendance at the Council of Clermont in 1095 retained the essential elements of the other pilgrimage churches but on a scale smaller than that of Santiago or Toulouse.

Returning to the vast basilica of Saint Sernin of Toulouse, the pilgrims would be told by the Augustinian canons who served the church that the bodies of no less than six of the apostles were buried there. This claim was based on a doubtful document that alleged that Charlemagne brought them from Spain according to the saying of an old Latin distich:

Sex vehit his rediens Hispanis ab oris
Carlus apostolici corpora sancta gregis.[54]

This number was eventually increased to eight, including the body of Santiago. The total length of the church was 115 meters, its width 32.5 meters, and it had double side aisles longer than those of Santiago of Compostela. It is likely that the only church longer than Toulouse was that of Cluny. The basilica of Saint Sernin was begun about 1060 and was in the thick of construction in 1080 when Raymond Gayrard was director of the works. According to a local chronicle the church and the high altar were consecrated by Pope Urban II in the presence of fifteen French bishops in 1096 and it can therefore be fairly assumed that the choir was then complete. The consecration of the secondary altar by Pope Calixtus II in 1119 must have marked the end of the works of the nave. Gómez Moreno thinks that the decorated part of the chevet, the crossing, the daring height of the nave, and the embossing of the ambulatory show the unity of a single hand "in whom we must recognise the sculptor of the cloister of Moissac" and this must be the same Bernard Gelduin who made the altar of Saint Sernin.[55]

Elie Lambert recognizes two distinct stages in the building of Saint Sernin. He argues that it may be that the primitive plan was an ampler version of the plan of Saint Martial of Limoges, but that later the Augustinian canons of Toulouse sought to rival the mother church of the Benedictines at Cluny with their double side aisles. This appears to be the case because there is uncertainty in the disposition and the joining.[56]

The monumental vastness of Saint Sernin can be imagined by comparing its dimensions with those of Saint James of Compostela. Saint Sernin was longer than Saint James by 18 meters but much narrower for it was only 32.5 meters wide while Saint James had a width of 65 meters from the north to the south porch. Saint James was perhaps the perfect pilgrimage church, and for the present we will leave it with the description from the *Codex Calixtinus* that its head is to be found in the altar of the Sacred Savior, its crown in the ambulatory, its body in the great central nave, its two members are the arms of the transept, while it has eight other little heads—the four radiating apsidal chapels and the four chapels in the crossings in each of which an altar is to be found.

After the visit to Saint Sernin, the pilgrim would be prepared for the similar pilgrimage basilica of Saint James of Compostela, his ultimate goal.

A second route to Compostela, according to the guide, begins at Le Puy and is frequented by Burgundians and Germans. The only relic mentioned by the author on this route is that of the martyr Saint Foi at Conques. But it is possible that some pilgrims might come to Le Puy by way of the greatest monastic church of them all at Cluny in Burgundy, with its relics of both Saint Peter and Saint Paul. Other pilgrims from Auvergne would be able to visit the shrines of Saint Nectaire, with its twelfth-century copper and gilt bust of Saint Baudime, Saint Austremoine of Issoire where his relics were to be venerated in the crypt and where a thirteenth-century reliquary chest in copper and enamel of Limousin work can be viewed today, and Orcival with its twelfth-century Virgin in majesty with Jesus looking like a little Roman emperor. Notre Dame du Port at Clermont would also be visited where a famous statue of the Virgin and Child was executed about 946 for Etienne II, the bishop of Clermont and also abbot of Conques (937–84).[57] Yet other pilgrims would have visited Chamalières whose pride it was to possess a holy nail donated by Charlemagne from the Cross of Christ.

Le Puy itself has an ancient history as a pilgrimage center, and it was Godescalc its Bishop who led the first notable pilgrimage to Compostela, as we have observed. In this dramatic area of volcanic craters, the very cathedral itself dedicated to the Virgin is a living example of the three-way traffic among Muslim Spain, Orthodox Constantinople, and Catholic France, with its stones of alternating color, its three-lobed arches, its octagonal cupolas in the nave, and its doors with Kufic characters. Pilgrims would certainly see the "Pierre des Fièvres,"[58] which may well have been a Druidic dolmen later Christianized,[59] and on which the sick lay while prayers for their recovery were made to the

Blessed Virgin. Probably the greatest attraction of the cathedral was its fame as a healing center, associated with the power of the Virgin. The earliest sacred image of her that was placed near the "Stone of the Fevered" has disappeared, but it may well be recalled in the leaden tokens of pilgrimage fabricated in the thirteenth century, which show a crowned Virgin holding a fleur-de-lis rod in her right hand like a scepter while she supports the Infant on her knee with her left hand. The second image was even more famous. Imported from the Orient, this image was mysteriously hieratic and was burned in 1794 during the revolution.[60] Another precious relic was one thorn from the Savior's crown of thorns donated by Saint Louis to the cathedral of Le Puy.

However, the most notable reliquary on this route to Compostela was undoubtedly that of Saint Foi at her abbey church of Conques in Rouergue. The monk who showed the pilgrims round this famous church must have been delighted to point out the facade of the tympanum of the west door. It depicts Saint Foi prostrate before the hand of God and a monk advancing toward Christ introducing a crowned king and a woman, certainly Charlemagne and probably his sister Berthe, and behind them acolytes bearing the legendary gifts of the emperor to the abbey. The monastic treasure in Conques is probably the most significant survival of the great medieval treasures of France and enables the modern visitor to understand how dazzled the eyes of medieval pilgrims must have been by these marvels of the goldsmith's and jeweler's art.

The majesty of Saint Foi is carved of wood and covered with gold and begemmed with pearls, intaglios, and rock crystal. Just as bronze statues honored emperors, and pagan divinities had marble or stone representations, it was felt at the end of the tenth century that the Virgin and the saints should have figural memorials or reliquaries like the Golden Virgin of Essen or the Majesty of Saint Foi.[61] This crowned image, with begemmed earrings, sits on a throne surmounted by rock-crystal balls added after Romanesque times and probably should be imagined as holding a golden dove in each hand, the symbols of purity and of the divine approval.[62] Her most striking feature is her penetrating gaze, formed by her enamel eyeballs. This may have been a deliberate way of recalling the famous act of healing attributed to her, in which she restored the eyes of a supplicant, which had been torn out by the roots. Certainly her church was thronged with those who had maladies of the eyes and other sicknesses.

The meaning and the placement of the enthroned martyr's reliquary were very important. The martyr by his or her relics was the designated president of the eucharistic meal. André Grabar has argued convincingly that it was the martyr chiefly who was called to this presidency because he by his (or her) sacrifice had shared in the Passion of Christ that renews the mystical agape of each Mass.[63] The martyr in a sense replaced Christ in the role as president since the martyr occupied the throne of Christ, having procured it by virtue of the sufferings that reflect those of Christ. Furthermore, this was the earthly image of the throne in heaven promised by Christ to his elect. Naturally this throne had its place in the apse, at once the place of the president at Mass and the site of relics. It was appropriate therefore that the majesty of Saint Foi should have appeared to the eyes of pilgrims in the year 1000 behind and above the main altar of the basilica. The attitude of this majesty was therefore that of the saint presiding at the Mass.

Conques, as we have indicated, had and has other precious relics. Included among them is the famous Pepin reliquary in the form of a chest, or purse made of wood, covered with gold and gems, which contained relics of the Virgin, saints Peter, Paul, Andrew, George, John the Evangelist, and Hippolytus, the prepuce and umbilical cord of Jesus, and relics of other saints including John the Baptist and Saint Martin. There was also a hexagonal table-reliquary made of wood, covered with engraved silver, enameled and gilded, which contained seventy-one fragments of relics. There was and is also the famous reliquary known as the "A of Charlemagne." It is of wood covered with gilded silver, and it probably contained a relic of the True Cross.[64] Another reliquary of the True Cross is also at Conques, bearing the inscription that Pope Pascal II in the year 1100 sent these relics of the Cross of Christ, of his sepulcher, and of several saints. The Begon portable altar contains similar relics and dates from the same period. A coffer of the relics of Saint Foi is also at Conques. It is of wood covered with copper and silver and decorated with thirty-one medallions of enamel work, with exquisite coloring of lapis lazuli, azure, green, turquoise, and yellow. This summary account of the treasures of Conques gives only a faint glimmer of the scintillations of medieval reliquaries, most of which have now disappeared, except at Conques itself. No wonder the sanctuary of the third-century martyr, Saint Foi, was popular for both the sightseers and the sick.

The last place that the author of the Compostela guide advised pilgrims to visit on the second route was the abbey church of Saint Peter of Moissac. It was renowned for its grand tympanum of the southern porch with the elders of the Apocalypse worshiping Christ in glory and for its exquisite cloister, neither of which was mentioned in the guide. There are extant no dazzling reliquaries to trap our gaze with gold, silver, enamel, and precious gems, as an important abbey such as Moissac must have had in keeping with its superb buildings. But reliquaries must have existed for we know that this abbey, supposedly founded by King Clovis, was enriched with important Carolingian relics.[65] The smaller religious houses in its environs such as Duravel[66] received the relics of three early hermits of Egypt—Saints Hilarion, Poemon, and Agathon—which had been given to Moissac by Charlemagne, the very king who had also sent relics to the cathedral of Saint Stephen of Cahors[67] in the same region. This great royal cache of relics, we may assume, was the gift of the grateful emperor of Constantinople for the services Charlemagne had rendered to the Eastern Church in pushing back the Muslim frontiers.

Pilgrims following the third route to Compostela began at Vézelay, with stations at Saint Martial of Limoges, Saint Léonard of Noblat, and Saint Front of Périgueux. The great abbey of Vézelay, originally under the patronage of the Virgin, was transferred in 1050 to the patronage of Saint Mary Magdalene, whose remains it was said to contain. It is almost certain that, despite the popularity of the pilgrimage to Vézelay in the eleventh and twelfth centuries, these were not the relics of the Magdalen, although in 1058 and again in 1103 (despite the disagreements of inhabitants of Provence) these relics were declared authentic by Rome. The death blow to this pilgrimage center was delivered in 1279 when it was revealed that the real bones of the saint had been hidden centuries ago through fear of Saracen raids and had been rediscovered. Pope Boniface VIII accepted this theory.[68]

Authentic or not, the conviction that the basilica contained the body of the famous saint who was the first to see the risen Christ drew vast concourses of pilgrims. It was here in 1146 that Saint Bernard preached the Second Crusade and where the soldiers of the Third Crusade assembled. Here also we can imagine world-spoiled pilgrims who identified themselves with the Magdalen who as a penitent sinner empathized with sinners. In the neighborhood, too, was the body of her brother Lazarus, whom Christ first raised from the dead and who was buried in the cathedral of Autun. The Compostela guide calls it "a most beautiful basilica," leaving its sculptural enrichments unsung, and declares that the saint not only assures sinners of absolution but cures the blind, the deaf, the dumb, and the insane.[69]

The next stopping place en route to Compostela was the church of Saint Martial of Limoges, who along with Saint Front of Périgueux was thought to be a disciple of Saint Peter according to *The Golden Legend*.[70] Almost nothing of the great abbey church of Saint Martial remains[71] except some illuminated manuscripts that show great verve and style. But this is the center of Limoges enamel work, and there are splendid chests and reliquaries of Limousin manufacture in the churches of Saint Michael of the Lions in Limoges, as of Ambazac, Bellac, Gimel, and of Gorre.[72] We may readily suppose that the great abbey with the remains of Saint Martial would have dazzled its pilgrims with its reliquary covers of champlevé, for this was one of the great cultural centers of France. Enameling consists in fusing a hard, vitreous compound onto metal surfaces. The glasslike compound is colored by various oxides that render the coffers brilliant in such hues as white, blue, green, red, turquoise, yellow, black, and purple. An interesting characteristic of Limoges enamels is a fondness for treating the heads of flat figures in relief. Where the enamel is missing, we see the heads, outlines, and backgrounds of the various figures standing out in brilliant bas relief, highly decorated. One can imagine how marvelously mysterious they would look in the half-light of the crypts of Romanesque churches in the Limousin area. We know quite definitely that a golden statue of Saint Martial, enthroned like that of Saint Foi of Conques, was made in 952.[73]

Close to Saint Martial was the church of Saint Léonard of Noblat, whose work in life and after death was concentrated in freeing prisoners. King Clovis is said to have held him during his baptism as an infant, and he is chiefly renowned for a life of austerity and humiliation as a deacon who founded an agricultural colony for prisoners whom he helped to rehabilitate. So immensely popular was he that five hundred churches or chapels dedicated to him remain in France and a third of that number remain in England.[74] The remarkable feature of Saint Léonard's church was that around his tomb there was a vast collection of fetters, chains, manacles, helmets, bolts and bars, and iron collars. These ex-votos were the tributes of those whom the saint had freed from their captivity.

The next pilgrim station would be at the great basilica of Saint Front of Périgueux. This disciple of Saint Peter who may even have been one of Christ's disciples himself, as the guide suggests, is most honorably buried in a round sepulcher imitating the shape of Christ's own. The church today is so entirely renovated that it is difficult to conceive how it looked to medieval pilgrims, except for the marvelous domes of the nave, which must have made it resemble some exotic Eastern temple. Saint Front's tomb must have been covered with gold because we know that a goldsmith, Théodelème of La Chaise-Dieu abbey, was brought to work on it.[75]

The fourth and last route to Compostela began at Orléans, though it must have been joined there by pilgrims from the coastal Mont-Saint-Michel, from England by the overland route, and from Saint-Denis and from the great Marian center of pilgrimage at Chartres, each worthy of a visit. Chartres, as is well known, boasted the possession (still retained) of the tunic (sainte chemise) worn by the Virgin Mary at the Annunciation. It had been given to the cathedral by Charles the Bald in 878 and was miraculously preserved when the cathedral burned down. Saint Denis, especially when ruled by the abbot Suger, the great regent of France and founder of Gothic,[76] was a royal treasury as notable for its collection of relics as for the splendor of its reliquaries. These relics included wood from the True Cross, a holy nail from the cross, and a crown of thorns, all of which had been in the original chapel of the royal Aix-la-Chapelle. Mont-Saint-Michel had its own pilgrimage in honor of the archangel who had defeated the devil in battle and was the defender of Christian souls. Being a bodiless angel he could not have had a relic, unless some featherbrained enthusiast invented one!

At Orléans in the cathedral of the Holy Cross the pilgrims could see the miraculous chalice of Saint Evurcus, which one day had been consecrated by the very hand of Christ himself, and could also view a portion of the True Cross. A rival eucharistic relic was to be found in the church of Saint Samson in the same city. It was supposed to have been the paten used at the Last Supper.

Moving down the Loire valley to the city of Tours the pilgrims would come to the great basilica of Saint Martin, most generous of saints, who shared his tunic with a beggar. The tomb itself was marvelously decorated with events from his holy life, and according to the guide, the sarcophagus was covered with gold and silver and coruscated with jewels.[77]

The next stop for pilgrims was to visit the body of the blessed Hilary, bishop and confessor, in Poitiers, where in 732 the Saracens were finally halted by Charles Martel. The bones of this champion of orthodoxy, Saint Hilary, were buried says the author of the guide in a reliquary that glittered with gold, silver, and the most precious gems. His large and lovely basilica was the scene of many miracles.[78]

The pilgrims would next reach Saint Jean d'Angély where a hundred monks sang the praises of the forerunner of the Messiah day and night and where the head of Saint John the Baptist was the chief relic.

The pilgrims on this route would also visit the relics of Saint Eutrope of Saintes in his basilica. There is much obscurity about the history of this confessor. When his relics were exposed his cranium revealed a cicatrix, and therefore he was probably a martyr.[79] The author of the guide provides a lengthy summary of the passion of Saint Eutropius and states that he is a very successful thaumaturge.[80]

The remaining shrines of the route in France are all associated with the *Chanson de Roland,* where the great Paladin and his peers and soldiers fought gallantly but vainly against the Saracens (but actually against the Basques). At Saint Romain of Blaye the body of the gallant Roland himself is to be found. He is according to the guide, "the blessed Roland, Martyr."[81] At Saint Seurin of Bordeaux his mighty horn was kept, which had been split by his last, desperate and rallying call. Drop-

ping down into the Landes the pilgrims would rest at Belin, where there
was a great tomb enclosing the remains of Roland's royal compatriots
slain by the Saracens, including Oliver, Gondebaud of Frisia, Ogier the
Dane, Arastain of Brittany, and Garin of Lorraine. All these warriors
were killed fighting for the Christian faith against the Muslims, and so
they were not only heroes but also were treated as saints.

Again one sees in the Benedictine abbeys on the four routes, and in
the sacred remains of Charlemagne's warriors on the fourth route, the
ecclesiastical and political commitment in the pilgrimage to Saint James
of Compostela. Though to our modern eyes there may appear to be a
confusion of the political and religious, the secular and the sacred, this
dichotomy would have been invisible to medieval eyes. For the emperor
Charlemagne and his successors ruled by the divine permission as was
symbolized by his anointing by the pope, as did the archbishops who
received the pallium of their authority from the pope, Christ's vicar,
while the *reconquista* of Spain by Crusader or pilgrim was winning back
a Christian land from the infidels. The confusion (or cohesion, depending on one's point of view) of secular and sacred is perfectly expressed in
the fact that Count Roland's sword, Durandal, contained in its hilt most
precious relics:

> Ah, Durandal, fair, hallowed, and devote,
> What store of relics lie in thy hilt of gold!
> St. Peter's tooth, St. Basil's blood, it holds,
> Hair of my Lord St. Denis, there enclosed,
> Likewise a piece of Blessed Mary's robe.[82]

The *Chanson de Roland,* an eleventh-century epic, is an embellishment
of ninth-century events, and it shows how powerful was the belief in
relics. Charlemagne's sword is called "Joyeuse" and his men rally to the
cry of "Montjoie" uttered by pilgrims when they first caught sight of
Rome, as later of Compostela. The epic also reminds us of the relic in
that sword:

> You know the lance—for oft we've heard the tale
> Which pierced Our Lord when He on cross was slain:
> Carlon possesses the lancehead, God be praised!
> In the gold pommel he's had it shrined and cased.[83]

The pilgrimage route resounded with Carolingian echoes after it
reached the Pyrenees at Ostabat, near Cize, where it joined the other
three routes toward Santiago of Compostela. On the mountain there
was an ancient cross supposedly erected by Charlemagne while his face
was turned in prayer toward Saint James of Compostela. Here the
pilgrims imitated the great emperor and each planted a cross of wood

beside Charlemagne's great cross of stone. The road then led to Roncesvalles where all could admire the huge rock that Roland was supposed
to have split with his sword.

The two most important names and influences on the pilgrimage
roads through France to Galicia in the Jacobite pilgrimage are Charlemagne and Cluny. The first gathered and generously donated the most
precious relics that he had collected from the Christian emperor of
Byzantium, and under the inspiration of the second, abbeys were built
to house these relics. To these the pilgrims were attracted, in them
housed, and from them sent on their journey to meet more of the
proven friends of Christ, the saints. Pilgrims honored them in their
daily liturgies as examples of the holy life and as intercessors for those
whose sins and sicknesses cried out for absolution and healing.

NOTES

1. Pierre Riché, *La vie quotidienne dans l'empire carolingien* (Paris: Hachette, 1974), pp. 316, 320. "It was the Judge of the Apocalypse more than that of the Incarnation."

2. Ibid., pp. 321–22.

3. The words of Raymond Oursel, a French authority on pilgrimage, deserve attention: *"Le culte des reliques charnelles est le trait le plus frappant peut-être de la dévotion populaire du haut Moyen Age"* (*Les pèlerins du moyen âge: les hommes, les chemins, les sanctuaires* [Paris: A. Fayard, 1963], p. 16).

4. Exodus 13:19 refers to Moses taking the bones of Joseph with him from Egypt.

5. See Revelation 6:11 and 14:13.

6. Acts of the Apostles 19:12 refers to handkerchiefs and aprons that had been touched by Saint Paul as curing the sick.

7. *The New Catholic Encyclopedia*, 17 vols. (New York: McGraw, 1966), Vol. XII, p. 235a. The Christians of Smyrna affirmed that "we took up his bones which are more precious than the costliest jewels and finer than refined gold, and laid them in a suitable place. There the Lord will allow us to assemble, as we are able, with joy and gladness, to celebrate the birthday [Gk. *hēmeran genethlion*] of his martyrdom" (Epistle to the Smyrneans, which is XVIII in J. B. Lightfoot, ed., *The Apostolic Fathers* [New York: Macmillan, 1885], p. 196). See also J. Hastings, ed., *Encyclopedia of Religion and Ethics*, 12 vols. (New York: Scribner's, 1908–26), X, pp. 653–54.

8. *New Catholic Encyclopedia*, XII, p. 253 a and b.

9. *Contra vigilantium*, in *Patrologia latina*, 221 vols., ed. J. P. Migne (Paris: Garnier, 1844–64), 23, pp. 346–48.

10. Bishop Eusebius of Caesarea, *Vita Constantini imperatoris ad sanctorum coetum*, III, cap. 25–26, in *Patrologia Graeca*, 162 vols., ed. J. P. Migne (Paris: Garnier, 1857–66), 20:10–1316. See also Heinz Kraft, *Kaiser Konstantins religiöse Entwicklung* (Tübingen: Mohr, 1955), pp. 119–21.

11. *Contra vigilantium*, cap. 8.

12. Oscar Cullman, *Peter: Disciple-Apostle-Martyr*, rev. ed. (Philadelphia: Westminster Press, 1962), pp. 113–57.

13. S. G. F. Brandon, *Man and God in Art and Ritual* (New York: Scribner's, 1975), p. 205.

14. The elaborations of the legends were treated in greater detail in chapter 2.

15. A. P. Stanley, *Historical Memorials of Canterbury*, 5th rev. ed. (London: J. Murray, 1882), pp. 230–33. See also Paul Alonzo Brown, *The Development of the Legend of Thomas Becket* (Philadelphia: University of Pennsylvania, 1930).

16. Cited in Sidney Heath, *Pilgrim Life in the Middle Ages* (Boston and New York: Houghton Mifflin, 1912), pp. 190–91.

17. Ibid.

18. Suger, *De consecratione s. Dionysii*, II, pp. 216–17 in *Oeuvres complètes*, ed. by Lecoy de la Marche (Paris, 1867), pp. 211–38. See also Jonathan Sumption, *Pilgrimage: An Image of Medieval Religion* (London: Faber & Faber, 1975), pp. 213–14; and E. Panofsky, *Abbot Suger on the Abbey Church of Saint Denis and Its Art Treasures* (Princeton, N.J.: Princeton University Press, 1946) is an English translation of Suger's work.

19. Sumption, *Pilgrimage*, p. 23.

20. Ibid., p. 22.

21. L. F. Salzman, *English Life in the Middle Ages* (London: Oxford University Press, 1926), p. 274.

22. Aimonus, *De translatione sanctorum martyrum, Patrologia latina*, Vol. 115, pp. 939–60.

23. Adam of Eynsham, *Magna vita sancti Hugonis*, 2 vols., ed. E. L. Douie and H. Farmer (London: Nelson, 1961–62), II, pp. 169–70. As a complete contrast it is worth reading how abbot Samson of the abbey of Edmundsbury translated the body of Saint Edmund in 1198. After unwrapping the coverings of the saint's body, he prayed: "Glorious martyr, turn not my daring to my hurt, in that I who am a sinner and wretched touch you. You know my devotion and my intention." Then with great reverence "he touched the eyes and nose . . . and afterwards touched the breast and arms, and raising the left hand touched the fingers and placed his own fingers between those of the saint" (*The Chronicle of Jocelin of Brakelond*, trans. L. C. Lane [London: Chatto & Windus, 1925], p. 178).

24. Raymond Oursel, *Living Architecture: Romanesque* (New York: Grosset & Dunlap, 1967), p. 62.

25. J. D. Mansi, *Sacrorum conciliorum nova et amplissima collectio*, 53 vols. in 58 (Paris: Welter, 1901–27), 22, col. 791, canon 17.

26. Jean Leclercq, F. Vandenbroucke, and L. Bouyer, *La spiritualité du moyen âge* (Paris: Aubert, 1961). English edition: *The Spirituality of the Middle Ages* (London and New York: Burns, Oates, 1968), p. 313.

27. Other surviving statue-reliquaries include those of Saint Baudime, companion of Saint Nectaire, in the church of Saint Nectaire in the Auvergne—for a reproduction see Bernard Craplet, *Auvergne romane*, 3d ed. (Yonne: Zodiaque, 1972), plates 68–70. Also that of Saint Théau of Solignac—for a reproduction see Melchior de Vogüé, *Glossaire* (Yonne: Zodiaque, 1965), "Nuit des Temps" series, p. 124.

28. *Liber miraculorum sanctae Fidis*, ed. A. Bouillet (Paris: Champion, 1897), I, cap. VIII.

29. This is reproduced in color in L. Grodecki, F. Mütherich, J. Taleron, and F. Wormald, *Le siècle de l'an mille* (Paris: Gallimard, 1973), p. 283.

30. The reproduction is to be found ibid.

31. A striking though not unusual example of multiple translations is that of Saint Philibert. His relics had been venerated at Noirmoutier from the seventh century. Since the island was threatened from 819 onward, the monks first moved with the relics to Deas on the rim of Lake Grandlieu, then as the Normans advanced they moved back to Cunault in 845 and retreated further to Messay. As that became unsafe they left for Saint-Pourçain in the central massif of Auvergne, and, finally the monks and their saint's relics reached the safety of Tournus in 875. Thus five major moves had been made in fifty-six years (cf. Ermentarius, *Miracula Philiberti*, ed. Poupardin [Paris: A. Picard, 1905], p. 60–61; and Riché, *La vie quotidienne*, p. 326). The more important relics of Saint Martin were also moved to Cormery before returning to Tours (cf. P. Gasnault, "Le tombeau de saint Martin et les invasions normandes" in *Revue de l'église de France*, 1961, pp. 51–66).

32. The anecdote is reported in Sumption, *Pilgrimage*, p. 153.

33. *Chronica monasterii de Melsa*, ed. E. A. Bond (London: Rolls Series, 1866–68), 3, p. 35, cited in J. J. Jusserand, *English Wayfaring Life in the Middle Ages*, rev. ed. (London: Unwin, 1925), p. 354.

34. *Liber sancti Jacobi*, V, cap. 8, p. 26 (in the Fita and Vinson transcription).

35. Ibid., pp. 29–30.

36. As early as the fifth century two heads of Saint John the Baptist were venerated, and in the eleventh century both were to be found in Constantinople during the time the third head appeared in Saint Jean d'Angély (Sumption, *Pilgrimage*, p. 27).

37. On the subject of stolen relics, see Patrick Geary, *Furta Sacra: Thefts of Relics in the Central Middle Ages* (Princeton, N.J.: Princeton University Press, 1978), passim.

38. H. Ellis, ed., *Original Letters Illustrative of English History*, 3d series (London: Harding, Triphook & Lepard, 1846), 3, p. 168.

39. Detailed iconographical studies of themes will be considered in our chapter 5.

40. If pilgrimage churches could not claim apostolic origins, as Compostela did, it was important for them to insist that they were founded by disciples of the apostles, if possible. It is significant that of the seven evangelists supposedly sent from Rome, six of them are patrons of distinguished pilgrimage churches en route to Compostela. The most notable (apart from Saint Trophime) were: Saint Denis, Saint Sernin of Toulouse, and Saint Martial of Limoges, also Saint Eutropius of Saintes. Trophimus was thought to be the disciple of Saint Paul mentioned in the Acts of the Apostles 20:4 and 21:29 and also in 2 Timothy 4:20.

41. *Liber sancti Jacobi*, V, cap. 8, p. 22 (in the Fita and Vinson transcription).

42. Ibid., p. 24.

43. Ibid., pp. 25–26.

44. P. Jaffé, ed., *Monumenta Germaniae historica scriptores*, XII (Hanover: 1861), pp. 316–23. For a modern life see F. Brittain, *Saint Giles* (Cambridge: Heffer, 1928).

45. Saint Gilles is supposed to have died in A.D. 725, but by the eleventh century he was venerated in many places as helper of those in spiritual anguish and as patron saint of nursing mothers (Vera and Hellmut Hell, *The Great Pilgrimage of the Middle Ages* [London: Barrie & Rockliff, 1966], p. 134). See also W. S. Stoddard, *The Façade of Saint-Gilles-du-Gard: Its Influence on French Sculpture* (Middletown, Conn: Wesleyan University Press, 1973).

46. The attractive cloisters of its abbey church have been reassembled in the Cloisters Museum at Fort Tryon Park, New York City. For its foundation in French epic poetry, see Joan M. Ferrante, *Guillaume d'Orange: Four Twelfth-Century Epics* (New York: Columbia University Press, 1974).

47. *Pèlerins*, p. 11.

48. *Liber sancti Jacobi*, V, cap. 9, p. 47.

49. See Vásquez de Parga, J. M. Lacarra, and J. U. Riú, *Las peregrinaciónes a Santiago de Compostela*, 3 vols. (Madrid: Escuela de Estudios Medievales, 1948–49), I, p. 547.

50. See A. Auriol and R. Rey, *La basilique st. Sernin de Toulouse* (Toulouse and Paris: E. Privat, 1930), pp. 296–97.

51. *L'art religieux du XIIe siècle en France*, 3rd ed. (Paris: Colin, 1924), pp. 291–93. Mâle said it was for the ancestors of Frenchmen what the temple of Delphos was for the Greeks.

52. The dimensions were obtained from Charles Lelong, *Touraine romane*, 3d ed. (Yonne: Zodiaque, 1977), p. 60, itself based upon plans made in the eighteenth century, two watercolors of 1798, and the dimensions of the remains today.

53. *L'abbaye de saint Martial de Limoges* (Paris: Colin, 1901). The Bibliothèque Nationale has a fine engraving made in 1726 of the church in longitudinal section.

54. Vázquez de Parga, Lacarra, Riú, *Peregrinaciónes*, I, p. 552.

55. *El arte románico español* (Madrid: Centro de Estudios historicos, 1934), pp. 138–39.

56. "La peregrinación a Compostela" in *Archivo español de arte*, 1943, pp. 273–309. The argument is summarized in Vázquez de Parga, Lacarra, Riú, *Peregrinaciónes*, I, pp. 553–54.

57. G. Gaillard, M.-M. S. Gauthier, L. Balsan, and A. Surchamp, *Rouergue roman* (Yonne: Zodiaque, 1963), p. 107.

58. It bears the inscription: *Plebs hac rupe sana fit sana sopore potita / Si quaeras quare, virtus adscribitur arae.* This can be very roughly translated: "Those people who sleep on this stone are cured. Do you wish to know why? Its virtue is attributed to the altar." See A. Faux, ed., *Guide du visiteur de la cathédrale du Puy*, 3rd ed. (Le Puy-en-Velay, 1971), p. 9.

59. Ibid., p. 2.

60. Reproductions of these images are to be found ibid., p. 40. See also O. Beigbeder, *Forez-Velay roman* (Yonne: Zodiaque, 1962), p. 45, for a reproduction of the first Virgin on a pilgrim token of a lead.

61. Gaillard, Gauthier, Balsan, Surchamp, *Rouergue roman*, p. 106. It seems that a lifesize corpus on a huge crucifix was the first example of a three-dimensional figure representation in the churches of the West. By a natural extension it was then applied to the beginning of the Incarnation, with representations of the Virgin in three dimensions as the *Sedes sapientiae*, forming with her limbs the throne for Christ as the Logos, or Wisdom of God. For a study of the second group of statues, see Ilene H. Forsyth, *The Throne of Wisdom: Wood Sculptures of the Madonna in Romanesque France* (Princeton, N.J.; Princeton University Press, 1972), which indicates that there were only sixteen statues of the Madonna and Child before 1100 (p. 133). Bernard of Angers reported in 1012 that Conques had a large crucifix of gold and silver as well as its majesty of Saint Foi.

62. Gaillard, Gauthier, Balsan, Surchamp, *Rouergue roman*, pp. 109 and 137.

63. His contentions are summarized ibid., p. 108.

64. Gaillard, Gauthier, Balsan, Surchamp, *Rouergue roman*, p. 141.

65. M. Vidal, J. Maury, and J. Porcher, *Quercy roman*, 2d ed. (Yonne: Zodiaque, 1969), p. 49.

66. Ibid., p. 147.

67. Ibid., p. 197.

68. Raymond Oursel, *Bourgogne romane*, 5th ed. (Yonne: Zodiaque, 1968), p. 257. The legend, dating from early in the eleventh century, asserted that a monk named Badilon had brought the saint's body directly from Jerusalem.

69. *Liber sancti Jacobi*, V, cap. 8, p. 29 (in the Fita and Vinson transcription).

70. *The Golden Legend of Jacobus de Voragine*, tran. and adapted by Granger Ryan and Helmut Ripperger (New York: Arno Press, 1969), p. 332.

71. Curiously enough the Compostela guide is silent on the pilgrimage church of Saint Martial of Limoges.

72. All are illustrated and most in color in J. Maury, M.-M. S. Gauthier, and J. Porcher, *Limousin roman* (Yonne: Zodiaque, 1960).

73. Ibid., pp. 114–15.

74. Joan Evans, *Art in Medieval France, 987–1498* (London: Phaidon, 1948), p. 21. It should be observed that Saint Léonard was thought of as the special patron of the mentally sick, who in the Middle Ages, were put in chains. See Vera and Hellmut Hell, *Great Pilgrimage*, p. 78.

75. Beigbeder, *Forez-Velay roman*, p. 9.

76. Suger wrote: "Men's eyes are set under a spell by reliquaries. . . . They see the shining image of a saint and in the imagination of the people his saintliness is in proportion to its brilliance" (Evans, *Art in Medieval France*, p. 21).

77. *Liber sancti Jacobi*, V, cap. 8, p. 33 (in the Fita and Vinson transcription).

78. Ibid., p. 34.

79. F. Eygun and J. Dupont, *Saintonge romane* (Yonne: Zodiaque, 1970), p. 38.

80. *Liber sancti Jacobi*, V, cap. 8, p. 42.

81. The Latin is *requiescit corpus Rotolandi, Martyris* (ibid., V, cap. 8, p. 43).

82. *The Song of Roland*, trans. Dorothy L. Sayers (Harmondsworth and Baltimore: Penguin Books, 1959), p. 141; stanza 173 of the original poem.

83. Ibid., p. 147; stanza 183 of the original poem.

—— 5 ——

Sermons in Stone: Iconography

DAZZLED by the glitter of gold and silver, as by the shimmering gems of the reliquaries, we turn now to the magnificent stone carvings of the Romanesque churches. Imagine, if you can, church walls and pillars painted ocher, blue, red, and green.[1] Some were carved, others uncarved. These carvings depicted scenes from the Old and New Testaments and the lives of the saints. The carvings can be found to this day on the exteriors and interiors of abbey, cathedral, and parish church. Usually they are on the half drums above the doors and on the tops of the columns supporting the roof and leading to the altar as well as in the apse.

The pilgrims were not the tourists of today, reading a guidebook or trailing behind a human guide. Tourism was not the aim in going on pilgrimage. Pilgrims did not visit churches as artistic curiosities. Also, the churches were not all centers of art and learning, although most towns and villages took pride in them. Their stones were embellished with carvings dependent upon local skills and the generosity of local donors. The carved images would delight and instruct the parishioners and the visiting pilgrims. The carvings would be all the more impressive since the vast majority (except the clergy, the upper nobility, and the wealthy merchants) could not read.

It would not be possible to take into account all the extant carvings of the pilgrimage churches. That would be both exhaustive and exhausting. It seems better to concentrate on the particular themes that were likely to capture the attention of our traveling ancestors, elicit their emotions, and improve their faith and morals by example or warning. Almost every single carving described or interpreted in this book, we have seen for ourselves on the pilgrimage roads to Compostela through France and northwestern Spain.

It was a delight to discover that many of the topics selected from the Bible for illustration were directly related to pilgrimage. However, this is hardly surprising, since the two major images for the religious life are a battle and a pilgrimage. In Bunyanesque terms, they would be called "The Holy War" and "Pilgrim's Progress."

Judaism and Christianity both picture humans as pilgrims redirected from the road to destruction to the right road to salvation. The very first man, Adam, was a reluctant pilgrim expelled from paradise and thereafter seeking his true fatherland; judicial pilgrims, paying the penalty of banishment, could easily identify with him. True pilgrims would follow in the footsteps of Abraham who answered God's call by pulling up his tent pegs and journeying from the far country of Ur of the Chaldees. Moses, too, led the children of Israel on a titanic pilgrimage lasting forty years.

The New Testament and the Church Fathers also advocate pilgrimage. Does not the first letter of Peter address Christians as "Dearly beloved, I beseech you as strangers and pilgrims"? The letter to the Hebrews says that the faithful confess that "they are pilgrims and strangers on the earth."[2]

The Fathers of the Church were true to the biblical tradition. Saint Augustine, the famous fourth-century bishop and theologian of North Africa, had good reason to think of Christians as refugee pilgrims. Fleeing from the supposedly eternal city of Rome, they thronged the beaches of Hippo Regius. He popularized the view that Christians were a peregrinating people, a company on the march, and that true followers of God found only temporary comfort as at roadside inns.[3] Two centuries later, the famous Benedictine, Pope Gregory the Great, reiterated this lesson. He wrote: "The righteous cannot settle permanently in this world. They understand that they are only pilgrims and guests in it. They long to rejoice where they belong and cannot be content in a foreign land."[4]

It was cheering for the pilgrims to see cockleshells, stars, palms, and figures of other pilgrims carved in stone but hardly instructive spiritually. It was the carving of the epochal events of pilgrimage in the biblical saga—such as the Exodus from Egypt to Canaan and the second exodus of Christ's resurrection from the dead and his meeting with the pilgrims on the Emmaus road—that taught the way and reward of pilgrimage. The churches en route to Compostela are to this day filled with such theological carvings. They are the testaments of the illiterate, the Bible of the poor.

For Christians as well as Jews, the Old Testament is Sacred Scripture. Hence it seems curious that greater use was not made of the pilgrimage theme in the earliest books of the Bible. The negative aspect—alienation from God and the ejection of Adam and Eve from Eden—is, of course, often depicted. Sometimes it is only an indispensable prelude to Paradise Regained and the recognition of Mary as a second Eve who bore the second Adam, Christ. Perhaps the loveliest of all Romanesque carvings of Eve in her frail and enticing beauty is found on a capital of Autun cathedral in Burgundy. A kinder version of the expulsion from Eden is depicted in the cathedral of Saint Maurice, Vienne, where God leads Adam out of Eden. The latter may very well have cheered the juridical prisoners whose clanking chains announced their presence.

It is rare to find any depiction of Abraham, the father of the faithful, traveling in hope to the far country at God's behest. Carvers preferred the more dramatic event of the testing of Abraham's faith when he was commanded to sacrifice his firstborn son Isaac and at the last minute God substituted a ram. The event was thought to be an anticipation of the sacrifice of the Cross and of the Eucharist.

Even the dramatic event of the Exodus in the crossing of the Red Sea is rarely pictured. The technical difficulty might have proved too much of a challenge. Exceptions can be found on the capitals of the elegant church of Saint Nectaire in Auvergne and in the abbey church of Saint George in Boscherville in Normandy. However, the giving of the Law to Moses on Sinai and the worship of the Golden Calf are commonly seen. These topics were probably chosen because the medieval penal system gave an important place to the Decalogue. Also, its second commandment forbade idolatry.

The themes most frequently depicted were naturally pilgrimage events associated with the life of Christ. One could rightly regard the historiated pillars of the Romanesque churches, which surrounded the choir, as liturgical commentaries. These commentaries were mysterious for the common folk in medieval days because Latin was an unknown tongue. This gave pilgrims undistracted opportunities for staring at images in stone or glass.

The first event in the prenatal life of the earthly Christ often carved is the Visitation. This commemorates the visit of the pregnant Mary to her cousin Elizabeth, the mother-to-be of John the Baptist. Mary's surprised joy is expressed in the Magnificat. Romanesque sculptures show the cousins embracing. There is a tender scene on the half drum over the entrance of the church of Saint Gabriel in Provence. Both saints look heavenward, their eyes enlarged with wonder, as the older Elizabeth hugs the younger Mary. More primitive carvings depict in Syrian fashion their interlaced bodies meeting in a kiss in the church of Rivière in Touraine. On the major routes to Compostela, the Visitation is carved as part of a sculptured frieze on Great Saint Mary's church in Poitiers and on a capital in the cathedral of Our Lady in Clermont.

The popularity of the Visitation theme in the pilgrimage churches is astonishing considering how short Mary's journey was. Its attraction could be explained by the ease with which a carver could depict it, and by the fascination of the twelfth century with the conception, birth, and humanity of the divine Jesus. Besides barren women, pilgrims who

longed for a child would rejoice in the fruitfulness of Mary and
Elizabeth and would pray that they would also be fulfilled.

Another popular theme for the carvers was that of the Three Kings,
or Wise Men, searching for the Messiah. There was a close parallel
between the Magi and the pilgrims to the tomb of Saint James. The
Kings were led by a star, as were the hermits who found the tomb of
Saint James in Galicia. Both Magi and pilgrims went in search of the
truest wisdom. Many kings and princes had emulated the Magi in bringing gifts to Jesus at the shrines of the saints. Also one of the major
pilgrimages of the West was that of Cologne where the relics of the
Three Kings were kept in a magnificent golden chest.[5] Pilgrims who also
had undertaken a long journey felt a great affinity with the Magi. Consequently there is hardly a cloister or an extensive low relief in
Romanesque France that does not include a representation of the Three
Kings.

The most elegant carvings of the Magi are to be seen in the famous
cloister of Saint Trophime of Arles and on the upper register of the half
drum over the eastern portal of Saint James of Compostela. Sometimes,
as in Autun, the Kings are shown three in the same bed wakened by an
angel; at other times they follow the star, as in a capital at Lescar
cathedral in the Pyrenees; most frequently they are depicted offering
their gifts to the Christ child, as in the admirable tympanum at Neuilly-
en-Donjon in Burgundy. One interesting variation is provided by carvings depicting the reception of the wise Kings by King Herod. The most
notable example is one of four panels dedicated to the Magi on the west
front of Saint Trophime of Arles.

The most unforgettable image, however, is not to be found in stone
carvings but in a painting. This glorious primitive masterpiece was
painted originally for the church of Saint Mary of Tahull.[6] It is now in
the Catalonian Art Museum of Barcelona. In the half dome of the apse,
in colors of blue, gold, green and brown appear the Virgin and Child in
glory. To the left and right of the Virgin's halo are seven-pointed stars.
To the left is Melchior, so named, an old bearded king, bending toward
the Virgin with his gifts contained in a bowl. On the right of the Virgin
are two younger kings, respectively Caspar and Baldasar, wearing
crowns surmounted by crosses, in the Byzantine manner. Each also
bends respectfully toward the Virgin and Child and carries a presentation bowl. It is an icon of profound reverence.

The next two events in the life of Jesus to be depicted are the Flight
into Egypt and Jesus' temptations in the wilderness. These events reminded pilgrims of the great physical and spiritual dangers they faced.
They also encouraged them with the assurance that their Master faced
and overcame the same and would help them in their difficulties.

No part of France was more successful in carving capitals with the

Flight into Egypt than Burgundy. Perhaps the most impressive of all is to be found today in the cathedral museum of Saint Lazarus of Autun. The resigned Virgin is riding sidesaddle with the Christ child on her knees. Both are on the back of a docile donkey that is led by a determined Saint Joseph bearing a sword over his left shoulder, ready for defense, as the Holy Family pushes toward Egypt. A subtle carving of the Flight into Egypt appears to the left of the great portal of Saint Gilles-du-Gard. No other carving shows so well the extreme exhaustion of the holy refugees. Many pilgrims must have felt the same.

The Flight into Egypt reminded the pilgrims of the physical dangers of their enterprise; Christ's temptations by Satan in the wilderness must have warned the pilgrims of the many spiritual temptations they would encounter on their way. The three temptations of Christ were to turn stones into bread, to cast himself down from the pinnacle of the Temple in Jerusalem, and to receive the kingdoms of this world by allegiance to the evil spirit. The temptations of pilgrims, unlike Christ's, did not involve the methods and motives by which the Messiah would establish his sway over the souls of humanity, that is, by materialism, miracle, and force. Yet they had one basic similarity—the temptations were to weaken their faith in the providence and grace of God. It must, therefore, have been a great consolation to know that Christ led the pilgrims through no darker places than he had been through before. In addition, these representations of the temptations of Christ were annual reminders of the fasting and prayers that should accompany the season of Lent and should symbolize a deeper devotion.

In the ambulatory of Saint Peter's church in Chauvigny near Poitiers there is a capital on which is carved an upright Christ threatened by a hideous Satan, with sharp teeth and pointed ears, wearing a crown of flames on his head. In his scaly hand he bears a stone, thus indicating that Satan is tempting Jesus to make a claim to popularity by changing the stones into bread.

It seems odd that this particular temptation should commonly have been picked for delineation. A temptation with much greater dramatic potential for the carver is the one in which Jesus is told to put providence to the test by flinging himself down from the top of the Temple. Yet in our travels only two images of this temptation come to mind, and both were seen on the major pilgrimage roads to Compostela. One is found in Autun cathedral of Saint Lazarus where the winged demon screams to Jesus to imitate him, for he seems to be making ready to throw himself off a two-storied tower. An even more impressive carving of the same event is in the abbey church of Beaulieu in Corrèze where a tall frieze allows room for a higher tower and a more dignified, erect Christ who raises his hands in horror at the devil's proposal. It may well be that the basic need to satisfy hunger seemed closer to humanity and so determined the commoner choice of that temptation rather than the two others. The most hideous and horrific carving of Satan is found on a capital in Saulieu church in Burgundy. Christ, who holds the Gospel book in his hand, is backing off from the grinning maw and ingratiatingly sinister smile of the devil, with simian limbs, and a sinuously smooth stone in his hand.

A more joyful and more popular theme for Romanesque iconography was furnished by the triumphal entry of Jesus into Jerusalem on Palm Sunday. The palms that his admirers waved at Jesus are the symbols of victory. This is made clear in the last book of the New Testament, which describes multitudes of the elect from many nations standing before the throne of Christ, "arrayed in white with palms in their hands."[7] The palm may have been selected as an emblem of victory and of the upright and righteous[8] because it is tall, flourishing, shades in intense heat, and bears fruit. Also, a palm has an attractive shape as an ornament.

Apart from being the symbol of martyrdom, which is the victory attained by witnessing to Christ through an agonizing death, the palm's chief importance in the liturgical calendar is its link with Christ's triumphal entry into the holy city. This marks the beginning of Holy Week, which ends with the commemoration of the Crucifixion on Good Friday and the joyful reversal and vindication through the Resurrection on Easter Sunday. The palm's immediate appeal to pilgrims was the reflection that the further south they traveled, the more palm trees they saw and that Compostela was their earthly Jerusalem, which they hoped to reach with joy.

In reality Christ's entry into Jerusalem is an event of the greatest ambiguity. The triumphal entry commemorates the recognition of Jesus by the crowds, yet it is a sign also of the mutability of the mob who cried "Hosanna" on Sunday and in four days shouted, "Crucify him!" Its deeper meaning was hidden at the time. It was later reflection that enabled Christ's interpreters to realize that he was, in riding on a modest donkey not a neighing warhorse, fulfilling the prophecy of Zechariah symbolizing his peaceful kingdom of reconciliation inaugurated by the Messiah.[9]

The triumphal entry is understandably a popular scene on stone and fresco. There is an animated version of it on a capital of Saint Trophime of Arles, in which children are vigorously waving the palm branches. One of them spreads a cloak on the ground while Jesus holds a bridle in his left hand and raises his right hand in blessing. In the same region of Provence there is an elegant frieze of the triumphal entry on the left of the main portal of Saint Gilles-du-Gard. It is the most impressive representation of the event we encountered in Romanesque sculpture. It palpitates with life and movement. On the right two figures bend in adoration as they fling cloaks to the ground before the advancing ass that is cantering beneath the Messiah. Two children have climbed a palm tree and are vigorously shaking its branches. Two disciples follow with a young foal and each holds palms.

A capital on the same theme also deserves mention. It is in the abbey of Saint Benoit-sur-Loire. Christ sits sidesaddle and advances from right to left, an obviously oriental trait.[10]

What could be more appropriate as a theme for the pilgrims than the meeting of the risen Christ with the two men on the Emmaus road? They, too, hoped to make a pilgrimage to eternity with the risen Christ and all the saints. Also, as the stranger hitherto incognito revealed his identity in the way that he blessed and broke the bread, so Jesus appeared to pilgrims in the Communion meal of every Mass. From the frequency of their appearance and the intensity of the art devoted to them, the Adoration of the Three Kings and the walk of the pilgrims to Emmaus impressed us as being the two most common and relevant events.

In the twelfth-century northern gallery of the cloister of Saint Trophime in Arles, the risen Christ is represented on a corner pillar, while two Emmaus pilgrims appear, one on each side. Each wears a Phrygian type hat (like that of a modern Santa Claus) and carries a breadbasket and a staff. The Compostela pilgrim would rejoice to see Christ carved as a pilgrim and to observe the cockleshell on the hat of one of the Emmaus pilgrims. The same theme is treated in two friezes at Saint Maurice of Vienne, also in Provence.

There is also a deservedly famous relief in the monastic church of Silos in northwestern Spain that derives from the first half of the twelfth century. The elongated, hieratic figure of Christ is depicted, carrying a staff, wearing a pannier suspended from his shoulder; on it appears the cockleshell of Compostela. Christ himself is depicted as a pilgrim to Compostela! What admirable advertising! The idea may have originated from the liturgical drama of that time.[11]

The central convictions of the Christian faith about our destiny are reaffirmed in the carvings of the half drums set above the vast doors of the largest Romanesque churches. We shall never forget the impact of the monumental facades of Autun, Beaulieu, Cahors, Conques, León, Santiago de Compostela, Souillac, Toulouse, and Vézelay, all on or easily accessible to the major roads to Compostela. It was these doors that provided the greatest opportunities for inspired carvers. They are the greatest glories of Romanesque art. The models were often found in illuminated manuscripts or in ivories. They record the ending of human history as described in the Apocalypse, the Ascension of Christ, and the donation of the Holy Spirit to the Apostles, and the dormition and the Assumption of the Virgin.

For the pilgrim the great west door of the church commonly served a triple function: it advertised by its size and decoration the importance of the house of God; it prepared the worldly minded for the reverence expected within as one crossed the threshold of the secular and demonic into the sacred domain. Further, it was an invitation by Christ who said according to Saint John's Gospel, "I am the door: by me if any man enter in, he shall be saved. . . . I came that they may have life and have it abundantly."[12] So the tympanum over the door often represents Christ as the King of Kings to whom full obedience is due or reminds the pilgrims of their ultimate destiny in the next world.

The purpose of the tympana celebrating the Ascension of Christ is to represent his triumph as he returns to his heavenly home. It is a theme of joy, though not unmixed with sorrow, since the disciples feel bereft of Christ's companionship. The greatest difficulty in representing it is due to its abstraction and the brevity of the New Testament accounts.

On the north portal of Cahors cathedral, Christ appears in a cloud as do two angels who lean toward the apostles and assure them that "this same Jesus who has just been raised to Heaven will return in the same manner."[13] Christ is a figure of grace and majesty. He is clearly rising with upraised arms and slightly bended knees. The court of heaven is detailed above, and below are the apostles in pairs, who with the Virgin Mother in the center seem to be deeply engaged in conversation. The scene on either side of Christ portrays in lively fashion the story of Saint Stephen, the first Christian martyr. As a sculptural achievement it invites comparison with the great apocalyptic tympanum of Moissac.

Another large depiction of the Ascension is the Miègeville tympanum of Saint Sernin cathedral in Toulouse, imitated in the great church of San Isidoro of León. It expresses some of the classical graces of earlier times although it was completed early in the twelfth century. The astonished apostles point explicitly upward toward the Christ above them whose hands are raised and who is supported by two small angels. Beside him are two pairs of larger angels. The two registers are divided by an ornamental band of repeated bunches of grapes. Elegant as this tympanum is, its Christ lacks divine majesty and it is too immobile for the event it describes. Nevertheless it remains a remarkable piece of stone carving.

The renowned tympanum of the Madeleine basilica at Vézelay is famous not only for its high artistry but also for its linking of the Ascension of Christ with the mission of the apostles. The great and magnificent narthex tympanum presents a triumphant Christ empowering his apostles and is, according to Emile Mâle, the most moving and profound of all the statuary carved in Romanesque Burgundy. However, the Ascension proper is portrayed on the smaller tympanum to the left of the great narthex portal. Here is an elongated Christ whose thin limbs are covered with a double garment, rustled by the rising wind. He is surrounded by highly excited apostles, some of whom appear to be dissuading Christ from leaving them. This emotional scene admirably expresses the perturbation of the apostles.

The fourth tympanum of the Ascension worth mentioning comes from the famous abbey church of Santo Domingo of Silos. This Christ is merciful as well as majestic, with all the concentration on his face, for the rest of him is swallowed up in clouds like a series of waves. It is thus an exact ideograph of the New Testament record that asserts that Christ was taken up and "a cloud received him out of their sight."[14]

The Virgin has to await her apotheosis in the many Gothic cathedrals of France built in her honor. In Romanesque iconography she plays a lesser role than that of co-mediator. Her importance is rather that of being the throne of wisdom as mother of the Word of God made flesh, the Messiah. But even in Romanesque art there is a recognition of her trust in the promises of God, as of her compassion and devotion to her Son. These qualities are shown in representations of her dormition and Assumption into heaven.

The first example of monumental art dedicated solely to the Virgin is in the abbey of Souillac in Quercy. This low relief portrays the celebrated miracle performed by the Virgin for Theophilus. Theophilus, a deacon, had determined to supplant his bishop by committing himself to the devil. But ultimately he was rescued by the Madonna.

The great Marian doorway of the cathedral of Senlis was begun in 1185 and completed in 1191. The Virgin in the first relief is dying amid a group of apostles. Three days later, angels lift her body from the tomb. The second part of the relief displays the resurrection of her body while a part of the lintel shows her in heaven crowned and sitting beside her son. The tenderness of the angels and the warmth of their welcome in heaven is a transcript of the devotion of the faithful. In the choir of Notre Dame du Port of Clermont, a series of capitals depict the role of Mary in the salvation of humanity. She is the good counterpart of the evil Eve.

Some of the greatest imaginative monumental works of Romanesque art are eschatological scenes on the tympana of pilgrimage churches. They represent in detail either the end of human history as depicted in the vision of Saint John in the Apocalypse, or the rewards and punishments of human destiny in the Last Judgment. The most famous among them are the tympana of Moissac, Conques, Autun, Beaulieu, and Saint James of Compostela. These scenes mark the ending of human pilgrimage in both senses: its earthly finish and its ultimate purpose.

Three out of the five of these great portals belong to Benedictine

THE SOUTHERN PORTAL OF BEAULIEU ABBEY. The victorious Christ between the apostles and the resurrecting elect; at his feet, the impious tormented by infernal beasts. *(Photograph: Zodiaque.)*

THE TYMPANUM OF SAINT PETER OF MOISSAC. The twenty-four elders worshiping the glorified Christ. *(Photograph: Zodiaque.)*

abbeys. The motherhouse of Cluny must have played an inspirational role since its first west portal (probably completed before 1130 when Innocent II consecrated the church) represented the vision of the Apocalypse. Nothing could be more appropriate for delineation in monastic art than the great goal to which the monks were dedicating their lives of ascetical contemplation: the enjoyment of eternal life and the avoidance of the miseries of hell.

It is at Beaulieu in Quercy that we first meet an adequate representation of the Last Judgment in monumental art. Angels sound the solemn summons by trumpet, and the elect raise the stone coverings of the tombs from which they emerge. Christ appears in the heavens in the company of the apostles and the elders, surrounded by the instruments of the passion. Hell is sculpted on two lintels, where monsters in the form of a three-bodied dragon, the seven-headed beast of the Apocalypse, winged lion, bear, and a griffin are seen threatening or devouring the damned. Behind the large and august Christ, with the dignity of a judge, is a huge Cross upheld by two angels. This tympanum might be named either the Triumph of the Cross or the Last Judgment.

The style of Christ's face and the ornamental roses of the lintel of Beaulieu show that it is derived from the more renowned tympanum of the abbey of Saint Pierre of Moissac. This great pilgrimage church was second only in rank to Cluny. This profound religious work is a commentary on the Book of Revelation. The divine Christ who fills the tympanum is of surpassing height and dominating presence—a veritable King of Kings or Lord of Lords. He is seated on a sumptuous throne whose jewels are seven stars. His right hand is extended in a generous gesture of blessing, while his left hand holds the Book of Life in which are recorded names of the saved. His majesty is enhanced by the presence of the three beasts and the man that form the Tetramorph of the Gospel witnesses, the two angels, and the twenty-four elders who surround him. The elders hold cups of incense, symbolizing prayers, and zithers, symbolizing praises. All faces in the hemicycle are turned toward Christ in adoration. This is a perfect transcript of worship— creatures gazing in gratitude on their Creator and Redeemer. It is also an admirable expression of the Benedictine Rule, for Saint Benedict gave worship priority over both contemplation and physical labor, calling it the *opus Dei*, or work of God. These churches were filled seven times each day with the prayers and praises of his monks rising to God.

The rest of the portal is filled with carvings of Isaiah, Jeremiah, saints Peter and Paul and John the Divine, and the narrative of Lazarus the pauper who ends in heaven and the mean rich man who ends in hell. It also contains the carvings of the Annunciation and the Visitation, the Adoration of the Three Kings, the Presentation in the Temple, and the

Flight into Egypt. Here is both the origin of the salvation that is confirmed in heaven in scenes from the infancy of Christ and the appropriate preparation for the Final Judgment, namely, in a compassionate charity to the poor such as Lazarus. The whole of the tympanum and its adjoining friezes provide a great summary of belief, worship, and behavior that would not be lost on visiting pilgrims.

The abbey church of Saint Foi of Conques is another great center of pilgrimage on the way to Compostela. Its intriguing tympanum is notable for its polychrome sculpture, for the famous men and women of God depicted there, for the great variety of sins punished by the torments of hell, and for its explanatory stone ribands.

The topmost of three registers has angels at each end blowing trumpets. Next to them are the sun and moon with human faces and in the middle two angels holding up the Cross, each with one hand while the other holds the lance and the nail, respectively. The inscription on the vertical arm of the Cross indicates that the judge is Jesus King of the Jews. The horizontal arm on the top line points out the sun, the lance, the nail, and the moon. The lower line states that this sign of the Cross will be manifest in the heavens when the Lord comes to judgment.

The second register is dominated by the large regal figure of Christ who is set within a glory of clouds and stars. His right hand is raised to welcome the elect, as he says, "Come, blessed of my Father, possess the kingdom prepared for you." His left arm is lowered to reject the damned to whom he says: "Depart from me, ye cursed."[15] Toward Christ advance the Virgin and Saint Peter, a third person with a hermit's staff, who may be the hermit founder of the abbey named Dadon or Saint Anthony of the Desert. Next come an abbot, who may be Saint Benedict, and a monk who introduces a crowned king almost certainly Charlemagne, and a lady. Behind are acolytes bearing presents, the legendary gifts of Charlemagne, still in the abbey museum. The procession ends with unidentified saints, possibly those whose relics the abbey possesses. Above the procession, angels hold scrolls listing the virtues of the elect: faith, hope, charity, perseverance, and humility. Another inscribed riband, below the procession of the elect, indicates that the elect, sharing in the joys of heaven, are given glory, peace, repose, and eternal light. Immediately beneath this inscription to the left is a prostrate Saint Foi, the young martyr to whom the abbey is dedicated and whose relics, kept in a golden bust, were its chief glory. The hand of God appears to bless her. Behind her are the fetters of prisoners whom she has liberated. A few of the righteous nearby are being helped by angels to remove the covers of their tombs.

On Christ's left (the viewer's right) one inscription above indicates that the perverse are thrown into hell, while another below asserts that the evil are tormented by chastising and tremble and groan perpetually

THE LEFT SIDE OF THE TYMPANUM OF SAINT FOI OF CONQUES. The saints and the elect. *(Photograph: Zodiaque.)*

THE RIGHT SIDE OF THE TYPANUM OF SAINT FOI OF CONQUES. The devils and the damned. *(Photograph: Zodiaque.)*

as they are burnt by flames in the midst of demons. Between these inscriptions of the second register, angels are separating the just from the unjust. Immediately below Christ, Saint Michael is weighing humans in his balance, while the devil opposite seems to be defying him. To the left of Christ is a horrifying scene of the punishment of the damned.

Just as there was a procession of the famous elect of God, so there is a chaos of the damned. These, according to Canon Bousquet's researches, are representations of real persons.[16] Rainon, arrogant horseman and lord of Aubin who had terrified the monks of the abbey, is thrown from his horse by an act of divine retribution and dispatched to hell as the excommunicated deserved. Next there is a chained couple awaiting torture: Hector, lord of the neighboring castle of Belfort, and the adulterous woman with whom he created a scandal on the day of the feast of Saint Foi. Three monks below are caught in a fishing net, held by a demon before whom a bishop, carrying his cross reversed, prostrates himself. He is Begon, bishop of Clermont, with his three nephews who were successively abbots of Conques at the end of the tenth century and who stole its treasure. Certainly God is seen as no respecter of persons for a king is uncrowned, and beside the crowned devil, Judas is hung with the money bag about his neck.

All the deadly sins are vividly represented. The chamber of horrors extends to the very lintel, while on the left side amid the paradisal arcades are unnamed souls at peace in the bosom of Abraham. The warning of the final inscription would not be lost on the pilgrims: "O sinners, if you do not mend your ways, know that you will undergo a harsh judgment!"

Another great church of pilgrimage is the cathedral of Saint Lazarus of Autun in Burgundy, where there is a tympanum of the Last Judgment. There, the saved express extraordinary joy as they enter heaven. Moissac showed the rapture on the faces of the angels and the elders of the Apocalypse; but neither Beaulieu nor Conques exhibits beatitude or bliss. At Autun a gigantic central Christ in an oval mandorla and seated on a throne reaches from the top to the bottom of the hemicycle. He is the world's impartial Judge, whose hands are spread equally to each side like the even scales of justice. Two bands divide the tympanum into three registers. Above, on Christ's right, is the Virgin, and on his left the prophets Enoch and Elijah. In the middle register, on Christ's right, paradise is represented by a group of apostles, including Saint Peter, who is leading one of the elect to heaven. On the left a tall Saint Michael is weighing souls. There are also horrible devils and the sinister palace of Leviathan. On the lintel there is a double procession of the resurrected: to the right of Christ the elect are seen in ecstatic jubilation, among

THE PORTAL OF GLORY IN THE CATHEDRAL OF COMPOSTELA. Christ in glory above, Saint James as a pilgrim below. (*Photograph: Zodiaque.*)

whom are two pilgrims and a monk; on the left, the reprobate cry out in their despair.

Like the central tympanum of the neighboring basilica of Vézelay, the figures of Autun are elongated and animated by an intense mobility. The elect rush out of their tombs toward the light. An abbot is already lost in contemplation. A husband takes the hand of his wife, but she lingers because her child sleeps in the sepulcher. The child, however, throws off his shroud and the three rejoice in their everlasting reunion. Children, trusting an angel as if he were a beloved parent, cling to his robe while he points them to God. The contrast with the damned is complete. Their backs are bent and some cover their faces in shame or plead in despair. The horrid beast Leviathan and his serpents torture the damned relentlessly. This haunting and memorable carving is the work of Gislebertus and bears his incised signature. The moral of this sermon in stone is not left to the imagination. Its engraved message reads in translation: "Alone I dispose of all things, and I crown the deserving. The penalty that I as a judge inflict curbs those who are harassed by vice. Therefore, whoever resurrects will never be the victim of a life of sins. For such the light of day will shine without end. Gislebertus made this. Let the same terror frighten those whom earthly error binds, for in truth the horror of these images tells what will happen to them." Nor are we allowed to forget that those most assured of salvation are the pilgrims now in paradise, clothed and bearing the emblems of Jerusalem and Compostela.

The goal of the pilgrims was the cathedral church of Compostela. In its Romanesque days, its three facades were the west front and the northern and southern ends of the transepts. The northern face displayed the Creation and the Incarnation, the southern, the manifestation of Christ to the world, and the western his glorious triumph.

In the third part of the twelfth century the old western facade was replaced by the portal of glory, the superb work of Master Matthew. It radiates elation: Christ's triumph and the joy of his elect in heaven. A vast enthroned Christ is preparing to show his wounds. To his right, supported by two angels is a huge Cross—the instrument of his glory and of the redemption of his mystical Body, the Church, which surrounds him. Those sharing in his glory include representatives of the holy people of God in the Old and New Testaments, who are depicted in the lateral arcades. The almost forty companions surrounding Christ are on their knees with hands joined in the attitude of prayer as they enjoy the vision of God in ecstasy. The archivolt is entirely occupied by the twenty-four elders of the Book of Revelation who are seated around the throne "arrayed in white garments and on their heads crowns of gold" and "having each one a harp, and golden bowls full of incense, which are the prayers the saints."[17]

Close to the Savior on each side are the symbols of the four evangelists. On the same register there are four massive angel figures linked with the instruments of the Passion: one carries the crown of thorns, two follow the Cross and the fourth kneels before the column of flagellation. Other angels to the left of Christ carry the lance, the nails, a pitcher, and a straw with a sponge.

On the left arch there are two series of statues half hidden in foliage. These represent the Church of the ancient Law. Below them with the Savior in the center, holding the Book of Life, are Adam and Eve together with the personages of the Old Testament. On the right arch above them are the reprobate, who are surrounded by monsters or given up to the passion of greed. By contrast the persons of the left are free and full of peace. We are meant to see the two cities coexisting on earth: the City of God and the City of Man. On the two lower borders of the arch, on the right, monstrous beings are about to torture or devour humans; on the left, angels hold the hands of little persons whom they cover with their mantels. These are symbols of the souls tenderly borne to paradise.

On the jambs of the portal are eight apostles and eight prophets thought of as the foundation on which Christ has built his Church. Angels in the corbels carry ribbons with inscriptions. The one near the apostles reads in translation: "These are victors whom God has made his friends." The inscription near the prophets reads: "Prophets foretold that salvation would be born of the Virgin Mary."[18]

The noble sculpture of Saint James of Compostela appears on the central trumeau supporting the tympanum. He fittingly occupies a position second only to Christ for he was the first apostle to die as a martyr and had witnessed with John and Peter the anticipation of Christ's glory in the Transfiguration.[19] His face bears a striking resemblance to that of Christ. He is honored with a begemmed aureole made of gilded copper. In his hand is a staff but no other distinctive sign of pilgrimage, least of all the cockleshell.

This splendid portal of glory, with its dependent arches, unites three iconographical themes: the triumph of the Cross as at Beaulieu, the joy of worship as in the Apocalypse at Moissac, and the Final Judgment as at Autun. These tympana, along with those of Cahors, León, and Vézelay are the most stunning sermons in stone of the entire Romanesque era.

Many pilgrims must have responded to these stupendous eschatological images in the way that the poet Villon's mother did:

> I am a woman, poor and old,
> Quite ignorant, I cannot read.
> They showed me at my parish church

A painted Paradise with harps and lutes
And Hell where the damned souls are boiled;
One frightens me; the other gives me joy.[20]

Our deliberate focus on the pilgrimage theme in iconography has forced us to exclude other concerns of equal importance to all Christians. Such concerns are, for instance, the rare representations of Christ's parables, and the commoner depictions of the Agnus Dei (Lamb of God) and the Last Supper.[21]

On similar grounds, we left out ornamental repetitive motifs: the struggle of virtues and vices, wild beasts and imaginary monsters, scenes of labors during the seasons of the year, and scenes from national or local history or legend.

Some of the scenes that pilgrims may have witnessed on the way will, in fact, appear in other chapters. For example, in chapter 7 we shall meet troubadours, dancers, singers, instrumentalists, acrobats, and others. In short, such representations will provide the flavor of the fun and fear of the vanity fair of life.

NOTES

1. The present-day pilgrim can see in Saint Savin-sur-Gartempe, south of Poitiers, a church accurately redecorated throughout in polychrome paint on walls and pillars exactly as it was in the twelfth century. Also at the former abbey church of Saint Austremoine in Issoire in the central massif of France there is a superbly carved set of capitals painted in various colors.

2. 1 Peter 2:11; Hebrews 11:13.

3. *De civitate Dei*, Liber XVIII, *P.L.*, 41:559–620; and *Sermo XIV, P.L.*, 38:111–16. For a fuller treatment of this concept in the Church Fathers and later, see Gerhart B. Ladner, *"Homo viator:* Medieval Ideas on Alienation and Order," *Speculum* 12 (April 1967): 233–59.

4. Saint Gregory the Great, *Moralia*, VIII, *P.L.*, 85:1005.

5. Following the sack of Milan by Barbarossa in 1162, the relics of the Three Kings were transferred by Rainald Von Aassel to Cologne. See E.-R. Labande, *Spiritualité et vie littéraire de l'occident, Xe–XIVe siècles* (London: Variorum Editions, 1974), p. 162.

6. It is reproduced in color in Sadea and Sansoni, eds., *I primitivi catalani* (Florence: Forma e Colori, 1965).

7. Revelation 7:9.

8. Psalms 92:13 reads "the righteous shall flourish like the palm-tree."

9. Zechariah 9:9 reads ". . . behold, thy king cometh unto thee: he is just and having salvation; lowly and riding upon an ass, even upon a colt, the foal of an ass." The triumphal entry is recorded briefly in Mark 11:7–10 and in detail in John 12:12–17.

10. See Emile Mâle, *L'art religieux du XIIe siècle en France* (Paris: Colin 1924), p. 75. A translation with greatly improved photographic illustrations was published by Princeton University Press in 1978.

11. Ibid., pp. 137–38.

12. John 10:9–10.

13. Acts 1:10.

14. Acts 1:9.

15. Luke 25:34 and Matthew 25:41.

16. See Louis Bousquet, *Le jugement dernier au tympan de l'église Sainte-Foy de Conques* (Rodez: P. Carrère, 1948), who uses the medieval account of the miracles of Saint Foi for identifications of several personages.

17. Revelation 4:4 and 5:8.

18. The originals read: *Isti sunt triumphatores facti sunt amici Dei and prophetae praedicaverunt nasci salvationem de Virgine Maria.*

19. The event is recorded in Matthew 17:1–13, Mark 9:2–13, and Luke 9:28–36.

20. The French original that we have translated reads:

> *Femme je suis povrette et ancïenne,*
> *Qui riens ne sçay; oncques lettre ne lus.*
> *Au moustier voy, dont suis paroissienne,*
> *Paradis paint ou sont harpes et lus,*
> *Et ung enfer ou dampnez sont boullus:*
> *L'ung me fait paour, l'autre joye et liesse.*
>
> from *Le Testament* of François Villon, lines 893–99

(See *The Works of François Villon, with Text, Translation, Introduction and Notes*, Geoffroy Atkinson, ed. [London: Scholartis Press, 1930], p. 128.)

21. Especially impressive examples of the Last Supper are found at Saint-Gilles-du-Gard where Peter de Bruys was burned for denying the Real Presence in the Mass, at Charlieu, daughter house of Cluny, and Saint Julien-de-Donzy, both of the latter in Burgundy. See also W. S. Stoddard, *The Façade of Saint-Gilles-du-Gard: Its Influence on French Scultpure* (Middletown, Conn.: Wesleyan University Press, 1973).

6

Spirituality

SEVERAL reasons may be given for being uncertain about the spirituality of the pilgrims en route to Compostela. The great dangers and difficulties encountered during the first three centuries of pilgrimage suggest that the spiritual aspect was important, even if the motives were mixed. As Dom Jean Leclercq reminds us, even in the twelfth century *"peregrinatio* remains a salutary mortification, but only for the secular clergy and the laity."[1] But the spirituality of later centuries was probably less intense, so we guess.

A further uncertainty is caused by our ignorance of how far literacy had spread from the higher clergy and royalty, down to the ranks of the parish priests and the nobility, and possibly also to the merchants, as we move from the ninth to the twelfth centuries. Even in the earlier days when the literati were found in the monasteries, there is evidence to show that several who had no intention of becoming monks were permitted to be educated alongside future postulants.[2] Charlemagne had urged that the people of God become literate by the establishment of schools[3] in both monasteries and in diocesan centers. But the execution lagged far behind the royal commands, and successive centuries saw good intentions broken by the invasions by the Normans and the Hungarians, all contributing to the difficulty in determining the extent of literacy. Nonetheless, even if the literate were few, oral tradition encouraged the greater use of the memory. For this reason we may assume that there would be among monks and those they had taught a profound knowledge of the psalms and of certain popular hymns and canticles, and an understanding of at least the responses in the liturgy of the Mass.

A third difficulty we face is to allow for the considerable change that came over the understanding of the liturgy during the centuries of the Compostellan pilgrimage.[4] The major transformation from a communitarian emphasis in which all shared to a spectators' Mass, and from concentration on the Resurrection, Ascension, and heavenly life of Christ celebrated with great splendor to a growing interest in the human tragedy of the Agony in the Garden, the betrayal, the Crucifixion and deposition, and the burial of Christ, prior to his glorification, is one that caused significant differences in both spirituality and its expression in art and architecture. Some guesswork is involved in its interpretation.

150

With these warnings about the tentative nature of our enterprise, we will proceed.

The pious pilgrims would most certainly use every opportunity to be present at each sanctuary they visited at the celebration of the liturgy. As Kantorowicz reminds us: "The liturgy constitutes today, at the very least, one of the most important auxiliary sciences for the history of the Middle Ages."[5] In the mid-tenth century many of the earliest pilgrims to Compostela or to the local sanctuaries in France on the four ways to Compostela were illiterate. Their means of expression were gestures and spoken words. Their joy or misery was commonly expressed in songs and dances that, however pagan or profane they might seem to some clergy, were charged with incantatory power. Before the Roman liturgy became standardized in Europe, there were many local variations and additions that characterized the Gallican rites and seemed positively to encourage popular participation. Charlemagne, however, did his utmost to replace the Gallican liturgies by the Roman, as did his predecessor Pepin.[6] Pope Hadrian I sent Charlemagne a copy of the Gregorian Sacramentary in 781, which the emperor had copied; he requested his clergy to use Roman chanting six years later. This reform was certainly initiated at Aix-la-Chapelle, Metz, Lyons, and Saint Riquier, the major centers, but it is probable that innate country conservatism succeeded in postponing it elsewhere. In fact, the need for Louis the Pious to send Amalarius of Metz to Rome in 831 to get a copy of a new antiphonary from Gregory IV in order to "restore the office and Gallican chants to the Roman rite" indicates the difficulties in imposing Romanization on the worship of the Franks.[7]

In this struggle between the old and the new, Amalarius, the pupil of Alcuin, was one of the leaders. He interpreted the Mass allegorically so as to give the greatest importance to the sacred gestures and ceremonial. The bishop's throne represented the throne of Christ in heaven, the censer the body of Christ from which emerged the prayers of the saints. The seven candlesticks carried by the acolytes symbolized the seven gifts of the Holy Spirit. The deacons standing behind the celebrant represented the apostles, and the subdeacons the women at the Cross, while the elevation of the Host and the chalice represented the removal of the body by Joseph of Arimathea, and so forth.[8]

Thus there were two kinds of liturgical experience that the pilgrims could share: the older Gallican and the newer Roman. And they were radically different. In the Gallican variations, as indeed in the Mozarabic rite used in Spain until the late eleventh century, there was a good deal of local independence from diocese to diocese. The prayers were longer and the seasonal and sanctoral prayers and lessons were far more numerous than the Roman rite allowed. But, most significantly, the canticles of the church gave the congregation an important part to play in the worship.

The newer Roman Liturgy made revolutionary changes in the worship to which the common people had been accustomed. First, and this is a paradox, while the earlier theology stressed the distance, serenity, and triumph of Christ and his saints over death, the newer theology stressed Christ's experience of sadness and agony and death. At the same time the distance of the clergy from the laity was increased by the sacredness of the space around the altar and the mysteriousness of the ceremonial. Aspersions, genuflections, censings, and the ciborium raised over the altar and supported by four columns illuminated by a crown of candles, together with the subsidiary altars in the nave and choir with their sacred relics (seventeen in Saint Gall and fourteen at Saint Riquier) increased the reverence and holy fear with which the chief sacrament was approached by the faithful. A holy meal became a heavenly miracle.

Sacred objects became particularly important. The bells that summoned the faithful to prayers were also believed to have the power to put the demons to flight. The lights, surrounding the altars and carried in procession, allowed the laity to feel a sense of triumph over the powers of darkness. The thuribles, or censers, whether portable or stationary, symbolizing the prayers of the saints, brought the exotic perfumes of the East.[9]

Most significant of all, however, was the fact that increasingly as the allegorical interpretation of the Mass prevailed, its Latin words became almost ignored because they were unintelligible to the illiterate, and the ceremonial gestures were subjectively interpreted. Not only nature, but human nature abhors a vacuum. For example, a threefold silence was observed in the Mass in the silent prayer, in the Canon, and after the Pater noster: this was interpreted as signifying the silence of Christ during his three days in the sepulcher. The people noticed that the celebrant turned himself toward them five times: this they interpreted as the five appearances of Christ after the Resurrection. At the end of the Middle Ages it was imagined that the whole life of Christ was represented in the Mass. They divided the Mass into the various prayers and actions, which added up to forty acts of the life of Jesus, or to thirty-three years of his life.[10] Sheer fancy could hardly go further because an exaggerated emphasis on mystery on the part of the clergy could only lead to ignorance and misunderstanding by the laity. The positive advantages of this ignorance, however, should not be ignored. One was that the church was the place of maximum security in a world otherwise populated by demons. The other was the recognition that the saints were powerful protectors and healers, and paradise would be the reward of the faithful for their successful struggles with temptations sent by Satan and his minions in this dualistic universe.[11]

The seasons were not only marked by times of sowing, maturing, and gathering the harvest—of which the peasant was well aware—but also by sacred time. Feasts marked the Christian year, with the beginning of winter indicated by Saint Martin's day, and the return of the spring by Eastertide, the start of summer by Saint John's day, and the gathering of grapes on Saint Rémi's day. Furthermore, the neighboring laity heard the bells of the monastery tolling every third hour to summon the monks to matins, lauds, prime, tierce, sext, nones, vespers, and compline. Pocketbooks of prayers, abbreviated breviaries for lay folk, or pocket psalters were produced in the eighth and ninth centuries and later for all who wished to join with the monks in prayer to God.[12]

Gregorian chanting with its monodic purity and emotional restraint might seem to Charlemagne and his advisers admirably suited for concentration on the meaning of the psalms, but the people of Gaul preferred their own clashing and dramatic rhythms. Many musical instruments were used from this time onward. Greeks visiting the famous emperor introduced Charlemagne to the organ. Thus both in palace and nave, the lyre, the harp, the flute, horns, cymbals, castanets, handbells, and drums resounded. All such instruments are shown in the illuminated manuscripts representing David singing the psalms.[13]

The special delight of the faithful who loved music was to join gladly in the church songs. Their musical preferences and innovations were often a source of embarrassment to the clergy because the laity liked popular religious ditties whose melodies were bad and whose unorthodoxy was worse.[14] The faithful were asked to confine themselves to the singing of the Gloria, the Kyrie and the Sanctus in the Mass. For the rest of the liturgy they had to remain silent and watch the ceremonial. This was extremely difficult for them for they did not understand the language of the Mass nor the significance of the ceremonial gestures, and they easily became bored. The result was that some left before the reading of the Gospel and then chattered in the entry, as we know from archbishop Hincmar of Reims asking his clergy to read a warning after the Epistle to prevent such irreverence in the service.[15]

A similar disturbance of worship took place during the offertory procession. When the sermon was ended, the faithful were invited to bring their offerings to the altar, which would include not only bread but also oil or wax for illumination, the first fruits of the harvest, and money. For this reason the people were asked to bring up their gifts before the Gospel lection or after the Mass was over.

Several reasons, among them the strangeness of the language, the ignorance of the ceremonial, the consequent lack of participation, the increasing sense of inadequacy, and the fear of sacrilege, led the people to communicate very infrequently and then no longer in two species, bread and wine. The consecrated Host was received at the most three times each year: at Christmas, Easter, and Pentecost. These receptions were prepared for by celibacy, fasting, and confession, whenever possible. Annual confession was required on Ash Wednesday.[16]

Penitence, in fact, became enormously important in the life of Christians from the eighth century onward, whether public for the graver sins committed by important personages[17] or private penitence for lesser sins for humbler persons. Penitentials appeared that attempted to tax individuals precisely for the amount of gravity of their sins, following the example of the Celtic monks. These took the form of fasting, almsgiving, and physical mortification. But the penitent could be freed from some of the longer penalties by prayers and payments. Three days of fasting, for example, were equivalent to a hundred psalms recited during the night and three hundred lashes of the whip, or three deniers.

It would be difficult to imagine a more dramatic ceremony than that of the dismissal of public sinners that took place on Ash Wednesday. It is vividly described by Francis X. Weiser:

> Public sinners approached their priests shortly before Lent to absolve themselves of their misdeed, and were presented by the priests on Ash Wednesday to the bishop of the place. Outside the cathedral, poor and noble alike stood barefoot, dressed in sackcloth, heads bowed in humble contrition. The bishop, assisted by his canons, assigned to each one particular acts of penance according to the nature and gravity of his crimes. Thereupon they entered the church, the bishop leading one of them by hand, the others following in single file, holding each other's hands. Before the altar, not only the penitents but also the bishop and all his clergy recited the seven penitential psalms. Then as each sinner approached, the bishop imposed his hands on him, sprinkled him with holy water, threw blessed water on his head, and invested him with the tunic of sackcloth.

This ceremony completed,

> the penitents were led out of the church and forbidden to re-enter until Holy Thursday (for the solemn rites of reconciliation). Meanwhile, they would spend time apart from their families in a monastery, or some other place of voluntary confinement, where they occupied themselves with prayer, manual labor, and works of charity. Among other things they had to go barefoot all through Lent, were forbidden to converse with others, were made to sleep on the ground on a bedding of straw, and were not allowed to cut their hair.[18]

We can be sure that in whatever church the pilgrims worshiped on Ash Wednesday, they would be profoundly moved by this ceremony, for they, too, were aliens in the wilderness, seeking amendment of life and the removal of their guilt.

The theatrical, visual, or allegorical Mass, as it developed in the Middle Ages did, in one respect, increase the appeal of the service for pilgrims. That was in reference to the symbolical importance of processions. One of the great exponents of the allegorical meaning of Christian ceremonies in worship was Richard of Saint Victor (d. 1173). He insisted that the three most important processions in the Church year, namely those of the feast of the Purification, Palm Sunday, and the Ascension, were all symbolical of pilgrimage, or the quest for God. His modern interpreter, Jean Chatillon,[19] makes much of the symbolism of the Christian procession according to the famous mystical theologian. The very word *procession,* which evokes a march, regains its true meaning in the liturgical procession. It has the sense of a pilgrimage and exhibits the distinctive character of a Christian: one who is in transit without being able to attend to terrestrial attachments. The procession also recalls the great marches of Israel and the crossing of the desert. Monastic rites provided occasions for processions before the Mass and were repeated during the different offices. According to Chatillon, the procession of the Purification in certain medieval parishes was accompanied with liturgical drama[20] in which animals were also included, presumably asses and colts for Palm Sunday. In any case, these and all other processions on all feast days would have a special meaning for devout and thoughtful pilgrims.

On Sundays, however, as on all feasts and fasts, it was the celebration of the Mass, the application of the benefits of Christ's eternal sacrifice, on every altar that overshadowed all else in importance. How important it was can be readily seen in the iconography of the churches on the four routes through France and the two major routes through northern Spain to Compostela.

The Mass was important for at least two reasons. In the first place, short of heaven it was the supreme privilege of the Christian life. Secondly, by this miracle the comforting physical presence of Christ was made available to the pilgrims and all other believers wherever they traveled and wherever there was a church or chapel. Here they could receive what Saint Ignatius, bishop of Antioch and martyr, called "the medicine of immortality." But, as Emile Mâle pointed out,[21] there was a special reason for the many representations of the Last Supper and of the Agnus Dei, (or Lamb of God in a mandorla, looking like the sacred Host).[22] It was to combat the heresy of those who denied the reality of the Eucharist, whether as Petrobrusians or as Albigenses.

The heresy of those who denied the reality of the Eucharist was powerful in Provence, Languedoc, and Gascony, where Peter de Bruys,[23] a deprived priest, preached against infant baptism and the

Mass, as well as against church buildings as necessary for worship and against the veneration of the Cross. His many followers ill-treated priests and encouraged monks to marry. Even the liberal theologian Abelard wrote against him, and his teaching was condemned by the Second Lateran Council of 1139. He himself was burned at Saint Gilles-du-Gard in 1143 by an incensed crowd who were infuriated by his burning of crosses. It is thought that his teaching was a major root of the Albigensian dualistic heresy.[24] Under the influence of Cluny, one may suppose since one of its great abbots, Peter the Venerable, wrote against the Petrobusian heretics,[25] an iconographic attempt was made to refute the heretics by insisting on the importance of the sacraments, and especially of the chief sacrament, the Eucharist. But even in areas where the heresy had not been notably successful, there was every reason to celebrate the pilgrim's, indeed the Christian's, iron ration, the Eucharist.

That the Eucharist was Christ's own institution was sufficiently emphasized by representations of the Last Supper at which he presided. At Saint Gilles-du-Gard the right side of the lintel of the central portal represents the Last Supper so that the heresy is denied where the heretic died, and the left side of the lintel portrays Christ washing the disciples' feet. Cluny's clearest refutation of Petrobrusianism occurs in the fine church of Charlieu, a daughter house in Burgundy. The north portal has a superbly realistic depiction of the Last Supper on a semicircular table.[26] And as if it were not enough to assert the primacy of the Mass, we see the Magdalen anointing the feet of Christ with perfume to represent the second important sacrament—Penance. The hand of the genius who sculpted this can also be seen in the Last Supper in another Burgundy church, that of Saint Julien-de-Donzy.[27] Here the table lies along the lintel; above it is Christ in a mandorla of glory. In this case the table is long and rectangular not semicircular. Here, too, the sculptor delicately reveals the feet of the disciples, which were hidden in the Charlieu tympanum. The Saint Julien depiction lacks the subtlety of the Charlieu, for the lintel of the latter displays a ram, a deer, and a cow, representing the bloody sacrifices of the ancient Law now, according to the Epistle to the Hebrews, superseded by the all-sufficient sacrifice of Christ made on Calvary but applied on each altar. A less delicately carved Last Supper, formerly in the abbey church of Saint Benigne of Dijon and now in the museum of Dijon, like Charlieu depicts both Penance and the Mass. Also, in the church of Neuilly-en-Donjon in Burgundy[28] there is an interesting lintel, which contrasts the false meal given to Adam at the Fall with the true meal given by the Second Adam, Christ, at the Last Supper.

There is, however, an even more subtle way of linking sacrifice in the

Old and New Testaments than was used at Saint Julien-de-Donzy. It is by depicting the incident of Abraham's readiness to sacrifice Isaac until a ram was found as a substitute, as an anticipation and foreshadowing of the oblation of the eternal Son of God, the Lamb, on the Cross and in the Eucharist. This, too, was a favorite theme of carving in Romanesque churches. It is delicately represented in a fine tympanum at San Isidoro of León on the route to Compostela where the Agnus Dei above is linked with Abraham's sacrifice dramatically depicted immediately below.[29] It can be found as far apart as on a high capital on Sainte Foi de Conques, on another capital in the cathedral of Lescar,[30] in the cloisters of both Saint Trophime of Arles and of the cathedral of Gerona.[31] There is also a dramatic capital of the event at Bommiers church in Berry,[32] in which a tall angel holds back Abraham's hand that grips the sacrificial knife and points to a ram. A badly mutilated capital on the same theme is one of the pathetic remains of Cluny[33] and one of the remains at Notre Dame du Port, Clermont.[34]

It is likely that the symbolism of the sacrificial lamb was made more meaningful to the faithful by the important blessing of the lamb, which ceremony terminated the long service of Holy Saturday in the Mozarabic rite as in all the contemporary Latin rites.[35] What made this service memorable was not only the fact that it was held on Easter eve but also the fact that it was long, lasting from nones on Saturday to Sunday matins.

The locations and frequency of the iconography make it clear that the centrality of the Mass was effectively stressed, especially in areas where heresy had been rampant. This was done by depicting the Last Supper, where the Eucharist was instituted by Christ, and by showing its Old Testament adumbrations in the readiness of Abraham to sacrifice his son Isaac. In the Abraham story, the substitute ram anticipated the Lamb of God, or Agnus Dei, so frequently carved on tympana in romanesque France and northern Spain[36] in a circle, thus indicating the Host. At the cathedral of Le Puy[37] there is a capital that perfectly expresses the meaning of the Agnus Dei to the initiated devout. The divine Lamb is lying on a cross and both are placed in a circular mandorla, supported by two adoring angels who present the scene to the admiration of the congregation at worship.

If there were still those who doubted, wondering how Christ's body could be on so many altars as an apparently inexhaustible supply of the soul's nourishment, it was always possible to point to the New Testament miracle of the few loaves and fishes that fed thousands and was recorded in all four Gospels.[38] As part of the antiheretical campaign it seems that this was, in fact, done at Saint Nectaire in an impressive capital in the choir. It is significant that the loaves that Christ and two apostles hold are circular and marked with the Cross so that they will resemble Hosts. The same miracle is also represented on a capital in the cloister of Sant Cugat de Vallès in Catalonia.[39] Oddly enough, in this portrayal Christ does not appear, but only the apostles delivering the loaves and fishes to the multitude. One may wonder why this miracle was not more frequently depicted, and one can only speculate. Technically it presented difficulties but not beyond the solving capacities of the sculptors of Burgundy, Rouergue, and Provence. Perhaps it created theological difficulties. For example, the miracle might seem to contradict the temptation that Christ had refused in the wilderness. Or, it might seem curious that the eucharistic Meal did not consist of loaves and fishes, both because of the miracle and because Christ's first meal with his disciples after the Resurrection comprised broiled fish. In any case, we have to note that this variation was infrequently shown.

Perhaps the most surprising development in the Middle Ages is the gap between the insistence upon the solemnity and importance of the Mass and the infrequency of reception of communion by the laity, and even by the religious.[40]

Put in another way, one might suggest that the emphasis was on the consecration rather than on the communion, on the miracle of transubstantiation rather than on eating and drinking the sacred elements of consecrated bread and wine, on being present at Mass and watching the ceremonies, rather than on receiving the Sacred Species.[41] In our view Dumoutet has convincingly demonstrated that particularly among the laity there was an eucharistic hunger in the central Middle Ages, which the official Liturgy of the Roman Catholic Church did not satisfy, and which only a growing appreciation of the closeness of Jesus Christ in his human nature to humanity helped to overcome.[42] How did this eucharistic hunger arise? Dumoutet believes that it was the risen, victorious, ascended and sovereign Christ, the supreme Judge at the end of history, who was presented in the Liturgy, while the human Word made flesh, Jesus, was the moving center of the Gospels, and the medieval laity preferred the concreteness and particularity of the Gospels to the universality and abstraction of the Liturgy. Other historians of the Liturgy would argue that Christ as the end of salvation is more important than Christ the means of salvation and that an excessive concentration on the Lord's humanity easily leads from the obedience of faith to psychological subjectivism. However, Dumoutet finds an impressive ally in Romano Guardini in the French translation of his masterly *The Spirit of the Liturgy.*[43] This excerpt affirms that the "eternal" Christ of the Liturgy presents a different image from the image of Christ in the Gospels:

In the latter all is individualised, and particularised life. The reader breathes
in the scent of the sun, receives the physical sensation of time and place. He
sees Jesus of Nazareth walking the roads, mixing with the crowd; he hears
his inimitable voice and its accents of persuasion, and catches the living
contagion of emotion that links heart with heart. The Saviour's image is
bathed in the magic of history, fresh and palpitating. . . . How different is
the image of Jesus in the Liturgy. Now he has become Priest, the Judge of
the living and the dead, the hidden God of the sacramental species who
mystically unites in his Body all believers in the immense family of the
Church, the Godman, the Word made flesh. It is thus that we find him in the
Mass and in liturgical prayer.

It is generally accepted that the leading feature of twelfth-century
spirituality is the emphasis on the humanity of Jesus Christ as the center
of concentration.[44] It had the curious effect, since it supplied what was
missing from the Mass, of increasing in the mystics especially of the
fourteenth century a devotion to the Blessed Sacrament and even
stimulated the visions of Christ himself appearing in the Mass to console
those who contemplated him in his sufferings.

It all arose, at least in part, from a concern less for an allegorical
rather than a literal and historical interpretation of the Scriptures. This
devotion on the part of the laity to the mystery of the humanity of God
incarnate, Jesus Christ, his lowly birth, the agony and bloody sweat of
his Passion, his death upon the Cross, and his burial—was strongly
supported by the teaching of Saint Bernard of Clairvaux in the prime of
the Cistercian renewal[45] and by the example of Saint Francis in the
springtime of the Franciscan foundation. Indeed, Saint Francis's experience of the stigmata was the ultimate authentification of his imitation of
God the Son incarnate.[46]

Our interest, however, is to see in what popular forms the spirituality
of the laity was formed (and hence that of the pilgrims in the central
Middle Ages) by meditation on the humanity of the Lord.

So far as it can be reconstructed the spirituality appears to have been
formed in three major ways. An early interest in the divine humanity
can be discerned in the early development of liturgical drama in the
eleventh and twelfth centuries. The nucleus of its development rested on
an amplification of those areas where the Liturgy was silent or reveren-
tially taciturn—that is, at the death and burial and anointment of the
body of Christ, and at his birth.[47]

Secondly, there developed independently from the Liturgy certain
practices—often part of private meditation—that stressed the relevance
of the Incarnation through the very frailty and weakness of the human
Jesus as baby, child, and dying man, while yet Savior. Such meditations
enabled the faithful to see in Jesus true *Emmanuel,* "God with us." This
was particularly the case when meditating upon his sufferings. Further-

more, we are thinking not only of prayers and meditations directed to Jesus as a child in the manger amid the beasts and to his Virgin Mother as she nursed him, which made a great sentimental appeal to the common people who marveled at the paradoxes of the Incarnation, with the Word of God as unspeaking infant, the King of Kings enthroned in a crib, the Creator as creature. We also refer to the development of the Cross and later the crucifix as objects of devotion, private and public. The latter particularly became a realistic reminder and focus of the sufferings of Christ on Good Friday.[48]

At the very beginning of his book on *Christ according to the Flesh and the Liturgical Life of the Middle Ages,* Dumoutet has included an illustration of a twelfth-century crucifix, now in the Louvre, said to come from Courajod, which perfectly illustrates his central thesis. This pathetic and dolorous representation of Christ shows the eyes closed in death and the exhausted head inclined to one side. It is a perfect image of the humiliated Christ who shared the agonies and disappointments, and the physical and mental sufferings of our humanity, and it is by his wounds that we are healed.

In the third place, in the Liturgy itself as time went on there developed an increasing veneration for the sacrament of the Eucharist, as characterized in two ways in the Mass itself. One was the importance of the gesture of the elevation of the Host, and the other was the institution of the Corpus Christi festival. The elevation of the Host (that is, the raising by the priest facing the altar of the consecrated round wafer above his head so that the people behind him may see it) was the climactic action of the Mass. It also led to the development of a series of prayers of which the most moving are the *Adoro te* and the *Anima Christi.*[49]

The reasons for the popularity of the elevation in the Mass are still shrouded in mystery. Some authors suggest that it was approved in order to affirm the moment of the miracle of consecration against such deniers as Berengarius of Tours (ca. 999–1088) or Peter the Cantor.[50] Others insist that it was introduced as a result of the attacks of Albigensian heretics in order to reaffirm the importance of the miracle of the transformation of bread and wine into the very Body and Blood of Christ. But whatever its rationale, it led to two significant though wholly disparate results. One was a desperate desire on the part of the laity to see the elevation of the Host, so much so that some desired that the chalices be made of glass rather than precious metal, presumably so that the miraculous change might be witnessed. (This, in fact, was impossible, because it was the substance that was changed, not the accidents or surface characteristics, so the official Aristotelian type of explanation went.) The English laity even rushed from church to church begging the priests to raise the Host "higher—higher!" This glimpse of the true Body of Christ was all they believed they needed for salvation, an idea that seemed to be worked out in the search for the Holy Grail in the Arthurian romances.

The second, more valuable, consequence was that here contact was established between the human Savior and his flock, resulting in the production of prayers at the elevation that stressed the sufferings of the Savior for humanity, in meditations on the five wounds on the Body of Christ, in an interpretation of the water and blood that flowed from the lance-riven side of Christ as prophecies of the institution of the sacraments of Baptism and Communion, and in visions of Christ in the Sacrament as a foretaste of paradise (seen either with the physical eyes by a miracle or by the eyes of faith). At any rate, the closeness of Christ to believers was the consolation to be derived from such prayers, meditation, or visions.[51]

Eventually the celebration of the feast of Corpus Christi, which should rightfully be celebrated on Maundy Thursday, when it was instituted by Christ, was held on the first Thursday after Trinity Sunday. This, with its impressive processions, which gathered crowds of the faithful in the streets, and the consequent ostensoria, led to a much deeper appreciation of the Blessed Sacrament. Thus the eucharistic hunger of the common folk was almost satisfied by these coordinate emphases on the humanity of the God-man. The feast of the Body of Christ (Corpus Christi) is believed to have originated from a vision of Saint Juliana of Cornillon near Liège (d. 1258), and it was instituted six years after her death by Pope Urban IV.[52] The services of the day were drawn up by Saint Thomas Aquinas, and they include the admirable hymns, *Lauda Sion*[53] and *Pange lingua gloriosi.*

Although this feast increased the appreciation of the Eucharist, yet it was still a visual communion not a manducation. The eucharistic hunger therefore found only partial satisfaction, only to be fully satisfied during the Catholic renewal of the sixteenth century. In our own days, however, the Mass has reestablished the Communion as both a commemorative sacrifice and a communal meal at the Lord's table.

It was, then, as an awe-inspiring miracle that the pilgrims to Compostela experienced the Mass, but one in which they had a profound sense, at whatever altar they received it, of being Christ's guests in his home, with a due appreciation of both the love of the Savior and its costliness to him. On the rare (three or fewer) occasions each year on which they received Holy Communion they knew it to be the soul's banquet and never more splendidly so than in the great cathedral of Santiago where the candles banished the shadows so that even on vigils it was as the day. Some pilgrims may even have felt that it was like paradise itself, which according to the Apocalypse was without night, for Christ is its everlasting light.

But what of the noneucharistic provisions for the pilgrim's soul? Here we must turn to an earlier indication of other spiritual nourishment. We indicated that the emperor Charlemagne was eager for Christian people to be literate, with the result that schools were formed in the major centers of his empire to teach letters to clergy and laity alike. It would not be unreasonable to suppose that both monks and secular clergy alike, when accompanying pilgrims, would encourage them to sing the psalms that were the very heart and soul of the Breviary and the Daily Office. Two further considerations reinforce this probability.

The first is, as we saw earlier, in the eighth and ninth centuries little books of private prayers, often abbreviated breviaries, were produced for the use of the laity. Understandably, they would wish to imitate the monks who were surer of salvation than they, and the inducement would be the greater if they lived near a monastery or were closely related to monks or nuns.

Our second consideration is that the psalms would prove to be a source of personal inspiration and encouragement to devout pilgrims, as they were to God's ancient pilgrim people, the Jews. An examination of the psalms in the light of the experience of pilgrimage will, we believe, show their astonishing applicability to almost all situations of hardship or joy that the pilgrims would be likely to face on their travels. This, of course, presupposes literacy on the part of some of the pilgrims or of the clergy accompanying them.[54] Our immediate task is to examine the psalms in light of the pilgrimage experience to determine the relevance of their spirituality to pilgrims on the way to Compostela.

If any readers are incredulous about this approach, let them try the most famous of the psalms, the twenty-third, and read it in light of the pilgrimage to Compostela. The psalm is essentially nomadic, and the double entendre of a shepherd-pastor would be particularly apt for a group of pilgrims led by their bishop, as Godescalc of Le Puy led the first known group of pilgrims to Santiago's shrine. The "green pastures" could be the meadows and plains before and after the mountains of the Pyrenees, and the "quiet waters" the rivers safely crossed or seas calm after storm for those who came from England to Bordeaux, or even, the rivers lacking the pollution that the editor of the pilgrim's guide warned them against. The guidance "in the paths of righteousness" would be the way of higher obedience in pilgrimage and the way to Compostela. The "valley of the shadow of death" could be a symbolical account of salvation by renunciation of the old Adam, or could describe the descent through the narrow defile of Roncevaux where Charlemagne's rearguard fell. The "rod and staff" are the very emblems of the pilgrim. The preparation of a "table before me in the presence of mine enemies" would perfectly express the situation of the pilgrim passing through Moor-occupied or -threatened kingdoms on the way to Compostela.

And the concluding "I will dwell in the house of the Lord for ever" would be the penultimate (Compostela cathedral) and ultimate hope (Heaven) of the pilgrim.

As we shall see, moreover, psalms of ascent,[55] which were originally sung by pilgrims to Jerusalem, were most appropriate for Christian pilgrims ascending great mountains and reaching the ascent of Montjoie overlooking the city of Compostela on the last stage of the pilgrimage.

Psalm 29 would comfort pilgrims even in the floods or the sea storms by the remembrance that God is "king of the flood."[56] When the searing sun of summer bore down on the pilgrims and drained their vitality, it would be interpreted by some as the divine displeasure against unacknowledged sin.[57] A greater consolation, however, would have been the thought that God is like a shade in the intense heat of midday or that the pilgrim may take cover "in the shadow of thy wings."[58]

The psalmist—God's interpreter, David (so scholars in the Middle Ages believed, with the exception of Saint Jerome who challenged the Davidic authorship of the psalter)—affirmed that God was more than a match for any calamity that could befall the pilgrim, such as the wicked who were like snakes, for "they have venom like the venom of a serpent, like a deaf adder that stops up its ears, so that it does not hear the voice of charmers, of a skillful caster of spells."[59] Snakes were real dangers en route, although bad companions might be more poisonous morally and spiritually. Other dangers envisaged in the psalms and known by the pilgrim were: ambushes in the afforested areas,[60] being taken prisoner by foreign armies,[61] great peaks to be scaled or formidable descents to be made through ravines,[62] getting lost in deserted wildernesses and solitary places,[63] or the sheer weariness and exhaustion that leads to carelessness, so that the pilgrim's bones are "scorched like a hearth" and "his bones cling to his flesh" and he seems an eccentric—"I resemble a pelican of the wilderness" or "an owl of the waste places."[64] We can imagine with what gratitude a pilgrim having emerged from the marshy area of the Landes beyond Bordeaux would recite the words: "He brought me out of the miry clay; and He set my foot upon a rock making my footsteps firm."[65] Equally, thirsty pilgrims reaching a crystalline river would gladly affirm: "Thou dost give them to drink of the river of Thy delight. For with Thee is the fountain of life."[66]

How vividly the psalms sing the praises of God the provider and protector! How encouraging this must have been for pilgrims who would present their varied petitions at Compostela asking for deliverance for captives, sight for the blind, or support for orphans and widows.[67] God's omniscience and omnipresence would be a consolation to good pilgrims and a worry to pilgrims of bad conscience as they sang or read Psalm 139 celebrating God the inescapable. The pilgrims would be grateful for the God "who covers the heavens with clouds" and who "provides rain for the earth" and "makes grass to grow on the mountains" and "gives to the beast its food."[68] Many, it may be recalled, made the journey on horseback, and their tired nags would be grateful for the lush new grass. The true pilgrims, paupers and afoot, would be grateful for even ground and would pray when in the mountains, "Let thy good spirit lead me on level ground."[69]

The pilgrims would be upheld by hope. Each, thinking of the end of his journey would say, "I will give Thee thanks in the great congregation; I will praise Thee among a mighty throng."[70] And the leader of a pilgrimage, recalling the past, could say: "These things I remember because I used to go along with the throng and lead them in procession to the house of God, with the voice of joy and thanksgiving, a multitude keeping festival."[70] Would the pilgrim not gratefully recall each hospice or abbey lodging he had accepted in the words: "I will lie down in peace to sleep for Thou, O God, hast established me in security"?[72] God's promises have sustained the pilgrim and his ultimate security has truly been God. Hence the words are precious that say: "You will not be afraid of the terror by night, or of the arrow that flies by day; of the pestilence that stalks in darkness, or of the destruction that lays waste at noon. For He will give His angels charge concerning you, to guard you in all your ways."[73] The rich pilgrim would remember his duty to give alms and the poor to receive them with gratitude unfeigned for the "righteous has given freely to the poor."[74] All pilgrims would be thankful for good companions on the way, as each said, "I am a companion of all those who fear Thee."[75]

The psalms would express the gratitude of many as they reached the end of their long journey, shared by so many from many nations: "Let all the peoples praise Thee, O God. Let the nations be glad and sing for joy."[76] Their unity with all Christians was deeply felt: "Behold, how good and pleasant it is for brothers to dwell together in unity."[77] How profoundly would the penitential pilgrims, weighed down with their chains and the scars they had made, reecho the words: "If Thou, O Lord, shouldst mark iniquities, O Lord, who could stand? But there is forgiveness with Thee."[78] They would, indeed, cry, De profundis.

As the grateful laid their ex-voto offerings at Santiago's shrine, they make the psalmist's words their own: "I will pay my vows to the Lord in the presence of all His people."[79]

Finally, the pilgrims having followed the Milky Way to Compostela—the legendary field of the star—must have felt that one particular psalm was meant for all of them on this particular pilgrimage route, Psalm 147. This psalm recalls that God "counts the numbers of the stars; He gives names to all of them" and, according to another psalm, the appropriate response is "Give thanks to the Lord, for He is good;

For his loving-kindness is everlasting; To Him who made the great
lights, For his loving-kindness is everlasting."[80]

This chapter has attempted to account for the spirituality of pilgrimage with special reference to attendance at the Mass and to the private
cultivation of spirituality with the aid of the psalter. But this was far
from being the whole of the spirituality en route.

In summing up, it should be recalled that on all saints days when the
pilgrims entered other sanctuaries on which the patron's feast was being
observed, a sermon would be preached celebrating the *passio* of the
martyr, if he or she was such, or the virtues of an apostle or confessor.
In any great monastic church that pilgrims visited, they would be taken
to the various altars to pay homage to the relics of the saints housed
there and taught something of the fame of these notable servants of
God. Not only so, but the pilgrims still had to spend their vigil in the
cathedral of Compostela, there to take part in the worship of God and
the cult of the saint on the next day, as well as present their offerings,
and kneel in tears at the tomb of Saint James and pray to him, as the
climactic gesture of homage. All this, so they hoped, would result in
their being better Christians.[81]

To be sure, there would be much dross of egotism mixed up with the
gold of pilgrims' devotion. With equal certainty there would be superstition mingled with genuine faith, J. M. Lacarra has rightly insisted
that the Compostela pilgrimage encouraged much devotion to Christ as
well as its own share of superstition. Legends about the miraculous
transportation of the body of Saint James from Palestine to Galicia were
swallowed wholesale by the overcredulous, until they were willing to
believe that the marble boat did not touch the waves but traveled over
them like a bird. They were willing to believe that the conch shells
picked on the beaches of Galicia would not only revive piety in them if
they listened intently, but had the magic power to still storms, put the
devil to flight, and dispatch hailstorms.[82]

But when all allowances are made for superstition and moral and
spiritual deviations on the way, it must be remembered that the journey
was undertaken as an act of *askesis*, or purification. It was begun with
the blessing of the Church and the sanctification of the symbols of
pilgrimage.[83] God would be remembered by the grace before every
meal eaten at every hospice en route, and by the carved stones of every
church and cathedral they entered.[84] The bejeweled reliquaries of the
saints they saw[85] would instruct or remind pilgrims anew of the saga of
salvation accomplished by God—Father, Son, and Holy Spirit—and the
continuing intercession of the saints on their behalf. Their entire jour-

ney, whether they came as voluntary pilgrims exiled from their homes, or as penitential pilgrims, or simply as vicarious ones, would be an entire waste if they did not return not only forgiven but also with proofs of the amendment of life. The proofs of their piety would be their capacity to endure danger, fear, privation, and other hardships such as loneliness and temptations, as pacific soldiers of Christ, who had taken up his Cross. As true pilgrims they should be eminent examples of trust in the living God, practicing charity to all they met, and sharing an unconquerable hope of living eternally with Christ the King of Kings in his supernal court in the company of the saints. In the profoundest sense they did not seek as pilgrims Jerusalem or Compostela but the New Jerusalem. They were eschatological pilgrims bound for paradise.

NOTES

1. *The Spirituality of the Middle Ages* (London and New York: Burns, Oates, 1968), p. 205. Two important articles by E. Delaruelle link popular piety with pilgrimage: "La piété populaire au Xᵉ siècle" and "La piété populaire à la fin du moyen âge" in *Relazioni del Xᵉ Congresso di Science storiche* 3 (Rome, 1956).

2. As early as 529 the Council of Vaison had ordered that a school should be founded in every parish with the priest as instructor, in which spelling and writing were to be taught, and the psalms were to be learned by heart. It is obvious also that all who took part in the offices of monastic churches would learn the psalms by heart, so that this part of spirituality can be generally assumed (see Charles Lelong, *La vie quotidienne en Gaule à l'époque mérovingienne* [Paris: Hachette, 1963], p. 155). Aelfric, the abbot of Eynsham in Oxfordshire (ca. 955–ca. 1020), published a colloquy, or manual of conversation, to teach children how to learn Latin, in the course of which the learner affirms that "I am a monk, I sing seven times a day with my brothers, and I am learning to read and to sing, but I am also eager to learn to speak Latin well" (Pierre Riché and G. Tate, *Textes et documents d'histoire du moyen âge*, 2 vols. [Paris: Sedes, 1974], II, pp. 519–29, Colloquy). One can assume that in monasteries and in the royal courts, as well as in diocesan schools, and as the bourgeoisie grew more powerful, literacy increased. For the need for schooling among merchants and the establishment of schools in Ghent, for example, in the twelfth century, see Jacques le Goff, *Marchands et banquiers du moyen âge* (Paris: P.U.F., 1969), pp. 100–101.

3. *Et ut scolae legentium puerorum fiant. Psalmos, notas, cantus, grammatici, per singula monasteria sint, vel episcopia et libros catholicos bene emendate* (Riché and Tate, *Textes et documents*, II, pp. 405.

4. Hermanus A. P. Schmidt, for example, in his standard *Introductio in liturgiam occidentalem* (Rome: Herder, 1960), distinguishes among the *Missa papalis* (6th and 7th centuries), *Missa affectus* (8th–11th centuries), and the *Missa dramatica* (12th–15th centuries).

5. E. Kantorowicz, *Laudes Regiae: A Study in Liturgical Acclamations and Medieval Ruler Worship* (Berkeley and Los Angeles: University of California Press, 1946), p. ix.

6. In 754 Pepin decreed the acceptance of the Roman Liturgy and the disuse of the Gallican liturgies and variations. See Theodor Klauser, "Die liturgischen Austauschbeziehungen zwischen der römischen und der fränkisch-deutschen Kirche vom 8. bis zum 11. Jh.," *Historiches Jahr Buch* 53 (1939): 169–89; and H. Netzer, *L'introduction de la messe romaine en France* (Paris: A. Picard, 1910), pp. 30–31. While there was a political concern to unite the Frankish kingdom with Rome, there was also a religious concern including a dissatisfaction with certain features of the Gallican Liturgy notably its excessively dramatic character, its tendency to vary from place to place, and its lack of clarity, sobriety, and concision. In contrast, the comprehensiveness of the early Roman Mass, as characterized by Edmund Bishop in *Liturgica historica* (Oxford: Clarendon Press, 1918), was appreciated. Furthermore, even in the Canon of the Mass, the anamnesis and the offertory were occasionally ignored in the Gallican masses.

7. C. Vogel, "La réforme liturgique sous Charlemagne" in *Karl der Grosse*, 4 vols. (Düsseldorf, 1965), II, p. 217–18.

8. Josef A. Jungmann, *Missarum solemnia: Eine genetische Erklärung der römischen Messe*, 2 vols. 2d ed. (Vienna: Herder, 1949), I, pp. 219–20. Amalarius's later influence was even greater than in his own time. See J. M. Hanssens, ed., *Amalarii episcopi opera liturgica omnia*, 3 vols. (Rome: Studi e Testi, 1948–50), pp. 138–40. The *De ecclesiasticis officiis*, which is Hanssens's second volume, is most relevant for our purpose. An admirable account of Amalarius's interpretation of the Mass is to be found in O. B. Hardison, Jr., *Christian Rite and Christian Drama in the Middle Ages* (Baltimore and London: Johns Hopkins University Press, 1965), pp. 45–79.

9. Riché and Tate, *Textes et documents*, p. 274. The entire chapter, "Civilisation de la Liturgie" (pp. 272–89), proved most helpful.

10. Schmidt, *Introductio in liturgiam*, pp. 364–66, summarizes the contents of the allegorical interpretations of the Mass that began in the eighth century and continued to the fifteenth century. His conclusion (p. 365) is that "the sense of the words of the Mass was wholly neglected" (*sensu autem verborum totaliter neglecto*) by "an incredible strength of the imagination and the utmost arbitrariness" (*incredibili vi imaginationis et arbitrio maximo*).

11. A brilliant analysis of the dualism of medieval society is provided in M. Bloch, *Feudal Society* (London: Routledge, 1961), pp. 134–35.

12. See J. Chazelas, "Les livrets de prières privées du IXᵉ siècle" in *Positions de thèses de l'école des chartes* (Paris, 1959); and Riché and Tate, *Textes et documents*, p. 278.

13. J. Hubert, J. Porcher, and W. F. Volbach, *L'empire carolingien* (Paris: Gallimard, 1968), p. 138. For a fuller account see J. Chailley, *Histoire musicale du moyen âge* (Paris: Rieder, 1950), pp. 61–79.

14. See Agobard, *Liber de correctione antiphonarii*, P.L., 104: 333; and Riché and Tate, *Textes et documents*, p. 280.

15. Hincmar, *Epistola VIII: Ad Egilonem archiepiscopum Senonensem*, P.L., 126: 60.

16. For the eighth century, see J. Chellini, "La pratique dominicale des laïcs dans l'église franque sous le règne de Pépin" in the *Revue d'histoire de l'église de France* (1956), pp. 161–74.

17. Reginon de Prüm, *De ecclesiasticis disciplinis et religione Christiana*, P.L., 132: 245, provides a ritual for public penitence in which the sinner, covered in sackcloth, presents himself to the bishop, who places ashes upon him and the hairshirt, informs him of the penance he must make, and expels him from the church. Not even the great were spared, for Louis the Good had to confess his sins publicly at Saint Médard's cathedral church in Soissons in 833.

18. *Handbook of Christian Feasts and Customs* (New York: Harcourt Brace, 1958), p. 175.

19. Richard de Saint-Victor, *Sermons et opuscules inédits*, ed. J. Chatillon (Paris: Desclée, Brouwer, 1951), pp. 50–51.

20. See our succeeding chapter for the origins of liturgical drama. Also, cf. Hardison, *Christian Rite*.

21. *L'art religieux du XIIe siècle en France*, 3d ed. (Paris: Colin, 1924), p. 421.

22. The church of the priory of Sainte-Trinité in High Provence has an Agnus Dei interesting in its location and representation. The bas relief appears on the archway marking the beginning of the apse and stresses the importance of the altar of sacrifice below, while the lamb itself is lithe and lean, almost a greyhound (see plates 112 and 114 of *Provence romane*, II, by Guy Barruol [Yonne: Zodiaque, 1977]).

23. See under "Peter de Bruys" in F. L. Cross, ed., *The Oxford Dictionary of the Christian Church* (London: Oxford University Press, 1963).

24. See E. Vacandard, "Les origines de l'hérésie albigeoise" in *Revue des questions historiques* 55 (1896): 50–83. The Albigenses, originating in the town of Albi, appeared early in the eleventh century. Inheritors of a Manichaean dualism stressing the value of the soul and the evil of matter, they interpreted the Scripture allegorically and hardly ever literally. In consequence, they denied the Incarnation, the Crucifixion, and the Resurrection of Christ in any physical sense, as well as the sacraments, and the Church's teaching on purgatory and hell. Their hatred of matter and their ethical rigorism led the "perfect" among them to reject marriage and to receive the *consolamentum*, or the baptism of the Holy Spirit. A second class of believers practiced less rigorous lives and were married and received the *consolamentum* only when in danger of death. Despite the austerity of their life (perhaps because of it) many were attracted by this heresy, especially in the region of Languedoc, where the failure to win them back to the Church by preaching and persuasion led to the cruelty of the Crusade against these impenitent enemies of the Church. The heresy did not die out until the end of the fourteenth century (see under "Albigenses" in Cross, *Oxford Dictionary*).

25. *Tractatus adversus Petrobrusianos haereticos, P.L.,* 189: 719–850.

26. Illustrated in Raymond Oursel, *Bourgogne romane,* 5th ed. (Yonne: Zodiaque, 1968), plate 128.

27. Illustrated ibid., plate 133.

28. Illustrated ibid., plate 130.

29. Illustrated in Antonio Vinayo Gonzáles, *L'ancien royaume de León roman* (Yonne: Zodiaque, 1972), plates 22 and 23.

30. Illustrated in L. Durliat and V. Allègre, *Pyrénées romanes* (Yonne: Zodiaque, 1969), plate 98.

31. See Edouard Junyent, *Catalogne romane,* 2 vols. (Yonne: Zodiaque, 1969), II, p. 98, for a description.

32. Illustrated in Jean Favière, *Berry roman* (Yonne: Zodiaque, 1970), plate 2.

33. Illustrated in Oursel, *Bourgogne romane,* plate 31.

34. Illustrated in Bernard Craplet, *Auvergne romane,* 3d ed. (Yonne: Zodiaque, 1972), plate 43.

35. See *Dictionnaire d'archéologie chrétienne et de liturgie,* 15 vols., ed. F. Cabrol and H. Leclercq (Paris: Letouzey & Ané, 1907–53), 12, pt. 1, col. 424.

36. The Agnus Dei is found among other places at Polignac, Girolles, Lichères, Saint Aubin in Anjou, and at Mezac in Auvergne—to take only a few widespread examples—and in Spain throughout Galicia as well as in León. There is also an impressive capital of the Last Supper at Issoire where the disciples gaze at Jesus with reverent eyes (see G. de Boussac, *L'église d'Issoire, st. Austremoine* [Clermont Ferrand: *Guide du visiteur,* 1971], pp. 17, 24).

37. Illustrated in A. Faux, ed., *Guide du visiteur de la cathédrale du Puy,* 3d ed. (Le Puy-en-Velay, 1971), p. 23. The adjacent Saint Michel d'Aigulhe, perched high on its needlepoint of rock, has on its tympanum over the entrance door an Agnus Dei between an adoring lion and angel, while in the immediately adjacent arcade on the right and on the left are the adoring elders of the Apocalypse. Evidently this is "the Lamb slain from the foundation of the world" symbolizing the predestined sacrifice of Christ (see the Book of Revelation 13:8).

38. The miracle is recorded in Matthew 14:13–21; Mark 6:30–44; Luke 9:10–17; and John 6:1–14.

39. See Junyent, *Catalogne romane,* II, p. 149, for a full description.

40. Henri Brémond, in *Histoire littéraire du sentiment religieux en France,* 12 vols. (Paris: Bloud & Gay, 1931), 9, p. 46, remarks on this despite the fact that so many intelligent and saintly persons had tried and failed to make the reception of Communion more frequent.

41. See E. Dumoutet, *Le désir de voir l'Hostie et les origines de la dévotion au sacré sacrament* (Paris: Beauchesne, 1926).

42. See this Benedictine scholar's intriguing work, *Le Christ selon la chair et la vie liturgique au moyen âge* (Paris: Beauchesne, 1932).

43. Published in French (Paris, 1929), pp. 169–70, which we, in turn, have translated into English. Cf. ibid., p. 2.

44. See, e.g., Dom François Vandenbroucke in Leclercq, Vandenbroucke, and Bouyer, *Spirituality,* pp. 243–50.

45. See *Sermones in cantica, Sermo 61, P.L.,* 159: 823–24. See also Didier, "La dévotion à l'humanité du Christ et saint Bernard," *Vie spirituelle ascétique et mystique.* (Aug.–Sept.; Oct.; 1930), pp. 1–19; 79–94. Saint Bernard said on one occasion, "The image of the God-man being born, being nursed, teaching, resurrecting, ascending to heaven, never ceases to be present to the soul in prayer" (Sermon XX, 6, on the Song of Songs). Important as the Nativity was for Saint Bernard, the Passion was absolutely central and dominating in his Christological thought and spirituality.

46. The twelfth century's stress on the humanity of Christ was not wholly new, since it was a feature of Antiochene, as compared with Alexandrian, theology, was central in Origen's theology, and was liturgically expressed in the fourth-century Church in Jerusalem during Holy Week at the sacred sites associated with the earthly life of Jesus.

47. The early development of liturgical drama is briefly traced in our chapter 7.

48. See L. Bréhier, *Les origines du crucifix dans l'art religieux* (Paris: Bloud, 1904); H. Leclercq in *Dictionnaire d'archéologie chrétienne et liturgie,* 3, pt. 2, cols., 3045–3131 for "Croix et Crucifix"; and *Enciclopedia Cattolica,* ed. P. Paschini and others (Rome: Il Libro Cattolica, 1949–54), cols. 964–80.

49. This moving eucharistic devotion begins, in English, thus:

Soul of Christ, sanctify me,
Body of Christ save me.

A very popular devotion found in many Books of Hours in the fourteenth century, though originating earlier in simpler form, it is even found in 1364 in a Moorish inscription on the gates of Alcazar in Seville.

50. See Dumoutet, *Le Christ selon la chair;* Paul Alonzo Brown, *Die Verehrung der Eucharistie im Mittelalter* (Munich: M. Huber, 1933); and A. Wilmart, *Auteurs spirituels et textes dévots du moyen âge latin* (Paris: Bloud, 1932), pp. 370–78.

51. Here reference is to be made to the vision of the Cross after the elevation of the Host vouchsafed to Elizabeth of Schöngau according to her *Vita (P.L.,* 195: 147), and later to others, including Saint Catherine of Siena (d. 1380) and Saint Margaret of Cortona, both of whom had visions of being invited by the Savior to kiss his wounded side, and these were received during Mass after the elevation.

52. See her *Vita* in *Acta Sanctorum,* I (April), pp. 435–76.

53. See in F. J. E. Raby, *A History of Christian Latin Poetry from the Beginning to the Close of the Middle Ages,* 2d. ed. (Oxford: Clarendon Press, 1953), pp. 405–8.

54. James Westfall Thompson's careful study, *The Literacy of the Laity in the Middle Ages* (Berkeley: University of California Press, 1939), dispels the myth that only the clergy were literate in Latin. He shows that many rulers and members of the aristocracy and nobility in Italy and France, and to a lesser degree in Germany, England, and Normandy, were often literate. Their numbers included learned women. Occasionally, there were also literate merchants. Thompson also shows that the study of Latin usually began by teaching the pupils to learn the psalms and the responses of the Liturgy by heart. For example, Blanche of Castile taught her son, the future saint and King Louis IX, to read from a Psalter which is extant (p. 130). He also assures us that "a knowledge of liturgical Latin was probably commoner among women than men" (p. 92). In these circumstances it is reasonable to assume that several upperclass pilgrims knew at least some of the most popular psalms by heart. Even if they did not, the pilgrims would have them read in translation to them by their accompanying chaplains.

55. See C. C. Keet, *A Study of the Psalms of Ascents* (London: Mitre, 1969). The term is generally applied to psalms 120–34 and may refer either to their inspiration through "the lifting up of the heart" or to the Jews "going up" from Babylon to Jerusalem after the Exile, or to the "going up" of pilgrims to Jerusalem for the annual festivals celebrated there, or even to the fifteen "ascents" or steps from the Women's Court to that of the men in the Temple area, for *Middoth* ii.5 describes these steps as corresponding to the fifteen songs of ascents in the psalms, implying that one was sung on each step.

56. See Psalms 29:10; 107: 23–30.
57. Psalms 32:3–4.
58. Psalms 57:1.
59. Psalms 58:4–5.
60. Psalms 59:5.
61. See Psalms 59:3. Pirates often took pilgrims prisoner on the high seas.
62. Psalms 95:3–4. Ravines are slippery places, see Psalms 121:3.
63. See Psalms 107:4–7: "They wandered in the wilderness in a desert region. They did not find a way to an inhabited city. They were hungry and thirsty and their soul failed within them. Then they cried to the Lord in their distress; He delivered them out of their troubles. He led them also by a straight way to go to an inhabited city." This must have been a frequent experience for pilgrims.
64. Psalms 102:3–6.
65. Psalms 40:2.
66. From Psalms 36.
67. All these categories of needy persons are recalled in Psalms 146:1, 6–8.
68. Psalms 147:8–9. See also Psalms 145:15.
69. Psalms 143:10; also Psalms 28:11.
70. Psalms 35:18.
71. Psalms 42:4.
72. Psalms 4:9, and Psalms 3:6.
73. Psalms 91:5–6, 11–12.

74. Psalms 112:9a.
75. Psalms 116:63.
76. Psalms 67:4.
77. Psalms 133:1.
78. Psalms 130:3–4.
79. Psalms 116:14. All could also say, "Ascribe to the Lord the glory of His Name; Bring an offering and come into His courts." Psalms 96:8.
80. Psalms 136: 1 and 7.
81. The ceremonies and duties at the end of the pilgrimage are considered in detail in our final chapter.
82. J. M. Lacarra, in "Espiritualidad del culto y de la peregrinación a Santiago antes de la primera cruzada" in *Pellegrinàggi e culto dei santi in Europa fino alla I^a Crociata* (Todi: Centro di Studi sulla Spiritualita Medievale, 1963), p. 137, bases his charges on the *Liber sancti Jacobi*, III, chap. 4.
83. These were described earlier in our chapter 2: "Preparation for the Pilgrimage."
84. See chapter 4: "Sermons in Stones: Iconography."
85. See chapter 3: "Resplendent Shrines and Their Relics."

——— 7 ———
Dangers and Delights

BOETHIUS, the sixth-century philosopher, anticipated the dangers and delights of pilgrimage. First, he advised the pilgrim not to be surprised if the journey was hard and if he encountered many difficulties.[1] Secondly, he warned the pilgrim against being side-tracked.[2]

It is now impossible to determine how many pilgrims reached their sacred destinations. It is interesting, however, to observe how the attitude of the Church as to how important it was to complete the journey changed over the centuries. At first the Church stressed the importance of reaching the sanctuary containing the saint's relics. Later, especially during the time of the Crusades in the twelfth century, it seemed almost as important to travel hopefully as it was to arrive. Dying on the way was not held against the pilgrim, provided, of course, that he had neither deviated by yielding to temptation nor had given up the quest. The truly steadfast pilgrim could count on being buried in holy ground and on receiving total or partial remission of his sins just as if he had reached the goal of his pilgrimage.

Many pilgrims were ill when they started from home. They hoped either that they would be cured or that they would die in a state of grace and receive remission of their sins. Few of them, especially if they were ailing, can have traveled the whole route on foot, unless, of course, they were on a judicial pilgrimage. Even though most pilgrims must have worn shoes or sandals, the journey was a grueling one. The road from Paris via Tours was the longest but also the easiest one. It was necessary to cross huge forests in which it was easy to get lost. There was always the possibility that the imprudent pilgrim might bathe in the Loire river, get sucked into one of its treacherous eddies, and disappear into its depths. Equally he or she might get sucked into the swamps of the Landes beyond Bordeaux.

Both Vézelay routes, joining at Neuvy–Saint Sepulchre and going through Périgueux, traversed hills and valleys. The entire journey would be slowed down by the necessary climbing, and some places, especially near Orléans, were dangerously marshy.

The route starting from Le Puy was short, but it was much steeper than the previous one because it went through the Massif Central. The dramatic views on this road would include glimpses of smoking craters of old volcanoes, but a consolation was the access to healthy springs and rivers.

The fourth and final route to Compostela from Arles would proceed through flatter country, but the climb to reach Saint Guilhem-du-Désert would be exhausting, and water would be hard to find.

A consideration of the four routes (see map, page 86) clearly indicates that the seriously ill, undertaking the pilgrimage in the hope of recovery, would have little hope of survival. Their greatest strain was yet to come: the crossing of the Pyrenees. These are the youngest mountains around France and Spain. Unlike the Massif Central they menace the traveler with towering, craggy peaks and valleys that are fearful narrow defiles. In the winter the pilgrim might die from exposure to the snows and ice, or from ravening wolves. In the spring he might be buried beneath an avalanche. In the summer the pilgrim would surmount the Pyrenees only to be smitten and scorched by the torrid sun on the long Spanish plateau. Only the fittest pilgrims would survive, especially as there were only five hospitals planted on the route in Spain in the tenth and mid–eleventh century, at Sahagún, Villa Vascones, Arconda, Najera, and Santo Domingo de la Calzada.

The roads themselves were often in deplorable condition. The pilgrim would be hindered by broken bridges and muddy roads like those between Rabanal and the bridge over the Miño, at one of the most difficult parts of the entire route.[3] Probably more pilgrims reached the goal than might be expected. Believers would insist that such were sustained by the Holy Spirit. Agnostics would argue that the fact that such pilgrims had a purpose delayed their deaths, or that those suffering from psychosomatic illnesses were cured by psychological means. Whatever the explanation, more of the sick reached Compostela than might be expected after so arduous a journey.

As a help to pilgrims, hospices were erected on the road at fairly frequent intervals. Only a partial picture of the hospices can be painted, because most of them are now only heaps of unregarded stones, and many documents about their foundation have disappeared. Some were founded as early as the sixth century, like Mérida whose founder was Bishop Masona. Some hospices in Gaul originated in the sixth and seventh centuries but fell into disuse in the eighth century, until Charlemagne had them resurrected from their ashes. But the era in which hospices flourished was that of the peak of the Jacobite pilgrimage, from the end of the eleventh century to the beginning of the thirteenth.[4]

Who were responsible for the foundation of these hospices? Some were Benedictine and others Augustinian establishments, for both religious orders were concerned to take care of the poor as well as pilgrims. In fact most of the hospices were not kept for the exclusive use of pilgrims, although their most frequent visitors might be pilgrims. This is clarified in the act of the foundation of the hospice of Montaigu in 1174.[5] Hospices were often annexed to an abbey or priory. The hospices of the Cluniac monks in Spain were located at Saint Juan de la Peña in Huesca; Leyre and Irache in Navarre; Najera in Logroño; Santa Coloma and San Pedro de Cardeña in Burgos; Carrión de los Condes and Benevivere in Palencia; Sahagún, San Pedro de las Dueñas, and San Salvador de Astroga, among others. Two hospices in Spain were Augustinian, the chief one being at Fuente Cerezo. The Antonines created several leprosaria in Spain on the way to Compostela. They had fourteen houses in Navarre and Aragon as well as that of Castrojeriz. The Antonines also took care of moderately sick people at their houses in San Boal and Baudillo between Hornillos and Hontanas, and at their great convent of San Antón, two kilometers from Castrojeriz.[6]

Other hospices were built by private initiative, either that of a wealthy lord or of a municipality. In Fontenay-le-Comte, for instance, the "Hôtel-Dieu," also called Saint James's Hospital, was founded by William X of Aquitaine in 1130. The records reveal that it was rebuilt by Philip the Bold with the help of the town, including several nobles, seven drapers, eight tanners, eight bakers, and some artificers. Other hospices were monarchical foundations. Hospitals were built by Ramiro III of León, Alfonso VI of Castile and the nobles of his court, and by Alfonso VIII of Castile. The great Royal Hospital of Burgos was built both for the glory of the king and for the celebration of the anniversary of the Jacobite pilgrimage.[7]

Hospices might be located near a bridge, in the desert, or near a mountain pass. Few of those holy places are extant. The *Codex Calixtinus* claims they were built wherever necessary for the comfort of the devout pilgrims, the feeding of the poor, the consoling of the sick, the salvation of the dead, and the good cheer of the living.[8] Others were built outside the walled-in towns characteristic of the Middle Ages. If the weary travelers arrived at night to find the gates of the town firmly barred against them, they could find lodging at the hospices. The poor received the bare necessities of bed and board. If needed, they might also be given a few pennies to take them through to the next stage en route. Also, if their begging plate was destroyed or lost, they would be given another.[9] The rich would receive more lavish treatment in the larger hospices and particularly in the great abbeys. The plan of the famous German abbey of Saint Gall indicates that at the entrance of the abbey there was a *domus peregrinorum et pauperum* (a house of pilgrims and paupers). This included a square room with forms, two dormitories and dependencies with an oven, a bakery and a malt house. On the left of the entrance was a guest house kept for the exclusive use of wealthy travelers. It comprised two heated chambers, rooms for the servants, and a stable for their horses. At Fleury-sur-Loire, at Jumièges, and at Lobbes, the same discrimination was to be observed.[10] In small towns the rich would often go to the inn, but if they stayed at a hospice their gifts to the foundation would be rewarded in all probability by the provision of food and drink of higher quality, with a straw mat and a log.

Twelfth-century travelers going from France to Compostela would find well-equipped towns. The most thorough study of this feature of medieval travel is that of M. L. Fracard on Low Poitou. Since that area of France had few pilgrimage centers, its chief function was to serve as a road to Santiago. Hence at the peak of the Jacobite pilgrimage many churches and hospices were dedicated to Saint James. Fontenay-le-Comte has a "Hôtel-Dieu" and a twelfth-century hostel as well, together with a leprosarium founded by the Knights of Saint Lazarus and a chapel of the hostel of Saint Thomas.

Another city in Low Poitou, Bressuire, has five priories with a hostel attached to each: one within the walled city and four beyond the walls. In Parthenay L'Archevêque on the Thouet several refuges were founded by William IV who went on pilgrimage to Compostela in 1169: the hospital of Saint Catherine, the hostel of Saint Sepulchre, and the Benedictine priory of Saint Paul.[11]

The viscounts of Thouars had close links with Spain and therefore built hostels and hospices in order to attract pilgrims to and from Spain. Although these were admirably equipped by the fourteenth century, they were started in the eleventh century. The hospice of Saint Michael was founded no later than 1026 and was the earliest of which there is a record. The house of God of La Madeleine was situated in front of one of the doors of the walled town, while underneath the south wall could be found the Benedictine priory, and near the Saint James's bridge and in front of the Saint James's gate was the Saint James's priory and hospice. In the city itself the churches were either dedicated to Saint James or to saints found on the way to Saint James. If they were large enough, the churches might have several altars dedicated to saints of the pilgrimage route. Thus, in Thouars, Saint Leon church had two altars dedicated to Saint James. Finally, to the south of Thouars there was a very small almshouse at La Roche de Luzay built for the Jacobite pilgrims. It may well have been one of the hospices that were erected right over the road to provide a shelter of maximum convenience.[12]

Niort is another city that was well equipped for pilgrims, although it was usually used only when floods made the normal route through Low

Poitou impassable. It numbered many hospitals and hospices and one military refuge. Also, there is a trace of a confraternity of pilgrims that was started in the early Middle Ages but disappeared at the time of the sixteenth-century wars of religion.

Though studies for other areas of France have not been conducted with such thoroughness as for Low Poitou, it can be assumed that many other areas of France would provide similar findings. One should perhaps recall that Compostela was the goal of the third great pilgrimage of the Middle Ages—after Rome, which was particularly in favor in the tenth century and Jerusalem in the eleventh. Since extant documents from the tenth and eleventh centuries are scarce, we might infer that some of the almshouses and hospices referred to might already have been built for the sake of other pilgrims in prior centuries, and that they were brought up to date for the needs of a new pilgrimage. Places in Burgundy, Nivernais, and down the Rhone might already have been equipped, especially since pilgrims often used the Roman roads that dated from the invasion of Julius Caesar. Some had been maintained, although others were in bad repair.

Some hospices were huge; others were only a shelter. Givry Maison-Dieu in Burgundy was a square edifice with a saddle-back roof, a tower, and four sloping buttresses. Another house in Burgundy, near to Cluny, was a private house given to Abbot Hugh so that it might be used as a hostel for the relief of the poor. The donor even provided one of his servants to take care of them and to ensure that they would get fire, water, and a decent meal.[13]

A huge hospice was founded at Pons in Saintonge at the end of the twelfth century. It prided itself on a monumental dungeon. At this point the road to Compostela became a tunnel and the hospice rode over it. On one side was the chapel, on the other the hall of the hospice, and both opened with richly sculpted doors. Between the two there was a long passage of three bays or spans, which had both ends vaulted in pointed barrel style, while the middle span was covered with an ogival vault. There were benches on which travelers who arrived too late to be admitted might rest, and under the passageway roof they would find shelter from wind and rain. A photograph of the remains of this hospice can be found in Raymond Oursel's *Evocation de la chrétienté romane*, plate 81.

Other hospices were very simple, such as that of Harembels in the Basque country. Originating about 1000, ruled by a prior in the twelfth century, and served by "donats," it included a covered porch for shelter. At right angles to it was a modest chapel, a mere rectangle. The half drum of the primitive door bore a sculpted monogram of Christ that was linked with the alpha and omega beneath a cross of Malta inscribed in a circle. The hospice was probably taken over by the Knights of Saint

John of Jerusalem, who ran all the hospices of the Templars in the fourteenth century.

The various origins of the hospices, whether an old construction restored, a gift from a wealthy man, or a new construction, meant that hospices did not conform to one architectural plan. Yet the new buildings of the twelfth century tended to span the road, as can still be seen at Pons, Cayac, Cadeac, Morlaas, Bardennac, Aubrac, Saint James in Bordeaux, and last but not least, the great hospice of Saint James at Roncevaux.[14]

The two great hospices and hospitals competing with each other were those of Saint Christine of Somport and of Roncevaux, both located on the two important passes of the Pyrenees. The pass of Roncevaux was located a little lower than that of Somport, but both were grim in those fierce mountains. The traveler would arrive weary of the ascent and of the encounters he might have had with wolves or robbers, and would need rest for his body and comfort for his soul. Little conversation would be exchanged among the travelers during the ascent as each would try to keep his breath for the tremendous physical effort. Lingering would be fatal, and one had to reach shelter before dark in order to survive.

Dependencies of Saint Christine of Somport were to be found at Ordios near Dorde, and at La Commande-Aubertin between Lescar and Oloron, with a church that had carvings representing the Three Wise Men and an aged Joseph, appealing to the old men who had succeeded in reaching the shelter. The commandery of Mifaget had a circular church, dedicated in 1114 to the archangel Saint Michael.

Roncevaux caused chapels and hospices to be built at Syarte near Ostabat and at the pass of Ibañeta. It also had a commandery for the defense of pilgrims at Bidarray and at Odiarp. The church of Saint Engrace was built at the pass of Osquich with a chapel dedicated to Saint Anthony, the patron of travelers.[15] From then on the pilgrims would start the descent toward the plateau of Spain. The hardest physical effort was over, all but the searing sun and the poisonous rivers, as the Codex warns. But more dangerous still were human encounters, for this was the land of the infidels, the Moors.

It must not be assumed that no human danger awaited the traveler on the journey through France. For one thing the pilgrims themselves were a mixed bag of characters. Some were sincere imitators of Christ, but others were working out a sentence, often for murder. Still others were mendicants for whom pilgrimage was a way of life. Hence danger might come from the very company pilgrims were mixing with. A fifteenth-century testimony relates that "borrowing" or stealing was a common thing among pilgrims, especially since many had sold most of their goods to obtain money that they needed for the journey: "Ofttimes divers men and women of these runners thus madly hither and thither into pilgrimage, borrow hereto other men's goods (yea, and sometimes they steal men's goods hereto) and they pay them never again."[16]

Several Church councils were concerned with the abuses of pilgrimage, and the *Admonitio generalis* of 789 suggested that penitentiary pilgrimage might be replaced by penance accomplished on the spot where the crime was committed. In 813 the Council of Chalons-sur-Saône denounced all false pilgrims. Sometimes heretics were disguised as pilgrims, sometimes as bawds who wanted change of clientele, and sometimes as robbers who saw a good way of getting into priories to steal the riches of the monks. Women took singular risks in becoming pilgrims. If they were weak, they might succumb to the temptation of the flesh; and the sirens represented on so many capitals in so many churches, and particularly at León, warn against debauchery. The sirens are depicted with a single tail, whole or split, or with two tails. The wine served in many taverns would help women to be frail. Even if they were constant, they might incur the danger of being raped, either by their fellow companions or by infidels. The life of Saint Altmann tells of a prioress who went on pilgrimage to Jerusalem despite warnings against it. She was raped and killed by the infidels.[17]

Men and women would also be taken in by pardoners and palmers selling pigs' bones instead of relics. They would be cheated by goldsmiths and jewelers, butchers and merchants;[18] and in the *Liber sancti Jacobi* the cupidity of the innkeepers is contrasted with the ideal of hospitality and charity given in the hospices.

Even the bravest of men could be killed. The *Book of the Miracles of Saint Foi* records that Raymond II, count of Rouergue, left for Compostela but did not reach it, as he had been assassinated on the way. This was in the early days of the pilgrimage, ten years after Godescalc, bishop of Le Puy, had led the first pilgrimage recorded to Compostela.[19]

Some murders were due to highwaymen, others to the inimical presence of the Norsemen and of the Moors. Until the greater part of the tenth century the Norsemen invaded Spain from the sea and up the rivers, so that in 859 Pamplona was in their hands. Inland Muslim raids constantly menaced the routes followed by the travelers. In 924 again the caliph of Cordoba, Abdurrahman III, in a great expedition against Navarre, captured and ravaged Pamplona, whose cathedral he destroyed. There was a lull up to the last two decades of the tenth century at the time of Alfonso VII, a mighty king of the Asturias, and when the kings of Navarre, enlarging their realm toward the south, favored the implantation of monasteries and hospices. But at the end of the century, the powerful al-Mansur swore that Christianity should be eradicated and pursued his holy war against anything that had to do with the pilgrimage. He even took and burnt Compostela in 997. There was a lull then in the pilgrimage until the cathedral was erected again. His death in 1002 and that of his son in 1008 ended the greater menace to the Compostela routes. The route to Spain was later fortified by the construction of bridges under the supervision of hermit saints.[20]

Such were the great fears of the early pilgrims. Their chance of escaping either the Vikings or the Moors was fairly slight so that pilgrimage was, indeed, like a small Crusade, an idea emphasized by the poets of the twelfth and thirteenth centuries in retrospect. The later pilgrims were mainly faced with the dangers any traveler met at the time. The *Codex Calixtinus* warned the pilgrim against the sort of people he would meet on the way. According to the author the people in Poitou are beautiful and generous, but those of Saintonge and Bordeaux are rough. Those of Gascony are nice except when they are drunk. In the Basque country the tax collectors are cruel and instead of letting you go scot free, as they ought to, they beat you until you pay the right amount. But the people of Navarre are the worst of all; they are disloyal, drunken, and perverted, and armed robbery and killing are frequent in those parts.[21]

Some pilgrims thought that they would avoid the worst part by taking a ship at Bordeaux and traveling by sea. But all risks were not avoided since the sea was treacherous, and sometimes the sailors or the mariners overloaded their boats so that they capsized in the water. The mariners often survived and enjoyed the spoils of those who had perished.[22]

The situation called for some measures to be taken by the Church so that the lambs of God might safely move to other pastures. Though some protection might have existed before, only in the twelfth century did the monks of war, as Desmond Seward calls the military religious orders, appear. Three main orders protected the pilgrims. A chronology of the foundation of these orders might be of interest. The Templars, recruited in 1115 by Hughes de Payens, were given the "Temple of Solomon" by the pope in 1118. The Hospitalers of Saint John were given a constable in 1126, and they were entrusted with the key position of Beit Jibrin in 1137. In 1312 the Hospitalers took over all the possessions of the Templars. A third order was indigenous to Spain; in 1164 a fraternity near Cáceres was given Uclés to defend. This was the origin of the Knights of Santiago.[23] As one can see, they arrived rather late in the picture.

The Templars were a military order from the very start. They were formed by knights, often excommunicated men who were granted pardon as they joined the order. They also included some married men, provided they gave the order half of their worldly possessions. Thus the order grew rich, all the more so as they served as bankers to kings: their main marketplace was the Temple in Paris. They were supported by

Saint Bernard of Clairvaux, who wrote the *De laude novae militiae*, praising them and addressed to their founder. Some of their best-known houses on the way to Compostela were La Couvertoirade, Saint Eulalie, and La Cavalerie, placed in the heart of the plateau of Larzac. They controlled the security of the mountain routes toward Rodez, Aurillac, and Aubrac in the Massif Central. These were not only castles or commanderies placed on the flatland but strong towns that the Templars guarded. At La Couvertoirade, there was a castle backing into a rampart close to the church. Outside the enclosure was a guarded pond for the sheep, a reminder of the pastoral duties of the commanderies. In fact, this commandery was located where the sheep actually had to be brought down from the mountains for the winter. The pride of the Templars was not only the fortresses they erected confronting the infidels in the Holy Land but also the strongholds they opposed to those of Spain still held by the Moors.

The foundation of the Knights of the Order of the Hospital of Saint John of Jerusalem is more obscure, but it was organized under the Augustinian rule by Gerard, who was succeeded by Raymond du Puy, also called Raymond de Provence.[24] He gave the real military impetus to the order. It was divided into two classes, the military brothers and the brothers infirmarian, to whom were added the brothers chaplains. All members were bound by the religious vows of poverty, chastity, and obedience.[25] They usually had hospices and hospitals as well as strongholds for the defense of the pilgrims. In the winter the only sound that would be heard from their houses would be the bell for the lost *(la cloche des perdus)*. The bell of Aubrac was engraved with the quatrain:

Deo Jubila
Clero canta
Daemones fuga
Errantes revoca.[26]

Places like Saint Gilles du Languedoc offered their protection to the pilgrims bound for Compostela. They also had commanderies in the center of France, like the Templars. The commandery of Paulhac controlled the desolate land of the Margeride, while that of Estrets surveyed the bridge of the river Truyère and that of Recoules d'Aubrac defended the whole of the valley of the river Bes, one of the leading roads haunted by the pilgrims to Santiago de Compostela.[27]

The main Spanish order of the late twelfth century was that of Saint James of the Sword. Two subsidiary orders were those of Alcántara and Calatrava. In the eleventh century there were only five Christian kingdoms in Spain: Galicia, León, Castile, Navarre, and Aragon. They lived in the dread of *razzias*. In the twelfth century a fraternity near

Cáceres had offered its services to the canons of Saint Eloi in León for the protection of pilgrims traveling to Santiago. In 1171 the papal delegate, Cardinal Jacinto, presented them with a rule, and Alexander III, then pope, recognized them as an order. Their rule was also Augustinian, and pilgrims were attended to in separate guesthouses.

Each *encomienda*, or commandery, contained thirteen brethren dressed in black. They also included, like the Templars, some married people and their families. The knights were dressed in white and bore on their shoulders a red cross, the bottom part of which resembled a sword. Imitators of Saint James the *Matamoros* who had led the Spanish to victory at the battle of Clavijo, their battle cry was *Santiago! y cierra España!* The bloodthirsty motto of the order was *Rubet ensis sanguine Arabum.*[28]

Another brotherhood, the Knights of San Julian de Pereiro, was recognized as an order in 1176. The three Spanish orders of Calatrava, Alcántara, and Santiago were all involved in the *reconquista.*[29]

From aversions we turn to diversions, from danger and fear to the consolations and compensations of pilgrimage. Despite all the dangers and the crusading quality of the pilgrimage to Compostela one should not infer that all was misery. Nor should one think that the only pleasure was the spiritual satisfaction of earning one's way to heaven by going along the *via dolorosa.* There were other joys and merriment as in smaller pilgrimages. Unfortunately we have very little information about them. But the *Roman de Mont-Saint-Michel,* written between 1154 and 1186, gives an idea of the kind of entertainment and spirit that the pilgrims found on the way to a shrine. As they left, says the manuscript, the young men and the maidens broke into verse or song and even the old joined in. The minstrels accompanied them with their viols, playing their lays and songs. Even the horses and the mules made melody, so pleased were they to go on pilgrimage, and the birds chirped gaily. Among these tidings of great joy, the merchants did not waste the opportunity to set up tents and sell their goods to the rich, thus transforming the paths of pilgrims into merchants' rows. Everyone was cheerful and feasted to his heart's content. Wine flowed and tongues wagged merrily.[30]

The pilgrimage to Mont-Saint-Michel was easy, but this scene of revelry was not typical of all the stages on the road to Santiago. Yet as there were melancholy times, so also there were merry days. For the rest of this chapter we will consider the mirth involved.

The pilgrims were far from always respecting of the vows of poverty, chastity, and obedience—Christ's counsels of perfection. Though the poorer pilgrims depended on the charity of the hospices, the richer ones went to inns. So little information is available about medieval inns that one would almost doubt their existence if the *Codex Calixtinus* did not warn us against them. First it says, you may be fooled by the innkeeper, who would not offer you a bed unless you also had a meal, or would let you off with the meal provided you paid the same money for the bed. He would cheat you on the quantity and the price of good cheer, and it might not even be good. The pseudo-Calixtine author complains about tumblers that looked large but contained very little, about food that made you sick because it was two or three days old, even about being poisoned by avaricious innkeepers. You may well ask, Where was the fun?

The fun was in the wine, even if it was diluted, as it sometimes was. Even the weary traveler at night could not obtain water from the inns. He had to have wine. The company became merry, told stories and jests. They started to be libidinous and finally quarreled and brawled as the weary pilgrims, drinking on an empty stomach, could least bear their wine. Of course all hosts were not as wily as those described by the medieval text.[31] Some were jovial like the Chaucerian host of the pilgrims to Canterbury, encouraging the company to be merry and to tell stories to amuse themselves.

No wonder some of the detractors of the pilgrimages thought that most of those who went to the shrines came back with far more sins to their discredit than merits acquired.[32] The strongly motivated pilgrim, traveling in silence behind his companions, thinking of God and Holy Writ, would avoid the temptations of worldliness, but the vicarious pilgrim or the tourist-pilgrim would meet Satan at all corners in the fun of the fair. The dangers the serious pilgrim encountered were worse than the fear of death for his immortal soul was imperiled.

Though Chaucer paints a pilgrimage of the fourteenth century, he still captures some of the festive atmosphere of the journey to the holy shrine. Pilgrims were often accompanied by jugglers, minstrels, and acrobats, who in turn were often mated with some lady of easy virtue who may have generously extended the use of her charms to some other member of the company. Here the iconography of the churches on the pilgrim roads tells us more than the manuscripts.

Jugglers and courtesans were often depicted at the entrance pillars of the churches to signify that they might remain on the doorstep but were not welcome inside. Jugglers had as a distinctive sign the permission to wear a red beard; one of them holds his beard on the north portal of Saint Martin of Tours, another in the choir of Briennon, and still another on the tribune at Charlieu. At Le Puy, he is depicted as a crowned king grasping leaves in front of a siren, the medieval symbol of lust with the inscription: *interdit le seuil au lubrique.* At Vézelay, the acrobat on the keystone signifies fallen man living for his carnal pleasure, also represented by the cur and the siren flanking him. In San Isidoro of León, four such sirens crowd the pillars of the church, north, east and south. At St. André-le-Bas in Vienne, a female juggler is represented.[33]

A number of medieval songs attest that jugglers were commonly present at festivities. They cheered the banquet at the wedding of the lady of Avignon to Ganor, who had Christianized his court for the love of her:

> Qui veïst jonglaors du païs assembler!
> Tantost qu'ils ont oÿ de ces noces parler,
> Tant en y est venus que nus nes puet esmer.[34]

They also swarm at the nuptials of Guibor and Guillaume.[35] They accompanied the pilgrims or distracted them at the various stages of their route under the worried eye of Mother Church, which did not look kindly on those who might deter the pilgrims from their holy purpose, and yet used them to spread her propaganda.

What were the functions of the jugglers? In fact, they were very diverse. Some were acrobats. In the eyes of the Church they represented fallen man, that is, the opposite of the resurrected Christ. As Christ ascended to heaven, head first with his body following, so the acrobat was the opposite. He resembled the fallen angel, Satan, as his head was pointing to the earth and what was below it, the fires of hell. The cartwheel was also one of the symbols used to express the tortures kept for those who followed the ways of the world. Acrobats formed them with many bodies and one head only showing. So acrobats symbolized the condition of man without God, having followed Satan—man defeated by the forces of the flesh and evil. At Bois-Sainte-Marie, the acrobat is shown clubbed; at Anzy-le-Duc he is battered by a dragon; and at Dorat he is maintained between two lions.[36] In San Isidoro of León two naked acrobats are kneeling backward holding their feet in their hands, while above a third is standing with a foot on each of their chests.[37]

The most valuable scene showing jugglers comes from the Bible of Roda. It illustrates the worshiping of the statue of gold by the inhabitants of the realm of Nebuchadnezzar. On the right a little party is organized comprising jugglers, acrobats, musicians, and sword swallowers. The acrobat is standing on his head, symbolizing the upset order of the world.[38] There is a similar scene in the twelfth-century church of Saint John of Boi in Catalonia, which has been moved to the museum of Barcelona. Here there can be seen three jugglers, all on stools; one is a funambulist on swords, another throws three balls and a knife, while the third plays the harp.[39]

Other jugglers displayed animals. One man exhibiting a monkey can be seen on a relief found in the cathedral of Bayeux; the man's dress is oriental, and the monkey sits on a pillar. Another juggler can be found in Cantal in France. At Dienne a female juggler puts a collar on the beast that she holds on a chain, while in the other hand she holds a flute and a drum. Though the symbolic interpretation of these scenes is dubious, others transmit a clear message. In the southeast, the monkey is regarded as the ultimate in sexual appetite and therefore an equivalent to the siren. On the tympana of Compostela and Conques, the demons have monkey heads. On a southern niche of the cathedral of León, a capital represents a crouching man with the face of a monkey. The sculpture might have been inspired by the Islamic belief that sinful men were crouching in purgatory in the company of animals.[40] On the facade of Saint Jouin-des-Marnes, two opposed monkeys are found on the top of a double column representing Samson and Delilah, themselves contrasted with the purity and virginity of the adjacent Saint Mary. At Saint Gilles-du-Gard also, chained and opposed monkeys evoke vices, damnation, and death.[41]

The connection between the jugglers and death is clearly found on the north side of the church of Anzy-le-Duc. The somersaulting and naked figure is threatened by two serpents that try to swallow his chest and his feet. The upturned head is a sign that the spirit will survive the death of the flesh, resembling that of the Hellenistic *ouroboros*.[42]

The more literary function of the jugglers was to sing the poems of the trouvères, or the troubadours, or compositions of their own. For this they were accompanied by musical instruments as was the female juggler of Dienne. Carved corbels in the palace of the archbishop of Compostela, which was rebuilt in the thirteenth century, show banquet scenes that must have been similar in previous centuries. While the guests are being served and are invited to wash their hands, jugglers and musicians entertain them with their organistrum, guitar, cithern, harps, aulos, and violas. The twenty-four elders of the Pórtico de la Gloria in Compostela, carved by Master Matthew himself, show the instruments used at the time: strings dominated, plucked rather than bowed, imitating the harp played by King David; brass announced the Day of Judgment; percussion instruments were excluded, since they had been introduced by the infidels.

Musicians were also numerous in the capitals of San Isidoro of León. On the portal of the Lamb, above the head of Isidoro and his executioner, David and six musicians appear; the whistle, the viola, and the triangular psalterion are being played. Musicians were popular. Minstrels used to haunt the courts and sang for the pleasure of noblemen and gentle ladies.[43]

Sometimes the singing was accompanied by dancing. Spain's fame for such shows as the flamenco is not of recent date. In the church of l'Estany, a twelfth-century capital on the east side of the cloister depicts a viola player accompanying a dancer with castanets in each hand.[44] Sometimes the musicians would accompany the pilgrims in their songs on the way. They would carry viols, tabors, and harps. Their songs would not always be in keeping with the holy purpose of the journey, which the Lollards satirized in the fourteenth century. By that time the pilgrimage was freer of the early Moorish dangers. Those who should have set an example of virtue to the inhabitants of the villages they crossed were often pointed at as hypocrites, reveling instead of praying.[45]

They sang historic songs in which the beautiful but unhappy woman was maltreated by her husband; dramatic songs setting up three characters, generally a husband, a wife, and a lover; songs of a nun who tried to leave the convent when she was unhappy; dancing songs that were extremely popular in the thirteenth century; also others, like "reverdies," pastoral and morning songs, and of course from the twelfth century onward, "courteoise" poetry. They often had stanzas and a refrain in which the pilgrims and the crowd could join in the singing.[46]

Some of those who recited not only love poems but also epic poems, which were called *chansons de geste,* are depicted (according to Emile Mâle) on the great door of the church of Ferrières and on a capital in the church of Souvigny in Bourbonnais. The pilgrims prayed there at the tombs of two great Cluny abbots, Saint Maieul and Saint Odilon.[47] The theory of Bédier, according to which *chansons de gestes* and pilgrimage were closely interrelated, has in recent years been modified, but not rejected.[48] It has been proven that around 1090 a monk of Saint Yrieux-de-la-Perche in Limousin falsified a text to bring to his abbey the name of Charlemagne. Around the same time the same thing occurred in the abbey of Saint Jean de Sordé near the Pyrenees, as the monks claimed that Turpin was buried there.[49] Later this legend was expanded by the editor of the *Liber sancti Jacobi,* Aymery Picaud, a priest from Poitou who may have been a monk for some time in Saint-Eutrope of Saintes. Near Vézelay, between 1135 and 1140, the Pseudo-Turpin was composed that for many centuries linked in the minds of the pilgrims the *reconquista* of Charlemagne and the pilgrimage to Compostela.

Though not historical, the legend should not be discarded as irrelevant to the life of the medieval pilgrim. The location of these songs on the roads to Saint James is a fact unquestionably true. At least some of the poems—*Entrée en Espagne, La prise de Pampelune, Anseis, Guy de Bourgogne*—were composed at the time of the pilgrimage.[50] As they went through various parts of France, especially through Blaye and the Pyrenees, the pilgrims would hear jugglers praising the local history or legend. Indeed some clergy and some monks would take up the profession of minstrelsy and encourage the idea of the holy war that lay behind the Pseudo-Turpin. As for the minstrels, many of them would be dressed in clerical manner with tonsure and shaven beard. And yet the Church often resented the presence of the sportive arts and some ecclesiastical councils banned the jugglers from the churches, so ambivalent was the attitude of the clergy.[51] Sometimes poets themselves would be found on pilgrimage, like Guillermo Aneliers, and would bring back to their hometown some of the legends heard abroad, which would be taken partly or entirely for historical truth.[52]

On the route that goes through the west of France, the pilgrims would therefore hear about Count Roland, the beloved "nephew" of Charlemagne slain at the rear guard by the treacherous Basques, or Moors, according to the version and the century. They would see the relic of the horn of Roland and weep on the tomb of Turpin. The French jugglers would keep telling the story in Spain, to the annoyance of the Spaniards who would feel humiliated by the French boasting. *La chronica silenze* was inspired by such a feeling of wounded patriotism; it is a counter story to the life of Charlemagne, the *Vita Karoli magni* of Eginhart.[53]

In the southeast of France, the pilgrims would hear about the deeds of Guillaume of Orange, followed by the stories of Girard of Roussillon. They would hear how Guillaume fought endlessly against the Moors, how he gave most of his sons a chance of success in life—all but the youngest whom he wanted to keep near him, but the latter rebelled and wanted to prove his might also. They would hear how Dame Guibourg, seeing her husband fleeing before the Moors, would not open the gates of the city for him because she throught him a coward and an impostor. Once he had put the Moors to flight, she acknowledged him and greeted him with the love that her valorous liege deserved.

Other stories would be heard in Spain, reflecting the history of the country. *La primera crónica general de España* narrated the adventures of a king of the Goths with the daughter of Count Don Julian. *La condesa traidora* told the story of Garci Fernández de Castilla and Doña Sancha. In *Los hijos del rey Sancho de Navarra*, the king, who reigned between 970 and 1035, accuses his mother of adultery, whereas Ramiro, the king's bastard son, defends her innocence.

Furthermore, A. D. Deyermond, in his *Epic Poetry and the Clergy*, counters the theory of the redoubtable R. Menéndez Pidal that the epics of Spain owe nothing to ecclesiastical connections in an annotated map indicating how they are all connected in one way or another with abbeys on or near the route to Santiago de Compostela.

Mio Cid, Roncesvalles, and *La peregrinación del rey de Francia* are all connected with the French *chansons de geste* for several reasons: the king was pro-French and married French ladies and many Cluniac monks were in key positions in the Church of Spain.[54] Bernard de Sédirac was abbot of Sahagún, and in 1085 became primate of Spain and archbishop of Toledo. Bernard d'Agen was the archbishop of Osma and Giraud de Moissac was archbishop of Braga. Pierre d'Agen was bishop of Segovia and Pierre d'Andougues bishop of Pamplona. The connection between French and Galician authors was also a close one. The "Prince of Troubadours," Duke William of Aquitaine, came as a pilgrim to Santiago and according to the legend died in the nave of the cathedral during Mass. Besides, many French princes brought their "jongleurs" in their retinue when they came on pilgrimage.[55]

Mio Cid, composed in 1140, boosts the Spanish pride in their heroes as La chanson de Roland had eulogized the French heroes. The Matamoros is the hero of the beginning of the reconquista, and Compostela is considered as the center of Christianity rather than Rome. This is clearly seen in line 731, when Santiago is compared to Mohammed: "Los Moros llaman Mafomat, e los cristianos Sant Yagü."[56]

All these epic poems were sung by the minstrels who crowded on the way to Compostela in the hope of some profit. They increased with the centuries as literature became formalized and codified. The jugglers were so numerous and sometimes so riotous that measures had to be taken against them. For instance Le moniage de Guillaume underlines their propensity to drink beyond reason.[57] In 1116 they were expelled from Sahagún to be pardoned again in 1117. And yet some of them gained the salvation of their souls like the peddler who turned sailor, then merchant, then professional pilgrim, and finally hermit. He was Saint Godric of Finchale, a former pirate, who visited Santiago after Jerusalem in 1102.[58]

The rejoicing on the occasion of a saint's feast is also connected with the history of the fairs. Though tenth-century Spain was mainly agricultural, yet it saw an increasing number of merchants taking advantage of the pilgrimage roads. Some of those joined in with the crowd of pilgrims and even some of the pilgrims themselves carried merchandise back home such as almonds, figs, pomegranates, and grapes. Since pilgrims were often protected by arms, this was the safest way for merchants to travel. Strangers of all countries crowded the streets of Compostela, and Spanish merchants were found in the fairs of Champagne. From France, Flanders, and England there arrived mainly fabrics, and in the twelfth century Spain exported "Spanish metal work." Compostela specialized in the sale of gold and silver chalices, embroidered vestments, shells, and objects of jet. Other places sold other souvenirs like hobnails for boots to climb the Pyrenees, penknives, and similar goods.[59]

The establishment of fairs seems to have been the privilege of the monarch. Charlemagne attempted to regulate them. In feudal times fairs like those of Champagne were established by the private initiative of lords. But fairs, like other fiefs, were ceded and bought. Many churches either bought or were given the right to hold fairs. They were a considerable source of revenue since tolls had to be paid on bridges and at the entry and exit of harbors and towns, and taxes were levied on the sales and on imports and exports.[60] The first goods sold were food and wines since the throngs gathering on the saint's day required more victuals that the town could usually provide without depriving its regular inhabitants. Miracles, translations of relics, or newly found bones and bodies would attract authorities from the churches and a crowd of new pilgrims, and a fair would arise. The abbey of Saint Denis owned the fair of Lendit; from Vézelay only a few hours on horseback would lead to the fairs of Champagne, especially that of Provins; in Languedoc, Beaucaire attracted the surrounding noblemen. All were extolled by the troubadours and the trouvères.

The church or the priory often lent its grounds for the establishment of the fair up to the twelfth century when instructions were issued from Rome to forbid this practice of bringing the secular within the grounds of the sacred. The monastery often found it expedient to sell its goods there as well as to make considerable profit. Sometimes a general fee was exacted; sometimes the merchants had to give one item of each kind of merchandise to the monks and to sell them merchandise at wholesale prices. But mainly the fair was an occasion of great rejoicing and a chance for the community to partake in competitive games and watch jousts.[61] Therefore, the guilds played very little part in the organization of the fair at first. Later, when mystery plays began to be enacted, the guilds usually took part in them.[62]

The main fairs used to last a long time, even several weeks. The fair of Saint Martin in Provins, for instance, would open on Saint Andrew's Day and last till the first of the New Year; the May fair would start on the Tuesday before Ascension Day. The fair of Saint Ayoul would start on the day of the exaltation of the Cross and last till All Saints' Day. In Saint Denis, the fair lasted four weeks.[63]

Since the fair often took place on a holy day, coinciding with the feast day of the patron saint of the church, it opened after Mass. The dignitaries would walk behind the ecclesiastical authorities in their beautiful robes, and the representatives of the guilds would follow in their liveries. They would bless the grounds and declare the fair open. Foreigners would come to the major fairs like those of Troyes in Champagne or Beaucaire in the south of France; whereas Compostela itself looked like a permanent fair since merchants sold shells in silver and jet in shops crowding around the church. Tournaments, lists, and contests would ensue, and the first flourished with unusual brilliance in the fourteenth century.[64]

The ladies would lose their hearts to the mighty contestants who in the twelfth century would try to vie with the heroes of the songs celebrating chivalric loves. Everyone in the crowd would join in the dancing, while the more bloodthirsty would watch bullfighting, bearbaiting, or cockfighting. Some carved depictions of men fighting animals symbolize virtue struggling againt the passions. But other carvings, as the bullfighting scenes (one showing a man carrying a bull) in San Isidoro of León, depict the entertainments of the era without allegorical intentions. From the twelfth century onward, there would also be mystery plays, with their secular counterparts in jests, mumming, and "sapiences."[65]

Profane entertainment never attained the magnificence of the spectacles provided by the Church. The vestments, the splendid setting, the incense, the melodious voices of the clergy and the brothers all proclaimed the glory of God to the edification of the people. Tropes, proses, and hymns sang of God the creator. *Omnia creas omnia, qui vivificas* declared his divine providence. *Creatio vera, gubernatrix pia* praised his goodness and forgiveness deserving eternal gratitude: *Alleluia perenne.* They invited the people to join in the Eucharist as in *Venite, populi, ad sacrum et immortale convivium;* and finally the *Dies irae* would warn them against the judgment and wrath of their angered Lord of Heaven.[66] The congregation would know some of the hymns by heart, but how many of the laity were literate enough to understand the subtleties of the Latin poetry remains very questionable. The monk was the main scholar of the Middle Ages, and the people were more sensitive to the music than to the new verse by Notker, King Robert the Pious, Abelard, or Richard of Saint Victor.[67]

The pilgrims on the road to Santiago probably heard the lives of the local saints, narrated by the monks whose abbeys they were visiting. They heard the life of Saint Mary Magdalene both in Vézelay and in Aix-en-Provence, of the generosity of Saint Martin at Tours, and of the feats of Saint James against the Moors in Spain. Three poems are of particular interest dating from the eleventh century.

At Autun pilgrims heard the life of Saint Léger. Lothair, it narrated, was the protector of Saint Léger, but the succeeding monarch, Chilperic, was suspicious of him. Saint Léger had to leave his Autun bishopric and enter a monastery at Lisieux. On hearing of the death of Chilperic, Saint Léger returned to Autun. A treacherous count then attacked the kingdom and laid siege to Autun. Thus Saint Léger met his fate as a martyr. He was defeated. His eyes were plucked out, his lips and tongue cut and, wonderful to relate, they healed miraculously. But the count did not heed the warning of God! Saint Léger was then beheaded and his feet were cut off.[68] This is incidentally an interesting account of the problems of France divided between the sons of Charlemagne and the relationship between the throne and the Church.

In Conques pilgrims learned from the life of Saint Foi how one should be prepared to die for one's faith. The *Song of Saint Foi* had 593 lines and was composed between 1030 and 1070. It used the *Liber miraculorum s. Fidei* of Bernard of Anger: the procurator Dacien was told by Diocletian and Maximilian that he should obtain the abjuration of Saint Foi. Because she refused to renounce her faith, she was put on a rack and finally decapitated. Later Maximilian was punished: he married his daughter to Constantine, a Christian prince, the better to rule and destroy him. But his daughter came to love her husband and refused to plot against him. Maximilian then took arms against Constantine and laid siege to Marseilles, but he was captured and ordered to be hanged. On hearing this, Diocletian died, so that both princes were punished. Not only did this song encourage Christians to live and die for their faith; it also showed them that the persecutors of the true faith would eventually be destroyed by the wrath of God.[69]

The importance of the vow of poverty was stressed in the narration of *The Life of Saint Alexis*. Alexis, like a true pilgrim, left the comforts of home and married life on the very night of his wedding to live an ascetic life. Eventually he returned home incognito to live like a pilgrim in his father's place. He dwelt underneath the porch and gave away most of the food brought to him to poorer people, which caused him to die of undernourishment.[70]

Other songs were codified rather than composed in the twelfth century. One of the most famous was *The Life of Saint Gilles,* in which Saint Gilles prays for Charlemagne who has not told him about his sins of the flesh, meaning his incestuous love for his sister. An act of 1046 shows that the monastery housing the remains of this healing saint was visited by many pilgrims, and official acts under Charlemagne and Louis the Pious acknowledged the saint's powers.[71] In 1173 a life of Saint Thomas was composed at Pont Saint Maxence, which was recited at the tomb of the saint when pilgrims came. By the thirteenth century, narratives of the lives of the saints were appreciated so much that Jacobus de Voragine, a Dominican and archbishop of Genoa, compiled the *Legenda sanctorum*, in which each saint was given a story and a locality. The whole volume was arranged in the order of the Church's calendar.

Edification and entertainment prompted the telling of the stories of the saints, while the carvings on tympana and capitals and the images on stained-glass windows and fresco paintings reminded the faithful of their examples. The same expository impulse prompted the birth of the liturgical drama, which eventually developed into miracle, mystery, and morality plays that were enacted outside the church walls.

About two centuries were needed for the gestation of the liturgical drama proper. The first stage was the embellishment of the services and Masses in the church at the time of festivities either by short lines called tropes or by longer sequences or proses. They started with the Carolingian revival in worship, when the Church had very little unity and the intellectual level of the clergy was low. Alcuin, Amalarius of Metz, and Rabanus Maurus reviewed the liturgy, and tropes took an important place in public worship in the ninth century. In Germany Notker Balbulus was the first author of extant sequences written for the Allelluia, whereas the French origin of the sequences can be traced back to Limoges, Luxeuil, Moissac, or Saint Benoit-sur-Loire. The earliest examples were generally pairs of sentences called strophes; though the sentences had to be of the same length, the pairs could differ. In the eleventh century, however, there was an attempt at giving them rhymes and regularity, as one can see from this extract in praise of Saint Nicholas, the patron of sailors, whom he saved from the perils of the sea:

> 6a   *Quidam nautae navigantes*
> *et contra fluctuum*
> *saevitiam luctantes*
> *navi paene dissoluta,*
>
> 6b   *Jam de vita desperantes*
> *in tanto positi*
> *periculo clamantes*
> *voces dicunt omnes una:*
>
> 7a   *"O beate Nicolae*
> *nos ad portum maris trahe*
> *de mortis angustia;*
>
> 7b   *Trahe nos ad portum maris*
> *tu qui tot auxiliaris*
> *pietatis gratia."*[72]

Embellishment in the tenth and eleventh centuries was generally reserved for the Mass; these embellishments were mainly expositions of doctrine and expressions of the liturgical year. Early pilgrims could attend an offertory in the Mass for the Epiphany codified in Limoges in the eleventh century: the Three Kings enacted by the monks would enter singing *O quam dignis,* point to a hanging star, announce their gifts singing *Hoc signum magni regis,* approach the high altar, and deposit their gifts singing *Eamus, inquiramus.* A boy dressed like an angel behind the altar would sing *Nuntum vobis fero de superius.* The singers would go through the door of the sacristy singing *In Bethlehem natus est rex coelorum.* In Besançon a representation of the Three Kings was usually associated with the recital of the Gospel, whereas in Bayeux an Epiphany antiphon introduced the Gospel.[73]

The Slaughter of the Innocents, commemorated as early as the fifth century, was celebrated in Limoges. A manuscript from the eleventh or twelfth centuries was found in Saint Martial, a great pilgrimage church. It included a lamentation by Rachel, but the angel of God reassured her that the young ones were living happily in heaven:

> *Ergo gaude*
> *Summi patris eterni filius,*
> *Hic est ille quem querit perdere,*
> *Qui vos facit eterne vivere.*
> *Ergo gaude!*[74]

Plays for the Passion and plays from the Old Testament generally came at a later date, about the twelfth century and afterward. Three plays were particularly interesting to the pilgrims during the Easter season. In Beauvais, *Ordo ad peregrinum in secunda feria pasche ad vesperas* followed the Gospel of Saint Luke though it spoke of Christ's reappearance to the disciples, their reporting to Saint Thomas the Resurrection of the Lord, and Christ appearing eight days later to all the apostles. The twelfth- or thirteenth-century version from Saint Benoit-sur-Loire, called the Fleury text, contains many stage directions, insisting on the hairiness of the pilgrims and of Christ. It contains the same elements as the Beauvais play with a flashback to Christ's descent into hell and the visit of the Maries to the tomb.[75]

In the fourteenth century a play on the journey to Emmaus was enacted at Saintes in France, and the two pilgrims were supposed to sing their parts. A chorus announced their arrival in the evening at the village. A dumb show depicted Christ breaking the bread as well as his disappearance and reappearance among the disciples.[76]

In the fourteenth century all sorts of plays were created, praising the local saints. Saint Nicholas was the oldest subject of plays: *Tres filiae* dates from the twelfth century. Saint Nicholas, by giving an indigent father some money, saved the daughters from prostitution.[77]

In the manuscript from Saint Martial of Limoges on the *Foolish Virgins* the vernacular is mixed with the Latin, a rare feature of medieval drama: the chorus and the virgins (both *prudentes* and *fatuae*) speak in Latin, whereas the merchants and Gabriel use the vernacular. Christ speaks both in Latin and in the vernacular. Devils carry the imprudent young ladies to hell.[78]

In Spain the liturgical drama did not flourish to the same extent as in France or in England. The oldest Spanish liturgical play dates from the eleventh century, and two versions were found in two breviaries in Silos. They are two different forms of the Easter *Visitatio sepulchri*. Both are in Mozarabic script and notation, but they belong to the Roman-French rite, which had been introduced by Charlemagne in Catalonia.[79] The play was of short duration in Silos, but it reappeared in Santiago in the twelfth century, where pilgrims would expect the same entertainments as they had in their native countries. The *Quem quaeritis* appeared on the second line, and it finished with a *Te Deum*.

In Aragon, in the Huesca cathedral library, two other liturgical embellishments were found: a Christmas trope and an Easter trope. Both start with *Quem quaeritis* and date from the eleventh or the twelfth century. In León, nothing can be found before the thirteenth century, though antiphons were used from the tenth century.[80] So, in short, the Spanish liturgical production seems to be limited to two *Quem quaeritis* tropes at Huesca and Zaragoza and a *Visitatio sepulchri* at Silos and Compostela.

Why was there such scarcity when the pilgrimage to Compostela brought travelers as eager for liturgical entertainment as for relics? On this highly controversial issue, Richard Donovan has proposed to account for it with three reasons. First, the Roman-French rite arrived as late as 1080 to change the liturgy. Naturally it would be concerned with basic changes rather than florid additions. Secondly, the change came from Cluny, and no such plays are found either at Cluny or at its main priories. Thirdly, at the time of the liturgical change, a strong vernacular tradition was already established; the development of this rather than old Latin plays could have impeded the liturgical drama from flourishing.[81]

If we are sure that the tropes and sequences were performed in the church in front of the altar, which could represent a table, a crib, or a grave, little is known of the performance of all liturgical dramas. Whether the play was stationary, or took a processional form, or was a combination of both; whether it was performed within the church or in the square before the cathedral, or in an open field, are equally subjects of controversy.[82] For one thing, it may have depended on climatic circumstances. Most plays are not as explicit as the Fleury text of the *Officium peregrinorum*. What is certain is that the liturgical dramas at their early stages were performed by monks and occasionally by young choristers, and that great feasting ensued.

The Ethelwold manuscript of the tenth century describes what happened during the performance of the *Quem quaeritis* play in Winchester cathedral. While the third lesson was being recited, four brothers would dress up. After having put on a white vestment, one of them came noiselessly to the site of the sepulcher holding a palm in his hand and sat down. While the third response was being sung, the three other brothers, enacting the Maries, proceeded dressed in copes and carrying burning censers, looking for someone. When the seated monk saw the three others, he would ask the *Quem quaeritis?* with soft melodious voice. All three would sing back in unison *Jhesum Nazarenum.* The angel then answered that Christ was resurrected. Then the three monks would turn toward the choir and sing *Alleluia, resurrexit Dominus.* The angel then invited them to see for themselves, singing: *Venite et videte locum.* He got up, lifted the curtain that had been hiding the altar, and showed that the cross was no longer there; only the shroud remained. The three Maries then would drop their censers and take the shroud, holding it out to the clergy, to show them that Christ was risen indeed, which anthem they then sang. Then the *Te Deum laudamus* was chanted while the bells chimed around four-thirty in the afternoon.[83] All was sung in plainsong, which maintained within an audible range the words to be heard, as opposed to the later laic drama, which emphasized the dramatic qualities of both music and actors.[84]

A good example of later performances of such liturgical dramas is found in the twelfth-century play of Daniel. The satraps' words indicate the noise made by various instruments:

Resonent jocunda turba solemnibus odis
Cytharizent, plaudant manus, mille sonent modis.[85]

Citherists appeared soon after. Other texts lead us to believe that in later times the number of the performers was also increased. For instance, in the eleventh-century manuscript of Saint Martial of Limoges, *The Prophets of Christ* included a Praecentor, Israel, a Response, Moses, Isaiah, Jeremy, Daniel, John the Baptist, Virgil, Nebuchadnezzar, and Sibilla, in this order. This certainly was a strange mixture of the sacred and the profane.

There were many detractors of such religious entertainments, not to mention the later sneers of the sixteenth century. We have only to turn to the contemporaries like Gerhoh of Reichersberg. In his *De investigatione Antichristi,* ca. 1162, he suggested that the clergy and the monks resembled the figures of the Antichrist that they represented in their plays, for they encouraged men to think of Antichrist. A direct allusion was made to the play of Limoges on the Slaughter of the Innocents.[86] A more qualified view was expressed by the abbess of the convent of Hohenburg, Herrad of Landsberg. She argued that though plays were good in themselves, they provided an occasion for drinking bouts and impiety and therefore they might as well be suppressed, as many evils often come from good things.[87]

From these testimonies one can infer that whatever the difficulties the pilgrims met on the road and however strong the desire to acquire more merits to go to heaven, their path was not always one of virtuous obedience to the laws of the Lord, of silence to hear the word of God, and of holy poverty. They might indeed resemble the cursed carloads or shiploads of modern tourists that pour upon the Greek Parthenon, speaking loudly in the restaurants of the Acropolis, and dumping their bottles of Coke or of retzina in the surrounding streets. There were some pilgrims, though, who imitated Christ, traveled behind in silence and even wore hairshirts to increase the pain and difficulties. As the pilgrimage became easier and less dangerous, it saw an increase in the worldly minded, all the more irritable and riotous as they were tired from the journey, sought relief in the pleasures of Venus or Bacchus, and contemplated heaven through the end of a bottle.

NOTES

1. Boethius, *The Consolation of Philosophy*, tr. Richard Green (New York: Library of the Liberal Arts, 1962), Bk. II, iii, p. 8: "You should not be surprised then, if we are blown about by stormy winds in the voyage of this life, since our main duty is to oppose the wicked."
2. Ibid., Bk. V, i, p. 101: "I should not want you to become so wearied by side trips that you would not be able to complete the main journey."
3. Jeanne Vielliard, *Le guide du pèlerin*, (Mâcon: Protat frères 1950) p. 12. Nor should the wholesale disasters of fire and plague be forgotten. The fire at Vézelay in 1120 killed a thousand pilgrims (Alan Kendall, *Medieval Pilgrims* [New York: Putnam 1970], p. 51).
4. P. A. Sigal, *Les marcheurs de Dieu* (Paris: Colin, 1974), p. 69. An indication of the normal expectation of the traveler at a hospice can be found in an interesting capital in the porch of the Hôtel-Dieu at Le Puy, which is illustration no. 215 in Emile Mâle, *Religious Art in France: The Twelfth Century* (Princeton, N.J.: Princeton University Press, Bollingen Series, 1978). One side of the capital displays the pilgrim being given bread, while another shows him being put to bed.
5. M. L. Fracard, "L'équipement hospitalier en Bas-Poitou sur les routes de Compostelle" in exhibition catalog: *Hôpitaux et confrèries des pèlerins de Saint Jacques* (Cadillac-sur-Garonne, May–September 1967), p. 16.
6. L. Vázquez de Parga, J. M. Lacarra and J. U. Riú, *Las peregrinaciónes a Santiago de Compostela*, 3 vols. (Madrid: Escuela de Estudias Medievales, 1948), I, pp. 302–4.
7. Vázquez de Parga, Lacarra, Riú, *Peregrinaciónes*, I, p. 300.
8. Vielliard, *Guide du pèlerin*, p. 10. Monastic hospitality was a duty. The *regula monachorum* of San Isidoro de León states that monks are to divide their goods into three parts and one of them is to be devoted to the succour of the poor (*S. Isidori opera omnia*, ed. Lorenzana (Rome, 1802, VI, xix, 5, pp. 551–52). In 886, Alphonso III authorized for the church of Orenze the privilege, conceding an area *pro susceptione peregrinorum et sustentationibus pauperum* (*España Sagrada* [Madrid: Rodriguez, 1795], vol. 17, appendix, p. 245).
9. Raymond Oursel, *Evocation de la chrétienté romane* (Yonne: Zodiaque, 1968), p. 244.
10. Pierre Riché, *La vie quotidienne dans l'empire carolingien* (Paris: Hachette, 1974), p. 318.
11. Fracard, "L'équipement hospitalier," p. 17.
12. Ibid., p. 18.
13. Oursel, *Evocation*, p. 252.
14. A. Masson, "Existe-t-il une architecture des hospices de Saint Jacques?" in *Revue historique de Bordeaux et du département de la Gironde* 35 (1942): 5–17.

15. Oursel, *Evocation*, p. 246.

16. "The examination of Master William Thorpe, 1407," in Edward Arber, ed., *English Garner*, 8 vols. (London: E. Arber, 1887–96), 6, p. 84; also in A. W. Pollard, ed., *Fifteenth Century Prose and Verse* (London: Constable, 1903), pp. 140–42.

17. Sigal, *Les marcheurs de Dieu*, pp. 41–44. English women pilgrims on the Continent were considered whores, as we see from Bonifaci's complaint to Cuthbert, archbishop of Canterbury. For this see Cyril Vogel, "Le pèlerinage pénitentiel," in *Pelegrinàggi e culto dei santi in Europa fino alla I^a Crociata* (Todi: Centro di Studi sulla Spiritualita Medievale, 1963), p. 75. For pilgrimage as an excuse for amorous encounters reflected in the Spanish traditional lyric, see A. Sánchez Romeralo, *El villancico* (Madrid: Editorial Gredos, 1969), pp. 65–66.

18. See *Codex Calixtinus*, pp. 164–67: *O vos falsi hospites et subdoli mummularii et negociatores iniqui, convertimini ad dominum Deum vestrum; postponite nequicias vestras, dimittite cupiditatem, auferte fraudas iniquas a vobis! Quid dicetis in judicii die, quando videbitis omnes illos quos fraudastis accusantes vos coram Deo?*

19. Elie Lambert, *Etudes médiévales*, 4 vols. (Toulouse: Privat, 1956–57), I, chap. 4.

20. Ibid. On al-Mansur, see also G. G. Hartley, *The Story of Santiago de Compostela* (New York, 1912), pp. 42–43; and R. Menéndez Pidal, *Historia y epopeya* (Madrid: Hernando, 1934), pp. 16–22.

21. Vielliard, *Guide du pèlerin*, chap. 7.

22. *Multociens etiam tantam peregrinorum turmam naute, accepto precio, intromittunt, quod navis subvertitur et peregrini in pelago necantur. Unde naute nequiter gaudent, captis mortuorum spoliis* (ibid., p. 20).

23. Desmond Seward, *The Monks of War: The Military Religious Orders* (Hamden, Conn.: Archon Books, 1972), p. 307.

24. Oursel, *Evocation*, pp. 272–73.

25. See F. L. Cross, ed., *Oxford Dictionary of the Christian Church* (London: Oxford University Press, 1963), pp. 658–59. Three interesting scenes on the dubbing of a knight can be viewed in the cathedral of Le Puy. Beigbeder suggests that these may be Templars. We think it much more likely that it may be a reference to Raymond and the Hospitalers, thus praising the local scene (see O. Beigbeder, *Forez-Velay Roman* [Yonne: Zodiaque, 1962] p. 49 and plates 8 and 9).

26. See Oursel, *Evocation*, pp. 255–57.

27. Ibid., p. 272.

28. Seward, *The Monks of War*, pp. 135–36; and J. S. Stone, *The Cult of Santiago* (New York: Longmans, 1927), p. 181. Their hospitals at Toledo Las Tiendas and San Marcos were carefully protected.

29. Seward, *The Monks of War*, p. 4.

30. See Joan Evans, *Life in Medieval France* (London: Phaidon, 1957), pp. 76–77. The presence of commercialism is particularly interesting and reminds us of the same in modern times on the road to Marseilles. Montélimar is such a town and the road is strewn with shops selling their famous nougat. We quote the manuscript:

> Entor le mont el bois follu
> Cil travetier unt tres tendu
> Rues unt fait par les chemins.

31. *C. C.* I, xvii, Whitehill, pp. 160–62.

32. Vázquez de Parga, Lacarra, and Ríu. *Peregrinaciónes*, I, p. 112, recalls the warning of the Berthold of Ratisbon, a Franciscan of the thirteenth century, to the women pilgrims. One also recalls the misogynist's proverb *Ir romera volver ramera*, cited earlier. Cf. Gonzalo de Correas, *Vocabulario de refranes* (Madrid: Rates, 1924), p. 250b.

33. See O. Beigbeder, *Lexique des symboles* (Yonne: Zodiaque, 1966), pp. 30–32.

34. J. J. Borg, ed., *Aye d'Avignon* (Geneva: Droz, 1967), pp. 179.

35. *La prise d'Orange*, ed. Blanche Katz (New York: King's Crown Press, 1947), line 1882.

36. G. de Champeaux and S. Sterckx, *Introduction au monde des symboles* (Yonne: Zodiaque, 1966), p. 361 and plate 140.

37. Antonio Vinayo González, *L'ancien royaume de León roman* (Yonne: Zodiaque, 1972), p. 94 and plate 43.

38. G. de Chambeaux and Sterckx, *Monde des symboles*, p. 169.

39. Edouard Junyent, *Catalogne romane*, 2 vols. (Yonne: Zodiaque, 1970), II, p. 198. Plate 64 shows the detail of the juggler throwing balls into the air and keeping the knife in his left hand.

40. González, *León roman*, p. 45a.

41. Beigbeder, *Lexique des symboles*, pp. 398–99; for Bayeux, see plate 139; for St. Jouin des Marnes, see plate 132.

42. Ibid., p. 31.

43. Marilyn Stokstad, *Santiago de Compostela in the Age of the Great Pilgrimages* (Norman: University of Oklahoma Press, 1978), pp. 43–44, 153. Also see Edmond Faral, *Les jongleurs en France au moyen âge* (Paris: Champion, 1910).

44. E. Junyent, *Catalogne romane*, II, plate 51.

45. Sidney Heath, *Pilgrim Life in the Middle Ages* (Boston and New York: Houghton Mifflin, 1912), pp. 63–64.

46. Pierre Aubry, *Trouvères et troubadours*, 3d ed. (Paris: Alcan, 1919), 34–35.

47. E. Mâle, *L'art religieux du XIIème Siècle en France*, 3d ed. (Paris: Colin, 1924), p. 312.

48. Ferdinand Lot denied that the old epic legends were born in the cloister, but admitted that they might have found an asylum there, or even a prison, but only after having wandered for a long times over hills and valleys (*Etudes sur les légendes épiques françaises* [Paris: Champion 1958], p. 259).

49. Robert Lafont, ed., *Nouvelle histoire de la littérature occitane* (Paris: P.U.F., 1970), vol. I, pp. 28–29. See also the Conference given by René Louis on April 24, 1972, at the University of Paris-X.

50. Brigitte Luc, "Un pèlerinage type: saint Jacques de Compostelle" in J. Madaule, B. Luc, G. Gaillard, and Abbé Branthomme, *Pèlerins comme nos pères: retour à Saint Jacques* (Saint-Mandé: La Tourelle, 1950), pp. 55–100.

51. Edmondstoune Duncan, *The Story of the Minstrelsy* (New York: Scribner's, 1907), pp. 18, 36–37. See also Faral, *Les jongleurs;* and R. Menéndez Pidal, *Poesia juglaresca y origenes de las literaturas romanicas* (Madrid: Instituto de Estudios Politicos, 1957).

52. Georgia Goddard King, *The Way of Saint James*, 3 vols. (New York: Putnam, 1920), I, pp. 295–96.

53. Menéndez Pidal, *Poesía juglaresca*.

54. Ibid., pp. 318, 340–41.

55. Jean Secret, *Saint Jacques et les chemins de Compostelle* (Paris: Horizons de France, 1957), pp. 6–9. See also Stokstad, *Santiago de Compostela*, pp. 149–50.

56. See *Poem of the Cid*, tr. and ed. Archer W. Huntington (New York: Hispanic Society of America, 1942), line 731.

57. See W. Cloetta, ed., *Les deux rédactions en vers du Moniage Guillaume*, 2 vols. (Paris: Firmin-Didot, 1906–11), lines 1917 ff.

58. E. B. Mullins, *The Pilgrimage to Santiago* (London: Taplinger, 1974) p. 61. For a modern imaginative reconstruction of his life, see Frederick Buechner's fine novel, *Godric* (New York: Atheneum, 1980).

59. Vázquez de Parga, Lacarra, Riú, *Peregrinaciónes*, I, pp. 76, 466–88, 499.

60. Felix Bourquelot, *Etudes sur les foires de Champagne*, 2 vols. (Portulan: Manoir de St. Pierre de Salerne, 1970), I, pp. 17–22.

61. Nigel Heard, *International Fairs* (Lavenham: Dalton 1973), p. 36.

62. Ibid., pp. 67–68.

63. Bourquelot, *Etudes sur les foires*, II, pp. 11.

64. Heard, *International Fairs*, pp. 77–82.

65. See on this topic A. Pauphilet, *Jeux et sapiences du moyen âge* (Paris: Gallimard, 1951).

66. Léon Gautier, *La poésie religieuse dans les cloîtres des IX–XIème siècles* (Paris: V. Palmé, 1887), pp. 5–20.

67. Ulysse Chevalier, *Poésie liturgique du moyen âge* (Lyon: E. Vitte, 1892), pp. 24–31.

68. P. J. Toynbie, *Specimens of Old French* (Oxford: Clarendon Press 1892), p. 4.

69. Lafont, *Nouvelle histoire*, I, pp. 30–31.

70. Toynbie, *Specimens of Old French*, pp. 12–13. The author quotes the text (p. 13) that describes the frugality of Saint Alexis:

De la viande qui del herberc li vient
Tant en retient dont son cors en sostient:

se lui 'n remaint, sil rent alas almosniers;
n'en fait musjode por son cors engraissier,
mais alas plus porres le donet a mangier.

71. *La vie de st. Gilles par Guillaume de Berneville: poème du XIIème siècle*, edited by Gaston Paris (Paris, 1881), sig. 72–89.

72. Karl Young, *The Drama of the Medieval Church*, 2 vols. (Oxford: Clarendon Press, 1933), I, p. 187.

73. Ibid., I, pp. 179–85.

74. Ibid., II, p. 109.

75. Ibid., II, pp. 33–37.

76. Ibid., II, pp. 102–9.

77. Ibid., I, pp. 467–75. The Saint Benoit version was enacted in the Princeton University chapel on Easter Monday, 1976, with some changes in the staging.

78. Ibid., I, p. 454.

79. Ibid., II, p. 311.

80. See British Museum Add. Ms. 30848 fol. 125v., and the newer version of British Museum Add. Ms. 30850, *Breviarium Silense* saec. xi, fol. 106v.

81. See Richard B. Donovan, *The Liturgical Drama in Medieval Spain* (Toronto: University of Toronto Press, 1958), pp. 51–65. For an alternative view see J. M. Regueiro, "El *Auto de los Reyes Magos* y el teatro litúrgico medieval," *Hispanic Review* 45 (1977): 139–64. See also Joan Evans, *Monastic Life at Cluny, 910–1157* (Oxford: Clarendon Press, 1931); R. Menéndez Pidal, *Cantar de Mio Cid*, 3 vols. (Madrid: Bailly-Ballière, 1964–69); and W. Sturdevant, *The Misterio de los Reyes Magos: Its Position in the Development of the Mediaeval Legend of the Three Kings* (Baltimore: Johns Hopkins University Press; Paris: P.U.F., 1927).

82. See A. M. Nagler, *The Medieval Religious Stage—Shapes and Phantoms* (New Haven, Conn.: Yale University Press, 1976).

83. See B. M. Cotton Ms. Tiberius A III, fol. 21–21v., cited in Carol Heitz, *Recherches sur les rapports entre architecture et liturgie à l'époque carolingienne* (Paris: S.E.V.E.N., 1963), pp. 187–88.

84. E. de Coussemaker, ed., *Drames liturgiques du moyen âge* (texte et musique) (Paris: Didron, 1861), p. x.

85. Young, *Drama of the Medieval Church*, II, p. 291.

86. *Exhibent praeterea imaginaliter et Salvatoris infantiae cunabula, parvuli vagitum, puerperae virginis matronalem habitum, stellae quasi sidus flammigerum, infantum necem, maternum Rachelis ploratum. Sed divinitas insuper et matura facies ecclesiae abhorret spectacula theatralia, non respicit in vanitates et insanias falsas, immo non falsas sed jam veras insanias, in quibus viri totos se frangunt in feminas quasi pudeat eos, quod viri sunt, clerici in milites, homines se in daemonum larvas transfigurant.* The parallel between women and the creatures of Satan is interesting to notice. A fuller excerpt is to be found ibid., II, pp. 392–93.

87. *Denique multa mala exempla de bonis orta sunt.* Then she proceeds to give the main popular plays of the twelfth century: *Igitur de Nativitate Christi, de eius manifestatione et Magorum mysticis muneribus, de circumcisione, de eius in laude populi et palmis virentibus Hierosolimam itinere in asino et de duobus in Emaus discipulis quaedam imitandi vestigia ecclesia praefixit per exempla quae in quibusdam iuxta traditionem antiquorum digna veneratione celebrantur ecclesiis, in quibusdam aut pro volontate aut pro necessitate vel mutata sunt vel neglecta. . . .* She goes on to describe the riotousness that occurred during these plays: *Mutatur habitus clericalis, incohatur ordo militaris, nulla in sacerdote vel milite differentia, domus Dei permixtione laicorum et clericorum confunditur, commessationes, ebrietates, scurrilitates, ioci inimici ludi placesibiles armorum strepitus, ganearum concursus omnium vanitatum indisciplinatus excursus.* Quoted ibid., pp. 412–13.

PART III
Journey's End

——— 8 ———

Reaching Santiago's Shrine

LIKE Moses some pilgrims died on the way to the Promised Land, but all who reached the approach to Compostela rejoiced as Moses did to catch the first glimpse of the goal of pilgrimage. There is no record extant from Romanesque times of the reaction of any pilgrim on reaching Montjoie (Mons Gaudii),[1] the eminence from which they saw the sky-piercing towers of the great cathedral of Saint James. But its very name suggests the rejoicing that the pilgrims felt, combined with relief after the long and weary journey taken, penitentially on foot, or more expeditiously on a mule. After all the pilgrims had, for the most part, crossed the natural barrier of the Pyrenees where they could only trudge about fifteen kilometers a day, whereas they could walk thirty kilometers a day on flat ground. Weariness, as well as devotion, must have entered into their rejoicing. Even those who had ridden most of the way dismounted at Mountjoie and walked the rest of the journey.[2]

We can gain some idea of the joy of foot-weary and saddle-sore pilgrims from the sentiments expressed by other pilgrims reaching other longed-for shrines. Saint Paula was a Roman matron who at the age of thirty-three set out for the holy places in Palestine, and in A.D. 385 found herself before the Cross. There, "prostrate before the Cross, she adored it as though she saw the Lord hanging upon it; entering the sepulchre of the Resurrection, she kissed the stone which the angel removed from the door of the tomb, and with faithful mouth kissed 'the very place of the body' on which the Lord had lain, as one who thirsts drinks long-desired waters. What tears, what groans, what sorrow she displayed, all Hierusalem is witness, and the Lord Himself whom she called upon."[3] Jusserand attempted to divine the thoughts of the pilgrims of the eleventh and twelfth centuries, both tough-minded and tenderhearted, as they reached the shrine of Saint Thomas à Becket at Canterbury. It is doubtful if the pilgrims to Santiago's shrine at the height of its popularity felt any different. The French historian writes: "Though the practical man galloping up to bargain with the saint for the

201

favor of God, though the emissary sent to make offering in the name of his master might keep a dry and clear eye, tears coursed down the cheeks of the poor and simple in heart; he tasted fully of the pious emotion he had come to seek, the peace of heaven descended into his bosom, and he went away consoled."[4]

Saint Paula's adoration and Jusserand's reconstruction of the appropriate emotions are more expressive than the words of the last stanza of the *Chanson itinérante des pèlerins de Compostelle*. However laconic it is, we glimpse the desire not only to see Compostela but also journey's end in heaven:

> *Hélas! que nous fûmes joyeux*
> *Quand nous fûmes à Montjoye,*
> *Tous mes compagnons et moi,*
> *De voir ce lieu tant désiré*
> *C'était de voir la sainte église*
> *Où rendîmes graces à Dieu,*
> *A la Vierge et à saint Jacques*
>
> *Prions Jésus-Christ par sa grace*
> *Que nous puissions voir face à face*
> *La Vierge et saint Jacques le grand.*[5]

Before they reached the great cathedral, however, the pilgrims had to perform important terminal rites. One median rite had already been enacted en route, for all pilgrims had to plant a wooden cross at the summit of the Pass of Cize in the region of Mount Bentarte. The cross was facing the direction of Spain whose patron saint was Saint James. All pilgrims prayed on their knees presumably for grace to complete the pilgrimage. It was claimed that Charlemagne had initiated this tradition.[6]

More important, however, at the approach to Santiago of Compostela was a double requirement. In the first place, at the Lavamentula River two miles from Compostela, the Pilgrims were to undergo a ritual purification. According to the guide there was a stream in which "the people of France on pilgrimage are accustomed, after having taken off their clothing, to wash off the dust from their entire bodies for the love of the Apostle."[7]

This symbolized a second Baptism—a return to innocence and holiness of life. Here, again, there was an experience parallel to that undergone by pilgrims to the Holy Land, for the latter would, in imitation of their Savior, plunge into the waters of the Jordan River.

The second requirement of all pilgrims on the *camino francés* was an eminently practical one. Having descended Mount Cerebro in Galicia, the road to Saint James passed by the limestone quarries of Triacastela, where the pilgrims each received a stone that they then carried to the furnaces established at Castagnola, probably at Saint Maria de Castañeda.[8] Thence the lime was immediately transported by carts to Saint James. Thus each pilgrim had the sense that he was adding to the building of the saint's shrine at Compostela. Even the poorest pilgrim was able to make this contribution of his or her labor. While a practical gesture, it was also symbolical. For was not the purpose of the true pilgrim in his travel to burn away his sins as lime does, and is not the faith of the Christian the binding element in the Church? In any case, the ritual bath and the transport of stone were exciting preparations and anticipations of reaching the pilgrims' goal.

Most of the pilgrims to Compostela would travel in companies, perhaps as many as thirty, and we must imagine the excitement increasing, especially on the eve of a Feast of Saint James, when the crowds increased as one got nearer to the cathedral. The crowds included representatives of many nations. The compiler of the *Historia Compostellana,* assuming that everyone would know about the varied nationalities, mentions them only in passing. From that source, however, we learn that Spanish kings,[9] Roman cardinals,[10] abbots and monks from Cluny and elsewhere,[11] as well as merchants from England and Lorraine[12] came to the city.

On the great feast days the pilgrims would be impressed by the international composition of the crowds and by the social variety and physical condition of the individuals comprising it. This is stressed by the author of the pseudo-Calixtine sermon for the Feast of the Translation of Saint James, who, after mentioning the predominance of French, Italians, and Germans, continues: "In the church one hears various languages and voices in barbaric tongues, conversations and songs in German, English, Greek, and the languages of other tribes and differing peoples of every part of the world." He adds: "To Santiago come the poor, the rich, criminals, knights, princes, governors, the blind, those missing an arm or hand, the nobles, the heroes, the primates, the bishops, the abbots, some barefoot, others penniless, others again carrying iron or lead for the work of the basilica of the Apostle; yet others, weeping for their sins, freed from the prisons of tyrants, carry the iron chains and manacles on their shoulders as penance. They have been liberated by the intercessory power of the Apostle."[13]

The guidebook enables us to picture the entry to Compostela in the twelfth century. French pilgrims would approach from the northeast, passing the leprosarium of Lazarus on their left, then going through a small glade, up a short hill, and entering the city by the Puerta Francigena, a gateway in the city wall, with two towers. Eventually they would reach the cathedral at the square fronting its northern transept, a busy market center with an impressive fountain in the middle. As they faced the cathedral there would be the archbishop's palace on their right, the pilgrims' hospice behind them, and on their left the church of the corticela, and the monastery and hospital of San Pelayo Ante-altares, as well as shops and houses. In the square "the pilgrims are sold the scallop shells which are the emblems of St. James, as well as wine-skins, shoes, satchels of deerskin, purses, straps, belts, all kinds of medical herbs, additional drugs, and much else. The money-changers, inn-keepers, and other merchants as well are in the Via Francigena."[14]

Surprising as it may seem to modern eyes, it was one thing to see the sanctuary and quite another to be able to enter it. The chief obstacle, especially on feast days, was the crowd itself. It was even hazardous to enter a center of pilgrimage when the press was great. Two poems written about Fécamp, a Benedictine shrine on the coast of Normandy, relate the dangers of overcrowding at Christmas. A woman pilgrim is said to have been seriously wounded as she was trampled on by the feet of other pilgrims.[15] It was not less dangerous inside the Fécamp sanc-tuary for the other poem tells how the pilgrims jostled one another to place their alms on the abbey altar. Indeed, one sensible pilgrim ap-pointed himself as policeman to prevent the monks from being suf-focated by the dense crowd, and in the push discovered that he had been relieved of his purse for the good deed.[16]

The crowding into sanctuaries frequently led to fights and even occa-sionally to a murder. The author of the Codex Calixtinus happened to be present at the sanctuary of Saint Gilles in Provence when a battle broke out between the Gascons and the Franks in which one person was killed.[17] Blood was certainly shed at Compostela because in 1207 a decretal of Pope Innocent III, issued at the request of the archbishop of Compostela, indicated in the clearest and most explicit terms how the sanctuary could be purified after being profaned by the effusion of blood.[18]

What was the cause of such jostling? It seems that the faithful were so eager to penetrate into the heart of the sanctuary and to be the first to reach the body of the saint and to touch the tomb because there was a superstition that the first to arrive would be the first to be cured.

One can hardly imagine the chaos that reigned in a pilgrimage center during a vigil of the saint. The pilgrims generally spent the night there, if they had not been there several nights before, and filled the church to overflowing. While the majority slept, several of the pilgrims were wide awake. The groans of the sick were intermingled with the sobs of the penitent, while others shouted in their cups or told ribald tales or sang vulgar songs. It is only a rose-colored idealism that depicts a pilgrimage church during a vigil as a scene of ascetical devotions analogous to that of the future knight during the evening prior to his dubbing. The author of the *Codex Calixtinus* does not disguise the fact that a great confusion reigned in the church of Saint James during a vigil. If one cried because of his sins, another read the psalter aloud, while many trivial and even shameful conversations took place. Mothers nursed their babies, and children and adults partook of roughly improvised meals, while musical instruments of every land and type were played to destroy the quietness. One is impressed by the variety of nationalities that had gathered to honor the Apostle James. Even if there was a veritable Babel of sound produced by woodwinds, horns, strings, and drums, it was a very vivid scene in which the tapers held in the hands of the pilgrims illumined the church so that it seemed day, not night.[19]

Nor was the crowd composed exclusively of pilgrims. Jugglers, pick-pockets, hawkers, beggars, confidence men, pardoners, thieves, and prostitutes were part of the motley multitude. Yet even the ranks of the exploiters could not dampen the enthusiasm of the pilgrims. For the enduring supernatural power of Saint James was made known in the miracles he performed for the faithful. High above the songs, the prayers, and the curses would be heard the ecstatic shouts of the cured. At each new miracle the crowd would thrust itself forward, and the clergy rushed to the patient to check on the claim for themselves. They were ready to interrupt worship to proclaim the latest miracle enacted by their patron saint.

These emotional outbursts are reminders that "violent antithesis is the essence of the Middle Ages."[20] For all life was exceedingly precarious, hideous diseases were widely prevalent, and murder and pillage were all too common experiences. The poor barely managed to survive, and the rich maintained their riches with armed vigilance. The fear of death was an ever present *danse macabre* with dangling skeletons and defiant demons, so that it was no wonder if moments of joy or relief were extravagantly expressed.

The *Codex Calixtinus* provides a most vivid picture of the interior of the cathedral on a vigil at the height of the pilgrimage in the mid–twelfth century, when miracles were frequent. In fact it states that "the many thousands of miracles that are worked daily through the intercession of the Apostle in the city of his glorious tomb increase the legions of pilgrims who carry back with them to the utmost confines of the world the name of Compostela." This bold advertising was, however, hardly an exaggeration.

The account continues by observing that rich and poor, prince and peasant, governor and abbot, all go to the shrine of Saint James. "Some come at their own charges, and others depend wholly on charity. Some come in chains to mortify their flesh; others, like the Greeks, bear an icon of the cross in their hands. . . . Some carry with them iron and lead for the building of the basilica of the Apostle. Many whom the Apostle has delivered from prison bring with them their manacles and the bolts of their prison doors, and do penance for their sins."[21]

Next the *Codex* describes the classes of those who were healed by the Apostle: "The sick come and are cured, the blind receive their sight, the lame walk, the dumb speak, the possessed are set free, the sad find consolation, and, what is more important, the prayers of the faithful reach heaven, the heavy weight of sin is removed, and the chains of sin are broken."[21]

Finally, we see that the lodestone of the distant pilgrims is the saint's sepulcher. "Thither come all the nations of the earth. The pilgrims travel right across Europe in great companies, and in companies they place themselves beside the sepulchre, the Germans on one side, the Italians on this side, the French on another. There they stay to worship the whole night long."[23]

After the vigil was over, pilgrims both decorous and indecent, pious and worldly, were forced to leave the cathedral at dawn on the feast day. They returned to their lodgings in the city. Meanwhile the cathedral was cleaned up and prepared for the celebratory services of the day of the saint. At these celebrations of the perpetual power of Saint James, the crowds were greater than at the vigil because the local inhabitants joined the throng of pilgrims.[24]

Before the pilgrims joined in the magnificent liturgy in which the feasts of the Apostle James were celebrated, we must suppose that sheer curiosity if not piety would impel them to visit the cathedral, its fourteen altars,[25] and, of course, the crypt in which the body of the saint was kept in a glorious coffer, or chest.

The descent to the crypt to view the casket of the Apostle was, of course, the climax of the visit. This might take place the day before the feast or on the feast day itself after the conclusion of the liturgy. In the latter case it would be the finale of the worship for the individual pilgrim, which is how we shall imagine it, when we describe the terminal rituals of the visit, with the descent into the sacred darkness, the flickering lights of the tapers and candles, the coruscations of the silver and gold of the shrine, with its brilliant gems representing the contributions of the centuries.

We must understand that whether the pilgrim arrived at Santiago's shrine in the ninth century, in the eleventh century, or in the twelfth century, he would have found a very different church. Alfonso III, the Magnanimous, built a relatively small basilica with marble columns of the ancient type still extant in the Asturian hills, but this was burned to the ground by al-Mansur leaving only the tomb of Saint James intact. It was replaced in the eleventh century by a Romanesque church, with three parallel apses and with western towers, which looked like a smaller version of Cluny. The great church of the twelfth century—that envisioned in the *Codex Calixtinus*, which gives four chapters to its description—was one of the greatest Romanesque pilgrimage churches of which the most notable examples were Saint Martin of Tours, Saint Martial of Limoges, Saint Foi of Conques, and Saint Sernin of Toulouse. In addition, it borrowed a dramatic west front from the cathedral of Le Puy and probably some of the decoration of Poitou. At the end of the twelfth century the west end was rebuilt by Master Matthew who also rebuilt the narthex or Pórtico de la Gloria.[26]

The church of the twelfth century contained the majestic representation of Saint James, which greeted the pilgrims as they entered the vast basilica. On the trumeau the Apostle was seated with his tau-staff and scroll, which formerly bore the inscription *Misit me Dominus* ("The Lord sent me"). This majestic figure was enthroned upon the backs of lions, but his unshod feet of a pilgrim rest upon cool green leaves. Above Saint James was depicted the great event of which he was a privileged witness—the Transfiguration, an anticipation of Christ's Resurrection and Ascension glory.

Time and space forbid a detailed account of the splendid iconography of the cathedral. But the wondering eyes of the pilgrims would find almost the whole biblical saga represented in its sculpture. The northern facade represented the Creation at the world's beginning, while the southern depicted the end of the world and Judgment Day. At the south transept the tympanum showed Christ's betrayal, the scourging, and Pilate sitting as judge; and above this was Saint Mary, God's mother, with her son in Bethlehem and the Three Kings bringing their offerings, led by a star—the central Compostellan pilgrim theme—together with the warning of the angel. The other tympanum reenacted the story of Christ's temptations in the wilderness.

The author of the Compostela guide was interested in iconography, but he also drew attention to other marvels, such as the fountain of Saint James with its bronze column and lions spouting water, the many doors and ten towers of the cathedral, the great altar with its silver table and the vast ingeniously decorated ciborium that covers the Apostle's altar, and the three great silver lamps in front of the altar. He wished to impress pilgrims with the great dignity of this cathedral, which had an archbishop at its head, ruling over the seventy-two canons living according to the rule of Saint Isidore.

One wonders whether the pilgrims would feel at home in this vast temple in a foreign land, hundreds or thousands of miles from home. In addition to recognizing their own place on the Christian historical continuum between the Resurrection and the Second Advent of Christ, they would hear their own tongue spoken among the companies of pilgrims from their own land. But, more significantly, in two other ways they would feel that they were in a sense "at home." The other great pilgrimage churches en route would have prepared them for Compostela, with its vast nave with side aisles, its double transepts, its radiating corona of chapels, and its crypt where the body of the saint was to be found in a glorious reliquary. Our contention, however, is that the pilgrims would feel at home at one of the altars in the twelfth-century cathedral, with their differing dedications to saints, each of which had its attraction for pilgrims coming from different regions.

Of these fourteen altars, nine were found on the eastern half circle of the apse, two in the middle of the apse, and three in the gallery above. Numbering from the left, we find in the northwestern transept first an altar dedicated to Saint Nicholas of Bari, who became immensely popular in the west after his remains were translated to Bari in 1084.[27] Italians, in particular, would feel a special attachment to the altar of Saint Nicholas, and since he was the patron saint of travelers in general and of sailors in particular, those groups would seek his aid. The adjacent altar was that of the Holy Cross, which almost certainly contained a relic of the True Cross, discovered in Jerusalem by Saint Helena, the mother of the first Christian Roman emperor, Constantine. Saint Helena was the patron saint of sailors and children. Both British and Germans would claim to have links with her, for Saint Helena was believed to be the daughter of the British King Cole, while another tradition associated her with Trier and its great German monastery.

In the apse proper the next altar was dedicated to Saint Foi of Conques. It must have made all the French pilgrims who had traveled from Le Puy and Rouergue feel very much at home. The next altar was dedicated to Saint John the Evangelist, the brother of Saint James. His link with Ephesus would have endeared him to the Greeks who, as the *Codex Calixtinus* observed, came gladly to Compostela. Since the English Saint Edmund had a special devotion to Saint John, it is possible that some English pilgrims prayed at his altar too. The very central altar of the apse had a universal appeal for it was dedicated to the Holy Savior, Christ. To the right the next altar was dedicated to Saint Peter of Rome, important not only to Italians but to all Catholics as the rock on which the Church was founded and the keeper of the keys to heaven. To his right was the altar of Saint Andrew, with whom the Ethiopians (if any such came), the Greeks, and the Scots would feel an affinity.

In the southeastern transept there were two other altars. One was dedicated to Saint Martin of Tours and was therefore a magnet for all French pilgrims. For centuries he was the patron saint of France and the supreme exemplar of charity among the saints. His pilgrimage church was the start of the westernmost route to Compostela. Next to his altar was that of Saint John the Baptist, the cousin of Jesus. French pilgrims who had passed through Saint Jean d'Angély on the way to Compostela would have a special place in their hearts for this ascetical saint.

On the chord of the apse was the altar of Saint James, Apostle, the first of them to be martyred, patron saint of Spain, inspirer of the reconquest from the Moors. Naturally, he was most beloved by Spaniards, but since the *camino francés* led to his shrine, he was also admired by the French. Then at a specially important altar dedicated to Saint Mary Magdalene, which was located between the altar of Saint James and that of the Holy Savior, the Mass each morning was celebrated for pilgrims. All those who had traveled via Vézelay and venerated her relics there would feel a sense of kinship.

Typically in the dualistic Romanesque era, with its hosts of angels and demons, the central altar in the tribune or gallery was dedicated to Saint Michael the Archangel, to whom Roland prayed to convey his soul to heaven. He was always honored in high places, as in Saint Michel d'Aigulhe on its pinnacle of rock near to the cathedral of Saint Mary of Puy, or on the sea-encircled Mont-Saint-Michel in Normandy or at Saint Michael's Mount in Cornwall. In some ways he was a substitute for Saint James since he fought and led the Christian armies against the heathen and helped individuals at the hour of death.[28] Frenchmen, sailors, and soldiers counted on his support. Another altar in the gallery was dedicated to the great Saint Benedict and was itself one other testimony of the great Cluniac impact on the *reconquista* and the very pilgrimage to Compostela. The fourteenth and last altar, also found in the gallery, had a double dedication to Saint Paul and Bishop Nicholas. Relatively little is known about the latter, since his fame has been eclipsed by Saint Nicholas of Bari. But Saint Paul, the great apostle to the Gentiles, was uniquely the apostle for strangers and was most admired by the preaching friars who would be founded a century after the *Codex* was edited by Aymery Picaud of Parthenay-le-Vieux.

Thus, apart from the attraction that individual saints would have for those persons who were baptized with their names, or born on their festivals, or were patrons of their parish churches at home, or were believed to have assisted them in a special way, we can see that the fourteen different altars in the cathedral of Saint James would have been for many pilgrims a bit of home away from home in a distant land.[29]

It is exceedingly difficult to try to imagine how the pilgrims must have felt when they entered the sanctuary of Santiago. Probably they would have feelings of gratitude and also of regret, of awe and also of inadequacy, and a marvelous sense of the unity of Christendom. Raymond Oursel quotes a modern poem, which we have translated. It conveys some of these feelings and may be an approximation to the sensibility of a Romanesque pilgrim arriving at Compostela.

> And the promised splendor
> Breaks into the evening of the last stage of the journey,
> Which almost exhales the fragrance of regret.
>
> Into the sanctuary, like a vast ship,
> Bedecked with glory,
> They entered religiously.
>
> The shadows came alive with murmurings,
> As if the great ship slowly wakened
> From a mysterious dream.
>
> They advanced past column after column,
> Altar after altar,
> Unthinking and vulnerable,
> As their fingers twisted the folds of their pilgrim hats.
>
> Ashamed to find themselves there,
> Dirty, destitute, stiff, and poor,
> Before this very great Saint, so very rich today
> So high up and so very generous.
>
> Their pace slackened; the nave was expanding
> To the infinite dimensions of the vault of heaven,
> And they walked open-mouthed in awe.
>
> They went like a fearful flock of sheep
> Driven back by the baying of a hound,
> Jostling one another.
> Two, three, four, ten, a hundred, a thousand,
> An innumerable multitude!
>
> This was all of Christendom as a single being,
> Advancing along the flattened pavement in an irresistible procession,
> To where love and the heart's vow were bent.
>
> The cathedral stretched out over the unique sanctuary
> A mantle of velvet and of night,
> As a mother watches over her child.
>
> Happy, she wrapped all her penitent children
> In the folds of shining glories
> She treated their tiredness
> As if it were the center and grace of achievement,
> And she rocked them to a tender lullaby.[30]

Twice each year, if not three times,[31] a splendid liturgy would honor the great Apostle Santiago in his own cathedral. The feasts, according to

Raymond Oursel, provided the powerful attractions of "an extravagant fair, an incredible combination of sacred and profane, of noisy emotionalism and exceptional color, this mixture of magnificent liturgies and of carnival.[32]

In the calendar of the Hispanic Rite[33] since the seventh century the unique Feast of James the Greater was fixed as the thirtieth of December, but when the Roman Rite replaced the Mozarabic from 1080 with the calendar of the Western Church, the Roman date of July 25 was accepted as the date of the festival of Saint James.[34] But the custodians of the sanctuary were reluctant to give up the original date, hallowed by two centuries of pilgrims honoring the Apostle. Consequently, it was decided to mark July 25 as the date of the martyrdom of the Apostle and to retain December 30 as the date of Christ's calling of Saint James and the translation of his body to Galicia, and therefore to celebrate him as patron of Spain, first preacher of the Gospel on the Iberian peninsula, and *Matamoros*.

The Mozarabic Mass, used until late in the eleventh century, had a relatively simple celebration of Saint James, but it is worth considering if only to mark the contrast with the later rite at Compostela,[35] with its high claims for the Apostle, its splendid ritual, and its glorious hymnody and musical farcing. The title of the Mass is significant: it is "The Mass of Saint James the Apostle, brother of Saint John." The prayers recall how Jesus called James to be his disciple when he was in a boat, and they ask for a similar faith, responding immediately as he did to Christ. They pray also that as Saint James was able to command demons, Christ may defend his Church from the assaults of the enemy. They also recall the legend that as James was being dragged to his beheading by the command of Herod Agrippa, he cured a paralytic who cried to him beside the road, and thus made his way to martyrdom through confessing Christ before his execution. They beg that, through the same Christ who gave his life for the redemption of many, their sins may be forgiven. The final prayer asks that, being taught by the Apostle James, if they lack wisdom they may receive it from Christ. They pray that wishing to come to Christ, who has the strength and wisdom of God, they ask for the forgiveness of Christ their advocate.[36] It is to be noted that in this Mozarabic Rite there is no mention of Saint James preaching in Spain and no suggestion that he is the great leader of the armies of the Christians against the Moors. Equally significant, there is no suggestion that he is the first of the apostles in the court of heaven, as is clearly the case in the Roman liturgy as developed in Compostela in the twelfth century.

In the twelfth century the celebration of the Office required the provision of biblical lessons, the narration of the passion of the martyr James, suitable sermons, homilies on the Epistle and Gospel of the

Mass, and the antiphonary. The latter would include the anthems, the hymns, the responses, and the versicles. It would be impossible to summarize the very considerable contents of these records, but a general impression of the ritual and ceremonial of these festivals can be provided.

Some sense of the soaring music is given most vividly by Georgiana Goddard King in her description of the Great Office for Saint James's Feast. She tells of the splendid passages in the hymns of the Office, and in the antiphons she particularly admires two pieces "one very pretty and lyrical, where the waves dance about the God-led boat, and the golden stars hang low" while "the other is a set of long sonorous triplets, in which the solemn chorus will have rung and rolled magnificently under the brooding vault."[37] Her description of the Introit deserves full citation:

> The Introit is astounding in its application of Scripture and its implication of adoration, and as these bull-voiced Boanerges, these hierophants of the Son of Thunder, bellowed out in antiphonal roaring that would rise and fall in the crowded darkness like the sound of great winds and many waters, the testimony which the heavens declare and the firmament showeth, the multitude would hear the very Voice which thundered out of a terrible cloud in the Mount of Tabor, proclaiming that this was His beloved Son. They had been summoned by the echoing and re-echoing choirs, Kings of the earth and all peoples, princes and all judges of the earth, young men and maidens, old men and children, to praise the name of their Lord, and to hear the word, how Jesus called James the son of Zebedee, and John the brother of James . . . and He called them Sons of Thunder. Then came the Voice out of the cloud that acknowledged the Sonship, and there followed like the breaking of a sea in storm, *Quod est filii tonitrui.* And when the heavens have declared, and the sea, and all creeping things, the calling comes again, and the sending to preach the Kingdom of God, and the thunder comes back, and a mighty Voice from heaven "In the beginning was the Word" and once more the word is the same, *Quod est filii tonituri.*[38]

The ceremonial was as splendid in color and as dramatic as the choral music. The *Codex* makes us spectators of the Feast of the Translation of Saint James on the last day of the year in the mid–twelfth century, with all its processional splendor. It reminds us, incidentally, that Compostela was renowned for its workers in precious metals.[39]

> In that day's procession the King marched wearing his crown and royal robes in the midst of his many knights accompanied by the different orders of his counts and commanders. He was holding in his right hand the silver scepter of the Spanish empire, embellished with gold flowers of various workmanship and studded with variegated gems. The diadem on his forehead, with which he was crowned for the greater glory of the Apostle,

was of beaten gold, adorned with enameled flowers *niello*, precious stones and glistening images of birds and four-footed creatures. A unsheathed two-edged sword, decorated with golden flowers and glistening inscription, with golden pommel and silver hilt, was borne before the King. At the head of the clergy, preceding the King, the archbishop walked in dignity surrounded by the other bishops. He was vested pontifically with a white mitre and gilded sandals and in his right hand, with white gloves and a gold ring, he held a crosier of ivory. The clergy advancing before him were bedecked in venerable ornaments, the seventy-two canons of Compostela were vested in begemmed silken copes with silver brooches, gilded flowers, and everywhere resplendent fringes. Some wore silk dalmatics which were embroidered in gold from the shoulder down and of exquisite beauty.

Others were adorned with golden necklaces studded with gems, bands laced with gold, the richest mitres, attractive sandals, golden cinctures, gold-embroidered stoles and maniples inset with pearls. What more is to be said? The clergy of the choir of Santiago displayed every kind of precious stones and as much silver and gold as can be told. Some carried candlesticks and others silver censers; and others again crosses of silver-gilt. Some carried gospel books with variously begemmed golden covers, others coffers with the relics of many saints; and others phylacteries. Finally others bore gold or ivory choir batons, their tips decorated with onyx, beryl, sapphire, carbuncle, emerald, or other gem. Others bore two tables of silver-gilt on silver cars which held the lighted tapers offered by the faithful. Following the clergy came the devout folk; that is, the knights, the governors, the magnates, the nobles, the counts of Spain and beyond, all wearing festal attire. Following them were choirs of honorable women who came dressed and adorned with gilded laced shoes with furs of marten, sable, ermine and fox; with silk petticoats, gray pelisses, with mantles of fine scarlet cloth, lined with squirrel. They were adorned with gold coronets, necklaces, hairpins, bracelets, ear-rings, chains, rings, pearls, mirrors, golden girdles, silken belts, veils, bows, headdresses and their hair was braided with filaments of gold, and they had other varieties of dresses.[40]

The splendor of the ceremonial continued to the very end of the Middle Ages. Master William Way, formerly fellow of Exeter College, Oxford and a fellow of the new royal college of Eton, reported on his visit to Compostela in the jubilee year of 1456 how impressed he was by the magnificence, wealth, and dignity of its cathedral. Its archbishop—one of three in Spain—had jurisdiction over twelve bishops and, having seven cardinals under him, seemed a second pope.[41] On May 23, Way attended the Feast of the Holy Trinity, when the town was crowded with pilgrims. He was most impressed by the processionals in the service that had reached the very apex of magnificence. It happened that not long before King Henry IV of Castile and León, who had been successful in his Crusade against the Moors, had donated a golden crown as a token of his gratitude to Saint James. The crown was placed on the image of the Apostle sitting enthroned on the high altar that very day. Way noted there were nine bishops and cardinals taking part in the dramatic procession.[42]

Earlier in chapter 2 we saw how the Metropolitan Church of Compostela tried to rival Rome and Jerusalem as one of the great patriarchates, as León and Toulouse tried to eclipse Compostela itself. For a while, with Jerusalem or the routes to it dominated by the Muslims, and with tenth-century Compostela isolated from a Rome with degenerate popes,[43] to say nothing of the fourteenth-century Babylonian Captivity of the papacy in Avignon, prisoners of the French king and the sorry sight of popes combating antipopes, the ambition seemed within reach. We can find an echo in the great claims for the Apostle James in the songs of the festival that are eulogies to him. He becomes much more than a tribal hero, though he is that as the Moor-slayer *(Matamoros)* and general of the Christian armies of the *reconquista*. He is more even than *Sol sanctissimus*, lord and life-giver, the great thaumaturge, and even the lord of the dead with the power of resurrection.

The pseudo-Calixtine sermon, *Vigilie noctis sacratissime*, distinguished three leading apostles from the rest of the twelve, observing that Peter, James, and John were *tres barones et magistros*,[44] together called by Jesus on the Sea of Galilee, together present at the resuscitation of the daughter of the leader of the synagogue by Jesus, and together witnesses of the Lord's Transfiguration. The second pseudo-Calixtine sermon, also to be read during the Office, celebrated the triumphs of Saint James and made a higher claim, namely, that Christ the Lord himself "offered the first place among the apostles in heaven to his beloved and blessed James because he first triumphed as a martyr."[45]

The claim for the preeminence of Saint James was renewed in the antiphon that begins:

> O James, Apostle of Christ, unconquered soldier of the eternal king, shining in the brilliant court of the apostles as the sun glittering amid the stars, you gleam in glory.[46]

If Saint James is the sun, then obviously the other apostles, including Saint Peter, are merely stars. And the *miles invictimissime eterni regis* is none other than the victor of Clavijo, the great *Matamoros*.

Perhaps this would have been expected by the crowd of pilgrims, for a hymn, attributed to Bishop Fulbert of Chartres, sung earlier had begun:

> Here is Zebedee's son James,
> called the greater and esteemed,
> who in Galicia made
> a thousand miracles . . .

and continued by rejoicing that to his splendid temple all the nations of the world come singing the Lord's praises, "Armenians, Greeks, Apulians, English, the Gauls, Dacians, Frisians, entire peoples, tongues and tribes thither coming with their gifts."[47]

The most common and most beloved responses, because they expressed the need and the faith of the pilgrims in their approach to Saint James, were the eleventh and the twelfth. The former reads:

O worthy James, brother of chaste John, who piously recalled the fierce Hermogenes[48] from his crimes to a pure heart to the honor of the All-powerful; we beg you to continue to pray for us all.[49]

It would not be surprising if Saint James were thought of less as an apostle than a magician and miracle worker. The desperate pilgrims hoped he would work a miracle for them.

The twelfth response was even more appropriate as a pilgrim's prayer because it combined two important petitions, one for safety in traveling and the other for entrance into eternity:

O Helper of all the ages, O glory of the Apostles, O bright light of those who live in Galicia, O protector of pilgrims, James the uprooter of vices, loosen the chains of our sins, and lead us to the haven of salvation. You who assist those in peril who cry to you both on sea and land, help us now and in the danger of death. And lead us.[51]

The anthems, responses, and hymns of both feasts of Saint James were identical. It was only the lessons and the sermons and an occasional collect that differentiated the Office for July 25 from that of December 30. But the stress in December was not on the passion of Saint James but on the translation of his body from Palestine to Galicia and on his choice by Jesus as an apostle beside the Sea of Galilee. The double aim of this feast was made clear in the first prayer: "O God, just as your only-begotten Son elected blessed James beside the Sea of Galilee into the order of apostles, and gave him to be an advocate for the people of Galicia, grant to us, we beseech you that, with his help, whose relics are all on earth, for he is the greater, we may deserve to follow him to heaven."[50]

The most reliable evidence on the official Church teaching on pilgrimage in Santiago's shrine can be drawn from sermons in the *Codex* that are attributed to Pope Calixtus II. The most significant of them all—it is, in fact, almost a treatise on pilgrimage—is the one that is entitled *Veneranda dies laudamus*,[52] to which we have frequently referred. It tells of Saint James's martyrdom, of the fame of his church and the miracles the Apostle performs, and of the people who come to Compostela from all over the world. It describes their excitement at vigils, the unending festival they keep, and the fruits of their worship in improved lives. For Saint James forgives sins, and changes the spirit and the character of those who come to him. His benefits to his petitioners are to give children to sterile mothers, to cure the sick, to release prisoners, to return voyagers by sea and land in safety to their homes. He can even perform miracles in places far away from his tomb in order to increase faith in him.

The sermon's teaching on pilgrimage recognizes that the pilgrim's way is hard, but it overcomes carnality and wins heaven through encouraging contemplation, humbling pride, and choosing poverty. Also pilgrimage rewards the abstinent who do good works. The sermon gives allegorical lessons on the pilgrim's equipment and reminds pilgrims of the formula of blessing they received at their initiation. Abraham is the patriarch of the pilgrim, and Jesus Christ himself was the first Jerusalem pilgrim on the road to Emmaus. When the happy pilgrim feeds the poor, then Christ recognizes him. Christ sent seventy out as pilgrims without money; with these should be contrasted the wealthy and worldly pilgrims of the present day—such are more properly regarded as robbers of God. The Lord rode into Jerusalem on a mule; what then of those who ride on horseback or on litters?

Much is said about moral and spiritual preparation for pilgrimage. Those setting out for Saint James's tomb must leave with a license and with a clear conscience after arranging their affairs properly, leaving with sufficient funds to enable them to live simply on the way and to feed the poor and give alms, as well as to attend worship on Sundays and feast days regularly, and always to pray, doing good works on the way. They must avoid disputes and divisions among pilgrims. There follows a diatribe against drunkenness as leading to quarrels, sleeplessness, insanity, and libidinousness.

Then evil innkeepers fleecing pilgrims are excoriated as Judases, for they are motivated by greed to overcharge, and to promise fish and flesh while providing neither. The sermon continues by exposing cheats at pilgrimage centers, including moneychangers who give poor rates, false pardoners promising forgiveness if several Masses are paid for in advance, fake beggars who exaggerate their deficiencies, and the healthy who pretend to be handicapped; the women who at the threshold of Saint James sell tapers and candles with reduced wicks, the merchants who overcharge for food; they will all end in hell for tricking pilgrims, and the preacher describes the miseries of the damned in detail just as if he were the sculptor of the tympanum of Conques.

The sermon warns pilgrims of other dishonest persons, such as silversmiths, goldsmiths, and jewelers of the city who sell rings, chalices, or candlesticks. The pilgrims purchase these items as gifts for the cathedral treasury but are given lightweight or alloyed metals or semiprecious as if they were precious stones. The cheating apothecaries, sellers of paints, false lawyers, false butchers selling pork or beef as if it were venison, are all condemned, and asked what they will say on the Day of Judgment when accused by all the saints whose bodies are in the sanctuaries of pilgrimage? As from charity all good things are born, so from greed all vices arise. The sermon ends with a prolonged and perfervid eulogy of fortunate Galicia and its patron, the Apostle James himself. He has not only exceeded Saint Peter in importance (as we have seen in the hymns and responses) but is actually hailed as if he had replaced Almighty God in the skies above Spain. The following are the exaggerated praises offered to him:

> Glory of Spaniards, refuge of the poor, strength of the weak, consoler of the troubled, safety of pilgrims, fisher of souls, eye of the blind, foot of the lame, hand of the paralysed, guardian of sailors calling upon you, intercessor of the people, father of all, destroyer of vices, builder of virtues, you we petition with humble heart.[53]

With such instruction, the pilgrims were prepared to honor the great Apostle's sanctuary at Compostela, to beware of the crooks who would cheat them even though they came as holy pilgrims, and to return to their homes with holier lives as a preparation for life everlasting.

Yet the attendance at worship on the vigil and on the feast day itself did not complete the duties of conscientious pilgrims. The ritual expected of them, as laid down by Archbishop Juan Arias in the thirteenth century, went as follows. Immediately after the morning service,

> The custodian of the altar and the priest, each standing erect with a rod in his hand, marshalled the bands of pilgrims in turn according to their nationality, and in their own language. The pilgrims now grouped themselves around the priest whose duty it was to deliver to them the indulgences they had gained by their pilgrimages. Then, the divine service having been participated in by them, they therewith proceeded to lay their gifts before the altar, after which it was their privilege to venerate the relics of the Holy Apostle: first came the chain, and after the chain the crown, the hat, the staff, the knife and the stone.[54]

Furthermore, the pilgrims were asked whether their offering was for Saint James, that is, for alms and general needs, in which case it was placed on the altar, or whether it was for the building fund, in which case it was put on a side table. Cash or jewelry alone was accepted, and the indulgence was given only after the donation was received.[55]

The pilgrim had come prepared to make his offerings at the saint's tomb; this was, after all, a feature of all sanctoral pilgrimage centers. They were a necessity for every great shrine of pilgrimage because they paid for the imposing church that housed the saint and for the support of poor pilgrims. Both the poor and the wealthy were expected to give according to their means. Saint Foi is supposed to have told the countess of Toulouse, "Come to my shrine at Conques and give me all your golden bracelets"; moreover, a woman who had brought a precious ring to Conques and failed to donate it to the saint was cursed with night-mares and fevers.[56]

Santiago de Compostela might be fussy in demanding money or jewelry. It is well known that at an earlier period and in many shrines the custodians were only too glad to receive the wax ex-votos of the pilgrims. These would be shaped as a healed member of the body or a lost object that had been found. For example, a citizen of Montpellier who had lost two oxen carried wax replicas of them in miniature to Rocamadour as a thank offering to Saint Mary the Virgin for their recovery.[57] Others would bring a candle having the same height or weight as the person cured. These objects of wax served a double purpose. They were, in the first place, reminders of the power of the saint and of the piety of previous pilgrims. In the second place, when melted down, they served as the means of illuminating the shrine during vigils and daylight services in the form of candles and tapers.

The offering or oblation of the pilgrim was entirely distinct from an ex-voto, for it was simply an acknowledgment of gratitude to the saint. The poor man might offer some coins, while the rich man could offer the title to lands or articles of gold.

It is interesting to note that gradually there developed a ritual of expected gestures accompanying the visit to the saint's shrine. The pilgrim would be required to do five things. First, after making his offerings, which would already immediately lessen the debt of his sins, he would touch the tomb of the saint, either the bare stone or the silver or gilt coverings of the tomb. It was as if he were imitating the Apostle Thomas, who touched the hands and side of the risen Christ. So must the pilgrim touch the container of the saint's body. Secondly, he would kiss the tomb while weeping. These tears were interpreted as proof of the pilgrim's joy and as a mark of sincere compunction. E.-R. Labande, stressing this aspect of the visit, points out that this gesture was even expected of a pope and, as evidence, gives the example of Pope Pascal II visiting Saint Denis as a pilgrim in 1107, who is described as *sanctorum pignoribus humillime prostratus, lacrimas compunctionis offerebat.*[58]

In the third place, the pilgrim was expected to pray earnestly at the saint's tomb, and sometimes he did so either by prostration or with his arms in the shape of a cross. In the fourth place, pilgrims were to feel that their sins were forgiven at the saint's tomb, so that this was a substitute for the sacrament of penance.[59] Finally, they knew that no compunction or confession was adequate without a succession of good works, and we may suppose that they promised that improved quality of life to Saint James at his revered tomb.

Some pilgrims might feel the need to visit the various monastic and parochial churches in Compostela and its neighborhood, whether inspired by curiosity or piety, but to all intents and purposes in completing their vow by visiting the saint's tomb, revering him by touching his tomb with fingers and lips while in tears and praying, and by receiving their indulgence, they had finished the formalities with only one exception. They still needed proofs that they had been to Compostela. This was, of course (in addition to the license), the essential pilgrim token of the scallop shell.

Each important center of pilgrimage had its own official souvenir, a public token that the returning pilgrim had indeed visited that shrine. If he had been to the Holy Land he returned with the palm of Jericho, which is the origin of the English word *palmer*. Canterbury had the mitered head of Saint Thomas à Becket between two erect swords. Rome had the crossed keys of Saint Peter. The badge of Mont-Saint-Michel was a standard and a shield with a representation of Saint Michael weighing souls at the Last Judgment,[60] while the Virgin was the emblem of the shrine of Rocamadour. Pilgrims who had been to several sanctuaries would cover the brims of their hats with leaden badges, such as Langland's pilgrim who had

> An hundreth of ampulles on his hatt seten
> Signes of Synay[61] and shells of Galice
> And many a cruche on his cloke and keyes of Rome
> And the Vernicle[62] before; for men shulde knowe
> And se bi his signes whom he soughte had.

They were not only souvenirs and charms, but they proved that the wearer was exempt from tolls and taxes as a pilgrim, while they were accepted in some courts as proof that the property of the pilgrim was immune from distraint for debts.[63]

Why was the scallop shell chosen as the token of Santiago? Probably in the first place because it was abundant on the seacoast of Galicia. Its significance was however enhanced by a legend that as the stone ship bearing the body of the Apostle James neared the land at Padrón, a horseman riding on the beach was carried by his bolting horse into the waves. Instead of being drowned, however, both horse and rider emerged from the deep covered with scallop shells.[64]

The shell was known as the *vieira*, a term derived from the latin *veneria*, as attested in Pliny, and from which comes the Spanish *venera*. From ancient times it was consecrated to Venus, as being emblematic of the female sexual organs.[65] Pilgrims of religions other than Christianity used them as amulets with which to ward off the evil eye. Leclercq insists that the first Christians used these shells to mark Christian tombs from those of others. They have been found in Punic, Roman, Merovingian and in Visigothic cemeteries, as in Pamplona.[66] Christians in the twelfth century still considered the shells to have magical powers. This is illustrated through the story in chapter XII of Book II of the *Codex Calixtinus* about the cure that came to a knight of Apulia who suffered from an illness of the throat and who was healed by the application of a cockleshell brought by a pilgrim from Santiago.

E.-R. Labande has suggested that at a late date, and as a result of the similarity of sound between *pacten* (cockleshell) and the *peigne* (liturgical comb), as well as a certain physical resemblance, it was regarded as a symbol of purity, since this should be the virtue evident in the new man, recreated by the pilgrimage.[67] The theory seems farfetched to us.[68]

The *Veneranda dies* sermon in the *Codex* considers the shells to have a deeper symbolic significance. It claims that near Santiago there are certain fish with two valves like plate armor, one on each side of their bodies. These shells the pilgrims of Saint James would gather and sew onto their cloaks for the honor of the Apostle and as a remembrance of him. They also served as a memento of the long journey when the pilgrims returned rejoicing to their kith and kin. The kind of armor the shellfish used for its protection symbolized the two precepts of charity—to love God above all and one's neighbor as one's self—which were spiritual protection for the pilgrims. Each valve of the shell resembled fingers in a hand and served as a reminder that the pilgrim should be continually doing good works.[69] Allegorical interpretation was often more ingenious than convincing and rarely more so than when the Dominican, Thomas of London, wrote in his *Instructorum peregrinorum* of ca. 1430 that the staff, satchel, and tunic of the pilgrim represent, respectively, faith, hope and charity.[70]

It seems that the pilgrims first extended their visit to Galicia by going on from Compostela to two marine sanctuaries. At Finis Terrae ("the end of the earth"), now known as Finisterre, there was a large mountain on which was built a hermitage dedicated to Saint Guilhem-du-Désert. Thence the pilgrims would follow the coast to El Padrón to the mouth of the small River Ulla to view the place where the stone ship bringing the body of Saint James, supposedly from Jaffa, had finally beached.

After seeing the relic of the stone ship, the pilgrims would then collect the scallop shells from the beach where they were plentiful.[71] By the twelfth century, badges were made of silver, jet, and lead in the shape of scallop shells and sold in the paraiso, or square, opposite the north transept of the cathedral. So flourishing was this business that in 1200 Archbishop Pedro Suárez restricted the number of official vendors of these badges to a hundred. This is itself an indication of the popularity of the pilgrimage at its peak.[72] Often the badges were perforated so that they could be sewn on to the tunics, wallets, and especially hat brims of the pilgrims.[73]

Apart from their symbolical value and their significance as testimonials or credentials of pilgrimage, the badges also had a strictly practical value. If they were ornaments cut of azabache jet or of silver, they became precious keepsakes that could be exchanged for money. Their most strictly pragmatic value, however, was they could be used as a drinking cup, spoon, or dish, or even as a small plate for the reception of alms.

The ultimate value of the pilgrim outfit—tunic, staff, wallet, and gourd, as well as the cockleshell—would be appreciated to the full only when the pilgrims returned to their own homes. They would be reminders of the higher standard of Christian obedience for which they had ventured on pilgrimage and of the wisdom, maturity, illumination, and grace they had received on the road. Furthermore, the outfits would serve as inspiration and incitation for their descendants to go and do likewise. And, finally, they might be worn for the last, most intrepid pilgrimage of all, which they would take alone—the pilgrimage through death to eternity.

In addition to the emblem of the pilgrimage sanctuary, the pilgrim was also expected to return if at all possible with a relic from the sanctuary. On a modest scale it might be a tiny fragment of the stone of the tomb itself, or oil from a lamp that had burned at the tomb. More ambitiously it might be an ampul containing some particle of the blood of the martyrs (as, for example that of Saint Thomas à Becket of Canterbury in the tenth and eleventh centuries). Better still would be a true fragment of the body of the saint, such as the tooth of Saint Nicholas that was brought back from Bari to Normandy by the knight and pilgrim, Guillaume Pantoul.[74]

Not all pilgrims were ecstatic at Compostela. Some were critical, especially by the end of the Middle Ages. Andrew Boorde, an Oxford-educated English physician, who was suffragan Bishop of Chichester, came to Compostela first in 1532 and again some years later. He was most skeptical about the legends of Compostela. He wrote:

I dyd dwel in Compostell, as I did dwell in many partes of the world, to se &
to know the trewth of many thynges & I assure you that there is not one
heare nor one bone of saint Iames in Spayne in Compostell, but only, as they
say, his stafe, and the chayne the whyche he was bounde wythall in prison,
and the syckel or hooke, the whyche doth lye upon the mydell of the hyghe
aulter, the whych (they sayd) dyd sawe and cutte off the head of saint Iames
the more, for whom the confluence of pylgrims restoreth to the said place.[75]

The skepticism that sounded the death knell of the popular medieval
pilgrimage to Compostela was found in one of Erasmus's *Colloquies*
entitled *The Religious Pilgrimage*. In it Ogygius has returned from
Compostela and is being questioned by his friend Menedemus about his
dress and experience. The friend's first comment is: "But what strange
Dress is this? It is all over set off with Shells scollop'd, full of Images of
Lead and Tin, and Chains of Straw-work, and the Cuffs are adorned
with Snakes Eggs [i.e. Beads for praying] instead of Bracelets." Ogygius
says that he went to fulfill a vow of his mother-in-law that she would
pay her respects to Saint James if her daughter should deliver a live son.
Menedemus pokes fun at this substitute paying of a vow and suggests
the family would have been just as well if they had not bothered to
"compliment" Saint James. He asks his friend what response Saint
James gave to his expression of thanks. Ogygius replies: "None at all;
but upon tendring my Present, he seemed to smile, and gave me a gentle
Nod, with this same Scollop Shell." Menedemus asks how well does
Saint James fare, to which Ogygius replies: "Why truly, not so well by
far as he used to." He adds: "And this is the Cause, that this great
Apostle that used to glitter with Gold and Jewels, now is brought to the
very Block that he is made of, and has scarce a Tallow Candle."
Menedemus makes the final comment: "If this be true, the rest of the
Saints are in danger of coming to the same Pass."[76] The "new opinion"
that has reduced the attraction of pilgrimage is the satirical spirit of the
Renaissance combined with the Reformation's insistence on the Christian's unmediated and direct relationship to Christ, together with the
emphasis on justification by faith instead of by good works.

However desperate the situation was in the early sixteenth century, it
was otherwise from the tenth to the fifteenth centuries. In that era
Compostela was a powerful magnet that attracted the devout to the
tomb of the Apostle. The delight of many pilgrims in reaching their
journey's end at Compostela made them reluctant to tread the pilgrim's
road for home. Delay presented no particular problem, for there were
other sanctuaries to visit in the vicinity in addition to the hermitage of
Saint Guilhem and El Padrón, already mentioned. The guide proudly
mentions that there are no less than ten churches in Compostela itself.
In addition to Saint James's glorious church, there was the monastic

church of Saint Peter, Saint Michael's church, the abbey church of Saint Martin of Tours, the church of the Holy Trinity which was the burial ground of pilgrims, the churches of Saint Felicity, Saint Benedict, Saint Pelagius the martyr (immediately behind the cathedral), and of Saint Mary the Virgin, which has a direct passageway to the cathedral. To view the iconography, the relics, and especially the precious objects in the treasuries of each of these churches would take considerable time, as the gifts and their donors were each pointed out.

But there was a more serious reason for the desire of several of the pilgrims to remain in the pilgrimage center much longer. It was not uncommon for devout pilgrims to wish to stay at a shrine for the whole period of Lent or even longer. Gerard de Corbie stayed only two days at Benedict's first foundation, the famous Monte Cassino, but he allowed himself eight days in Rome.[77] Joachim of Fiore, that ardent visionary, stayed throughout the forty days of Lent at Mount Tabor, the supposed Mount of Transfiguration.[78] Martin of León spent two whole years at Jerusalem.[79]

It must have been tempting for the Jacobite pilgrim, especially after the difficulties of the journey over the Pyrenees or through the Bay of Biscay and the contemplation of the return, to prolong his stay in the city where he felt the protective and miraculous power of the Apostle James so near. A specially pious pilgrim might stay on with the express intention of accumulating good works, perhaps by serving the poor in the hospital of Compostela. Others who were old and enfeebled hoped they might die and be buried near the saint's shrine. There were dangers in remaining, particularly so for valetudinarians of the spirit who lived on moods and would not be able to maintain the enchantment indefinitely. The very wish to stay might be an evasion of diurnal duty and of family responsibilities. The temptation to cast aside heavy responsibilities while going on pilgrimage was not unknown to the personages of the period. Archbishop Hildebert had to dissuade Foulques, count of Anjou and Maine, from pilgrimage by insisting that even if he had made a vow to go on pilgrimage, "God laid on you the charge of governing your people" and advising that the discharge of this responsibility was a greater good than pilgrimage. He urged the count, therefore, "then stay in your place, live for your state, do justice, protect the poor and churches."[80]

Others, whether motivated by duty or delight, postponed the return home by alternative routes or by additional pilgrimage. Some chose to return by the Asturias through the ancient cathedral center of Oviedo, with its famous reliquaries in the *Camera Santa,* which remains to this day an extraordinary treasure house. Others passed by the abbey of Silos, then climbed the route traversed by eagles to the jagged mountainous abbey of Montserrat, where in a last generous medieval gesture

Saint Ignatius, the founder of the Jesuits, was to become the soldier of Our Lady before whose blackened shrine he spent a night in vigil. Others, again, pressed on to the central shrine of the Catholic Church, the great Saint Peter's of Rome.

Eventually the pilgrims reached home to be received with new honors among their kith and kin and friends. They were better prepared for the last pilgrimage of all through the dark doors of death to where Christ and his friends (and theirs), the saints, held unending festival in everlasting light, not in the field of one star *(Campus stellae)* but beyond the Milky Way with all the stars ablaze.

NOTES

1. The first Montjoie, according to Joseph Bédier in *Les légendes épiques*, 3 vols., 2d ed. (Paris: Champion, 1917), p. 247, was Mount Mary outside Rome. There were others at Le Puy and Vézelay.

2. E.-R. Labande, *Spiritualité et vie littéraire des XIe et XIIe siècles* (London: Variorum Reprints, 1974), article XIII, p. 109.

3. *The Pilgrimage of the Holy Paula* (London: Palestine Pilgrims' Text Society, 1887), I, pp. 5–6. For the best critical and annotated edition of Saint Jerome's 108th letter, from which the citation is taken, see F. Stummer, "Monumenta historiam et geographicam Terrae Sanctae illustrantia," in *Florilegium Patristicum* 41 (1935): 27–49.

4. J. J. Jusserand, *English Wayfaring Life in the Middle Ages*, rev. ed. (London: Unwin, 1925), pp. 357–58.

5. Cited in Georgiana Goddard King, *The Way of Saint James*, 3 vols. (New York: Putnam, 1920), I, p. 91.

6. Raymond Oursel, *Les pèlerins du moyen âge: les hommes, les chemins, les sanctuaires* (Paris: A. Fayard, 1963), pp. 85 ff. See C.C. V, Fita and Vinson, p. 15.

7. *In eo gens gallica peregrina ad sanctum Jacobum tendens . . . totius corporis sui sordes Apostoli amore lavare solet, vestimentis suis expoliata* (C.C. V, Fita and Vinson, p. 10).

8. Oursel, *Pèlerins*, pp. 85 ff. See also C.C. V, Fita and Vinson, pp. 6–7.

9. The *Historia Compostellana*, which was written at the request of Diego Gelmirez, was first printed in the series *España Sagrada*, vol. 20, to which these references are made. Spanish sovereigns are referred to on pp. 60, 124, 194, 206, 448, 586.

10. Ibid., pp. 267, 557, 571.

11. Ibid., pp. 140, 313, 318, 324, 407.

12. Ibid., p. 505.

13. C.C. I, xvii.

14. Ibid., V, ix.

15. O. Kajava, *Etude sur deux poèmes relatifs à l'abbaye de Fécamp* (Helsinki: Imprimerie de la société de littérature finnoise, 1928), p. 66.

16. Ibid., pp. 66, 73.

17. C.C. I, xvii, Whitehill, p. 158.

18. Labande, *Spiritualité et vie littéraire*, article XIV, p. 284.

19. *Nimio gaudio miratur qui peregrinantium choros circa beati Jacobi altare venerandum vigilantes videt. Theutonici enim in alia parte, Franci in alia, Itali in alia catervatim commorantur, cereos ardentes manibus tenentes, unde tota ecclesia ut sol, vel dies clarissima, illuminatur. Unusquisque cum patriotis suis per se vigilias sapienter agit. Alii citharis psallant, alii liris, alii timphanis, alii tibiis, alii fistulis, alii tubis, alii sambucis, alii violis, alii rotis britannicis vel gallicis, alii psalteris, alii diversis generibus musicorum cantando vigilant, alii peccata plorant, alii psalmos legunt, alii elemosinas cecis tribuunt. Ibi audiuntur diverse genera linguarum, diversi clamores, barbarorum loquele et cantilene Theutonicorum, Anglorum, Grecorum ceterarumque tribuum et gentium diver-*

sarum omnium mundi climatum (*C.C.*, Whitehill, p. 149). At Conques the long hours of the vigil were shortened by singing rustic songs—*tam cantilenis rusticis quam aliis nugis longe noctis solantur fastidium* (*Liber miraculorum sanctae Fidis,* ed. A. Bouillet [Paris: Champion, 1897], III, p. 12).

20. D. J. Hall, *English Medieval Pilgrimage* (London: Kegan Paul, 1966), p. 4. See also Paul Rousset, "L'émotivité romane," *Cahiers de civilisation médiévale* 2 (1959), who speaks of "ses contrastes véhéments."

21. Our translation of the *Codex Calixtinus,* Whitehill transcript (Compostela, 1948), p. 148.

22. Ibid., p. 149. . . . *alii pudis pedibus, alii sine proprio, alii causa penitencie liguati ferro. Alii crucis signum ut Greci manibus portant alii sus pauperibus tribuunt, alii ferrum aut plumbum ad opus apostoli basilice manibus deferant, alii ferreos uectes et manicas e quibus per apostolum liberantur de iniquorum erga tulis humeris portant, penitencia agentes, delicta lugentes.*

23. Ibid.

24. Jonathan Sumption, *Pilgrimage: An Image of Medieval Religion* (London: Faber & Faber, 1975), p. 21.

25. *C.C.,* Book V, chapter IX, para. 11, p. 54 (Fita and Vinson transcript), titled *De altaribus basiliae.*

26. Information for this succinct summary of the different churches of Saint James in Compostela was taken from King, *Way of Saint James,* III, p. 67. For a fuller account of the subject see Kenneth T. Conant, *The Early Architectural History of the Cathedral of Santiago de Compostela* (Cambridge, Mass.: Harvard University Press, 1926).

27. For the history of the development of the cult of St. Nicholas of Bari, see A. Gambacorta, "Culto e pellegrinàggi a San Nicola di Bari fino alle prima Crociata," in *Pellegrinàggi e culto di santi in Europa fino alla Iᵃ Crociata* (Todi: Centro di Studi Sulla Spiritualita Medievale, 1963), pp. 485–502.

28. F. L. Cross, ed., *The Oxford Dictionary of the Christian Church* (London: Oxford University Press, 1963), "Michael, The Archangel," p. 897.

29. An attempt was made to distinguish the functions of each saint honored at Compostela by reading their thirteenth-century hagiographies in the *Legenda Aurea* of Jacobus de Voragine. Since, however, many of the saints duplicated the functions of other saints, and Saint James himself was thought at Compostela to have all the powers of the other saints combined, the effort proved fruitless. Hence a topographical approach was found to be more useful, even if often speculative in character.

30. See R. Oursel, *Pèlerins,* pp. 94–95; a poetic but florid modern translation into English can be found in Victor Turner, "The Center Out There: The Pilgrims' Goal," in *History of Religions* 12 (1973): 203–4.

31. In Book I of the *Codex Calixtinus,* which contains sermons to be used on the feasts of Saint James, there is a pseudo-Calixtine sermon, *Celebritas sacratissime,* which on the first page instructs when the feasts are to be celebrated and states the Apostle's miracles are to be recalled on October 30. But otherwise no provision is made in the services at Compostela for this date in the *Codex,* even though there is an important Book II devoted exclusively to the miracles of the saint, which proved exceedingly useful advertising.

32. This passage is translated from Oursel, *Pèlerins,* pp. 100–101.

33. The Hispanic Rite would vary considerably in the alternatives and the ceremonial that would be used in cathedral, monastic church, or country parish. In general, the Mozarabic Rite is remarkable for the abundance, variety, and richness of its prayers, as for the many different votive Masses. Its prayers were long but also often redundant and prolix, and if the Mass were recited or sung, it would last several hours. Its mosaic of borrowing comprised such diverse sources as passages from sermons, acts of martyrs, hagiographies, and treatises of theology (especially those of Saint Isidore, archbishop of Seville, who lived ca. 560–636, and Saint Ildefonsus, archbishop of Toledo, who lived ca. 607–667). It is a highly dogmatic liturgy, very consciously theological, presumably to combat both the fourth-century Arian and the fifth-century Priscillianist heresies. In origin and in structure it was predominantly Roman, but in the fifth and sixth (Visigothic) centuries, its lections, prayer formulas, and melodies were the work of bishops and theological doctors of the peninsula, with borrowings from the African, Gallican, and Byzantine liturgies. See Fernand Cabrol, "La liturgie mozarabe," in *Dictionnaire d'archéologie chrétienne et de liturgie,* vol. 12, pt. 1, cols. 376–491; especially cols. 465–66 and 483–87.

34. *Liber Mozarabicus sacramentorum,* ed. Marius Ferotin (Paris: Firmin-Didot, 1912), makes

no reference in columns 72–75 or 812 to the translation of the Apostle to Galicia. We must therefore assume that the feast of the election and translation of the Apostle was a way of maintaining the original Mozarabic festal date for a second celebration of St. James—one at the height of summer and the other in the dead of winter. For details, see Pierre David, *Etudes sur le livre de saint Jacques attribué au pape Calixte II*, vol. II: *Les livres liturgiques et le livre des miracles* (Lisbon: Institut français des études portugaises, 1947), pp. 2, 18–9, and 24 ff. There was a precedent in the cult of Saint Martin of Tours for a winter and a summer festival. See E. Delaruelle, "La spiritualité des pèlerinages à Saint Martin de Tours du Ve au Xe siècles," in *Pellegrinàggi e culto di santi in Europa fino alla I^a Crociata*, p. 222. The two dates of Saint Martin's festivals were July 4 and November 11. The Mozarabic Mass continues to be used to this day in one chapel of the cathedral of Toledo.

35. It should be made clear that in reconstructing the worship at Compostela, we cannot rely entirely on the *Codex Calixtinus* in the twelfth century, except for the Gospels and Epistles of the Masses and for some of the responses that were used. Pierre David has argued convincingly in *Etudes sur le livre de Saint Jacques*, II, pp. 43–47, that the liturgical information in the *Codex* is derived from a monastic not a cathedral milieu. What we have, then, is a description of the worship at the feasts of Saint James as they might have been celebrated in a French Cluniac monastery of the twelfth century, which is not too remote in outlook from what would be going on in Compostela, but is not to be equated with it.

36. This summary of the prayers is taken from *Liturgia Mozarabica vetus*, ed. Marius Ferotin (Paris: Firmin-Didot, 1912), cols. 72–75.

37. *Way of Saint James*, III, pp. 156 f.

38. Ibid., pp. 156–57.

39. Compostela was famous in the twelfth century for its goldsmiths, silversmiths, and artificers in enamel work and jet, as well as its illuminators of manuscripts. See Marilyn Stokstad, *Santiago de Compostela in the Age of the Great Pilgrimages* (Norman: University of Oklahoma Press, 1978), Chapter 6, "Cultural Life: The Arts and the Humanities," especially, pp. 140–42.

40. *Codex Calixtinus* I, chapter xvii.

41. Three German and two French dioceses shared the privilege with Compostela, according to Stokstad, *Santiago de Compostela*, p. 100.

42. The paragraph is a summary of the relevant part of Way's *Itineraries*, of which the original manuscript is in the Bodleian Library, Oxford, and which was published by the Roxburghe Club in 1847.

43. Pope John's pontificate (955–964) was characterized by vengefulness and unbridled lasciviousness. He attained the triple tiara at the age of eighteen and during one orgy ordained a deacon in a stable. See F. Gregorovius, *History of the City of Rome in the Middle Ages* (London: Bell, 1895), III, pp. 321, 336; Luigi Salvatorelli, *L'Italia medievale* (Milan: A. Mondadori, 1938), pp. 530–42; Américo Castro, *The Structure of Spanish History* (Princeton: Princeton University Press, 1954), p. 132; and Henri Pirenne, *Histoire de l'Europe* (Paris: Alcan, 1934), p. 115. The later eleventh-century papacy under Gregory VIII, a Cluniac monk, recovered the lost moral prestige.

44. *Codex Calixtinus*, Whitehill, p. 25, Compostela ms. folio 13 verso.

45. C.C., Whitehill, p. 39, Compostela ms. folio 20 recto. Cf. also a repetition in equally strong terms on p. 40, folio 20 verso. The citation we have translated reads: *Christus enim dominus . . . ipse beato Iacobo dilecto suo per martirii primum triumphum, inter apostolos primatum prebuit in celis.*

46. C.C., Whitehill, p. 209, and Compostela ms. folio 111 verso reads: *Apostole Christi Iacobe, eterni regis miles invictissime, qui in preclara apostolorum curia ut sol micans, inter astra refulges in gloria.*

47. C.C., Whitehill, p. 194, and ms. folio 101 verso reads:

Hic Zebedei Iacobus
Major vocatur et probus
Qui facit in Gallecia
Miraculorum milia.

Ad templum cuius splendidum
Cunctorum cosmi climatum
Occurent omnes populi
Narrantes laudes domini

Armeni, Greci, Apuli,
Angli, Galli, Daci, Frisi,
Cuncte gentes, lingue, tribus,
Illuc pergunt muneribus.

48. Hermogenes, according to the Eusebian Passion of James, was a magician sent by the Pharisees to confound James whom James confounded in turn and converted.

49. C.C., Whitehill, p. 208, Compostela ms. folio 110 verso, reads: R. *Iacobe virginei frater preciose Iohannis, qui pius Ermogenem revocasti corde ferocem ex mundi viciis ad honorem cunctipotentis.* V. *Tu prece continua pro nobis omnibus ora.*

50. C.C., Whitehill, p. 208, Compostela ms. folios 110 verso and 111 recto reads: R. *O adiutor omnium seculorum, O decus apostolorum, O lux clara Gallecianorum, O advocate peregrinorum, Iacobe supplantor viciorum, solue nostrorum catenas delictorum, et duc nos ad salutis portum.* V. *Qui subvenis periclitantibus ad te clamantibus in mare quam in terra, succurre nobis nunc et in periculo mortis. Et duc nos.*

51. C.C., Whitehill, p. 242, Compostela ms. folio 129 verso reads: *Deus cuius unigenitus secus mare Galilee beatum Iacobum in ordine apostolatus elegit, quique illum Gallecianis populis advocatum dedit, da nobis quesumus, ut ipso opitulante relictis omnibus in terris, quod majus est assequi mereamur in celis.*

52. The sermon occupies about 18 pages of Whitehill's transcription, and is chapter xvii of Book I of the *Codex Calixtinus.*

53. The Latin of the C.C., Whitehill, p. 176, Compostela ms. 93 recto and verso, reads: *Tu decus Yspanorum, tu refugium pauperum, uirtus debilium, consolator tribulancium, salus peregrinorum, piscator animarum, occulus cecorum, pes claudorum, manus aridorum, tutor nauigancium te inuocancium, intercessor populorum,* pater omnium [our emphasis] *destructor uiciorum, edificator virtutum, te humile corde petimus.*

54. Translated from a Latin instruction and published in J. S. Stone, *The Cult of Santiago* (New York: Longmans, 1927), p. 248.

55. See also A. López Ferreiro, *Historia de la Iglesia de Santiago de Compostela*, 11 vols. (Santiago: Imp. del Seminario conciliar central, 1898–1909), vol. 5, pp. 64–67 (Appendix 25).

56. See Sumption, *Pilgrimage*, p. 159.

57. See E. Albe, ed., *Les miracles de Notre-Dame de Roc-Amadour au XIIe siècle*, 3 vols. (Paris: Champion, 1907), III, 8, p. 204; referred to in Labande, Article XIV, p. 285 of *Spiritualité et vie littéraire.*

58. Ibid., p. 287, citing Suger, *Vita Ludovici grossi regis*, ed. H. Waquet (Paris: Champion, 1929), p. 54.

59. For evidence, see C.C. I, Whitehill, p. 150.

60. Sumption, *Pilgrimage*, p. 174; and Jusserand, *English Wayfaring Life*, p. 365.

61. Sinai, in reference to the visit to Saint Catherine's Monastery on the place where Moses is supposed to have received the Decalogue.

62. The Vernicle was the headband supposed to have belonged to Saint Veronica, who offered it to Jesus as a sudary on the way to the Cross, and which was returned to her with his features imprinted on it. The original was supposed to have been in Rome since the eighth century and was translated to Saint Peter's by Boniface VIII in 1297.

63. Sumption, *Pilgrimage*, p. 174.

64. Stokstad, *Santiago de Compostela*, p. 6.

65. L. Vázquez de Parga, J. M. Lacarra, J. U. Riú, *Las Peregrinaciónes a Santiago de Compostela*, 3 vols. (Madrid: Escuela de Estudios Medievales, 1948), I, p. 129.

66. *Dictionnaire d'archéologie chrétienne et de liturgie*, 3, 1, cols. 2, 905–2, 907.

67. Labande, *Spiritualité et vie littéraire*, p. 344.

68. Oursel, *Pèlerins*, rejects Labande's philological and homonymous argument on p. 99. Labande's theory is farfetched in our view because the liturgical comb was unimportant in medieval worship.

69. C.C. I, xvii, Whitehill, pp. 155–56.

70. Sumption, *Pilgrimage*, p. 173.

71. Oursel, *Pèlerins*, p. 99.

72. Stokstad, *Santiago de Compostela*, pp. 89, 95.

73. Jusserand, *English Wayfaring Life*, p. 365.

74. Orderic Vital, *Historia ecclesiastica*, ed. Le Prévost and Delisle (Paris: J. Renovard, 1855) III, p. 220: *Quidam miles de Normannia, Guillelmus cognomento Pantulphus in Apuliam abiit, et quod sanctum Nicolaum valde diligebat, de reliquis ejus multum quaesivit, Deoque juvante procurationem ejus, a reliquiarum translatoribus unum dentem et duo frustra de marmoreo tumulo obtinuit. . . . Dentem itaque tanti baronis nactus, Normanniam rediit.* Cited by Labande, *Spiritualité et vie littéraire*, article XII, p. 345.

75. Cited in Stone, *Cult of Santiago*, pp. 342 ff.

76. *The Colloquies of Erasmus*, 2 vols. trans. N. Bailey, ed. E. Johnson (London: Reeves, 1878), II, pp. 2 ff. For a modern translation see Craig R. Thompson, ed., *The Colloquies of Erasmus* (Chicago: University of Chicago Press, 1965), pp. 287–89.

77. *Acta sanctorum* (April 1), pp. 414–15.

78. Jacobus Syllaneus, *Vita beati Joachim de Fiore*, in *Acta Sanctorum*, I (May 7), p. 95.

79. Luke of Tuy, *Vita beati Martini legionensis*, *P.L.*, 208: 18.

80. *Acta Sanctorum*, XXI, p. 290; also King, *Way of Saint James*, I, pp. 120–21.

Bibliography

ABBREVIATIONS

A.A.S.S. *Acta sanctorum.* Antwerp: Johannes Meurisus, 1643–.

C.C. *Codex Calixtinus* (see below).

C.E. *Catholic Encyclopedia.* 16 vols. New York, 1907–14.

D.A.C.L. *Dictionnaire d'archéologie chrétienne et de liturgie.* 15 vols. Edited by F. Cabrol and H. Leclercq. Paris: Letouzey & Ané, 1907–53.

E.C. *Enciclopedia Cattolica.* 12 vols. Edited by P. Paschini and others. Rome: Il Libro Cattolica, 1949–54.

H.E.R.E. Hastings, J., ed. *Encyclopedia of Religion and Ethics.* 12 vols. New York: Scribner's, 1908–26.

M.G.H. *Monumenta Germaniae historica.* Stuttgart: Hiersemann, 1938–.

N.C.E. *New Catholic Encyclopedia.* 17 vols. New York: McGraw, 1966.

P.G. *Patrologia Graeca.* 162 vols. Edited by J. P. Migne. Paris: Garnier, 1857–66.

P.L. *Patrologia Latina.* 221 vols. Edited by J. P. Migne. Paris: Garnier, 1844–64.

PRIMARY SOURCES

Codex Calixtinus, or *Liber sancti Jacobi:*

Ms. *Codex Compostellanus* in the archives of the cathedral of Santiago de Compostela;

Ms. Latin 12 in the Bibliothèque Nationale, Paris;

Additional Mss. 12213 in the British Museum, London;

Ms. C. 128 in the Biblioteca Vaticana, Rome;

Ms. O. 634 y P. 120–4305 in the Biblioteca Real, Madrid;

Ms. 99 of the abbey of Ripoll, Spain;

Alcobaca Ms. in Lisbon.

The five books of the *Codex Calixtinus* were transcribed by Walter Muir Whitehill in *Liber sancti Jacobi, Codex Calixtinus, texto transcripcion.* 2 vols. Compostela, 1944.

A facsimile of the *Codex Calixtinus* was published as *Libro de la peregrinación del codice Calixtino,* vol. 1 of *Medievalia hispania,* edited by Charles Romera de Lecca. Madrid: Joyas Bibliográficas, 1971.

Book V (misnumbered as Book IV) of the *Liber sancti Jacobi* was published by F.-J. Fita and J. Vinson as *Le codex de saint Jacques de Compostelle* in Paris, 1888.

Another edition of Book V, containing a Spanish translation from the Latin, is that of the Marqués de la Vega Inclán: *Guía del viaje a Santiago.* Madrid: Real Academia de la Historia, 1927.

A critical edition in Latin, with French translation, is that of Jeanne Vielliard: *Le guide du pèlerin de saint Jacques de Compostelle.* Mâcon: Protat frères, 1950; reprint 1963.

Other Primary Sources

Adam of Eynsham. *Magna vita sancti Hugonis.* 2 vols. Edited by E. L. Douie and H. Farmer. London: Nelson, 1961–62.

Agobard. *Liber de correctione antiphonarii. P.L.,* 104: 329–40.

Aimon. *De translatione sanctorum martyrum, Georgii monachi, Aurelii et Nathaliae. P.L.,* 115: 939–47.

Amalarius. *Amalarii episcopi opera liturgica omnia.* 3 vols. Edited by J. M. Hanssens. Rome: Studi e Testi, 1948–50.

Augustine of Hippo, Saint. *De civitate Dei.* Liber XVIII. *P.L.,* 41: 559–620.

———. *Enarratio in Psalmum 46. P.L.,* 36: 34–395.

———. *Sermo XIV. P.L.,* 38: 111–16.

Benedict, Saint. *The Rule of Saint Benedict in Latin and English.* Translated and edited by Justin McCann. London: Burns, Oates, 1952.

Bernard of Clairvaux, Saint. *Apologia ad Gullielmum sancti Theodorum abbatem. P.L.,* 182: 895–919.

———. *De laude novae militiae ad milites templi. P.L.,* 182: 895–919.

———. *Sermones in cantica, Sermo 61. P.L.,* 159: 823–24.

Bible moralisée (a thirteenth-century French illuminated manuscript). Ms. Latin 11560 in the Bibliothèque Nationale, Paris. Published as *Bible moralisée,* edited by A. Laborde. Paris: Société des bibliophiles français, 1912.

Boethius. *The Consolation of Philosophy.* Translated by Richard Green. New York: Library of the Liberal Arts, 1962.

Borg, J. J., ed. *Aye d'Avignon.* Geneva: Droz, 1967.

Chaucer, Geoffrey. *The Canterbury Tales.* Edited by W. W. Skeat. London: Oxford University Press, 1950.

Cid, El Campeador. *The Poem of the Cid.* Translated and edited by Archer W. Huntington. New York: Hispanic Society of America, 1942.

Cloetta, E., ed. *Les deux rédactions en vers du Moniage Guillaume.* 2 vols. Paris: Firmin-Didot, 1906–11.

Collins, Fletcher, Jr. *Medieval Church Music-Drama: A Repertory of Complete Plays.* Charlottesville: University of Virginia Press, 1976.

Dante Alighieri. *Convivio.* Critical edition by Maria Simonelli. Bologna: R. Patron, 1966.

Egeria. *Egeria's Travels.* Translated and annotated by J. Wilkinson. London: S.P.C.K., 1971.

Ellis, H., ed. *Original Letters Illustrative of English History.* 3d series. London: Harding, Triphook & Lepard, 1846.

Erasmus. *The Colloquies of Erasmus.* Edited by Craig R. Thompson. Chicago: University of Chicago Press, 1965.

———. *The Colloquies of Erasmus.* 2 vols. Translated by N. Bailey. Edited by E. Johnson. London: Reeves, 1878.

———. *Pilgrimages to Saint Mary of Walsingham and Saint Thomas of Canterbury.* Translated by J. G. Nichols. London: J. B. Nichols and Son, 1848.

Ermentarius. *Miracula Philiberti.* Edited by Poupardin. Paris: A. Picard, 1905.

Eusebius of Caesarea, Bishop. *Vita Constantini imperatoris ad sanctorum coetum.* P.G., 20: 10–1316.

Eutychius. *The Book of the Demonstration (Kitāh-al-Burhān).* Translated by W. M. Watt. Edited by P. Cachia. In *Corpus scriptorum Christianorum orientalium, scriptores Arabici.* 2 vols. Louvain, 1960–61.

Faith, Saint (Foi, Sainte). *Liber Miraculorum sanctae Fidis.* Edited by A. Bouillet. Paris: Champion, 1897.

"The Fleury Playbook." Ms. 201 of the Orléans Bibliothèque de la Ville (contains several liturgical dramas, including the *Officium peregrinorum*).

Gairdner, James, ed. *The Paston Letters.* Vol. 1. London: Constable, 1872.

Giles (Gilles), Saint. *La vie de st. Gilles par Guillaume de Berneville: poème du XIIième siècle.* Edited by Gaston Paris. Paris, 1881.

Glaber, Rudolf. *Historiam sui temporis quinque libri.* P.L., 142: 614–98.

Gregory the Great, Saint. *Moralia.* P.L., 75: 515–1162; 76: 1–782.

Hincmar. *Epistola VIII: Ad Egilonem archiepiscopum Senonensem.* P.L., 126: 60–68.

Historia Compostellana. Edited by Florenz. In *España Sagrada.* Vol. 20. Madrid: Rodriguez, 1795.

Isidore of León, Saint. *S. Isidori opera omnia.* Edited by Lorenzana. Rome, 1802.

Jaffé, P., ed. *Liber miraculorum sancti Aegidii.* In *M.G.H.,* vol. 12.

Jerome, Saint. *Contra vigilantium.* P.L., 23: 354–68.

————. *Epistola 108. P.L.*, 22: 878–906.

Jocelin. *The Chronicle of Jocelin of Brakelond.* Translated by L. C. Lane. London: Chatto & Windus, 1925.

Katz, Blanche, ed. *La prise d'Orange.* New York: King's Crown Press, 1947.

Langland, William. *Piers the Ploughman.* Translated by J. E. Goodridge. Harmondsworth and Baltimore: Penguin, 1959.

————. *The Vision of Piers the Plowman.* Edited by W. W. Skeat. London: Oxford University Press, 1873.

Langton, Robert. *The Pilgrimage of Robert Langton.* Translated and annotated by E. M. Blackie. Cambridge, Mass.: Harvard University Press, 1924.

Liber Mozarabicus sacramentorum. Edited by Marius Ferotin. Paris: Firmin-Didot, 1912.

Liturgia de la peregrinacion from the Missal of Vich, Ms. 66, fol. 56–68v., in the chapter library, Vich, Spain.

Liturgia Mozarabica vetus. Edited by Marius Ferotin. Paris: Fermin-Didot, 1912.

The Martyrology of Adon. Ms. Latin 3879 of the Bibliothèque Nationale, Paris.

Melsa, monastery of. *Chronica monasterii de Melsa* Edited by E. A. Bond. London: Rolls Series, 1866–68.

Panofsky, E. *Abbot Suger on the Abbey Church of Saint Denis and Its Art Treasures.* Princeton, N.J.: Princeton University Press, 1946. This is a translation into English of Suger's *Libellus de consecratione ecclesiae s. Dionysii.*

Paula, Saint. *The Pilgrimage of Holy Paula.* London: Palestine Pilgrims' Test Society, 1887.

Peter the Venerable. *Liber de miraculis. P.L.*, 189: 851–954.

————. *Tractatus adversus Petrobrusianos haereticos. P.L.*, 189: 719–850.

Reginon de Prüm. *De ecclesiasticis disciplinis et religione Christiana.* Liber duo. *P.L.*, 132:175–399.

Richard de Saint-Victor. *Sermons et opuscules inédits.* Edited by J. Chatillon. Paris: Desclée, Brouwer, 1951.

Rituale monasticum of San Cugat del Vallès. Ms. 72, fols. 23–24. Now in the Archivo de la Corona de Aragon.

Roland. *La chanson de Roland.* Analytical edition by G. J. Brault. 2 vols. University Park: Pennsylvania State University Press, 1978.

————. *The Song of Roland.* Translated by Dorothy L. Sayers. Harmondsworth and Baltimore: Penguin, 1959.

The Sarum Missal Edited from Three Early Manuscripts. Edited by J. Wickham Legg. Oxford: Clarendon Press, 1916.

The Sarum Missal in English. London: De La More Press, 1911.

Suger. *De consecratione s. Dionysii.* In *Oeuvres complètes.* Edited by Lecoy de la Marche. Paris, 1867.

————. *Vita Ludovici grossi regis.* Edited by H. Waquet. Paris: Champion, 1929.

Toynie, P. J. *Specimens of Old French.* Oxford: Clarendon Press, 1892.

Villon, François. *The Works of François Villon, with Text, Translation, Introduction and Notes.* Edited by Geoffrey Atkinson. London: Scholartis Press, 1930.

Vital, Orderic. *Historia ecclesiastica.* Edited by Le Prévost and Delisle. Paris: J. Renouard, 1855.

Voragine, Jacobus de. *The Golden Legend of Jacobus de Voragine.* Translated and adapted by Granger Ryan and Helmut Ripperger. New York: Arno Press, 1969.

Way, William. *The Itineraries of William Way, fellow of Eton College, to Jerusalem, A.D. 1458 and A.D. 1462; and to Saint James of Compostela, A.D. 1456.* London: Roxburghe Club, 1857.

Zamora Vicente, A., ed. *Poema de Fernán González.* Madrid: Gredos, 1946.

SECONDARY SOURCES

Albe, E., ed. *Les miracles de Notre-Dame de Roc-Amadour au XIIe siècle.* 3 vols. Paris: Champion, 1907.

Anderson, M. D. *The Imagery of the British Churches.* London: Murray, 1955.

Arber, Edward, ed. *English Garner.* 8 vols. London: E. Arber, 1887–96.

Aubert, M.; Pobe, M.; and Gantner, J. *L'Art monumental roman en France.* Paris: Braun, 1958.

Aubry, Pierre. *Trouvères et troubadours.* 3d edition. Paris: Alcan, 1919.

Auriol, A.; and Rey, R. *La basilique st. Sernin de Toulouse.* Toulouse and Paris: E. Privat, 1930.

Backes, M. *Art of the Middle Ages.* New York: Abrams, 1970.

Balsan, Louis. *Conques et son trésor.* Rodez: Editions de la cité, 1956.

Barret, Eugène. *Espagne et Provence: études sur la littérature du midi de l'Europe.* Geneva, 1970.

Barruol, Guy. *Provence romane.* Yonne: Zodiaque, 1977.

Beckwith, John. *Early Medieval Art: Carolingian, Ottonian, Romanesque.* London: Praeger, 1964.

Bedier, Joseph. *Les légendes épiques.* 3 vols. 2d ed. Paris: Champion, 1917.

Beigbeder, O. *Forez-Velay roman.* Yonne: Zodiaque, 1962.

————. *Lexique des symboles.* Yonne: Zodiaque, 1966.

Berlière, U. "Les pèlerinages judiciaires au moyen âge." In *Revue Bénédictine* 7 (1899): 525 ff.

Biggs, Anselm G. *Diego Gelmirez, the First Archbishop of Compostela.* Washington, D. C.: Catholic University of America Press, 1949.

Bishop, Edmund. *Liturgica historica.* Oxford: Clarendon Press, 1918.

Bligny, Bernard. *L'église et les ordres religieux dans le royaume de Bourgogne aux XIe et XIIe siècles.* Grenoble: P.U.F., 1960.

Bloch, M. *Feudal Society.* London: Routledge, 1961.

Bourquelot, Felix. *Etudes sur les foires de Champagne.* 2 vols. Portulan: Manoir de St. Pierre de Salerne, 1970.

Bousquet, Louis. *Le jugement dernier au tympan de l'église Saint-Foy de Conques.* Rodez: P. Carrère, 1948.

Brandon, S. G. F. *Man and God in Art and Ritual.* New York: Scribner's, 1975.

Bréhier, L. *Les origines du crucifix dans l'art religieux.* Paris: Bloud, 1904.

Bremond, Henri. *Histoire littéraire du sentiment religieux en France.* 12 vols. Paris: Bloud & Gay, 1931.

Brittain, F. *Saint Giles.* Cambridge: Heffer, 1928.

Brown, Paul Alonzo. *The Development of the Legend of Thomas Becket.* Philadelphia: University of Pennsylvania Press, 1930.

———. *Die Verehrung der Eucharistie im Mittelalter.* Munich: M. Hüber, 1933.

Buechner, Frederick. *Godric.* New York: Atheneum, 1980.

Cabrol, Fernand. "La liturgie mozarabe." In *D.A.C.L.*, vol. 12, pt. 1, cols. 376–491.

Castro, Américo. *Santiago de España.* Buenos Aires: Emecé, 1958.

———. *The Structure of Spanish History.* Translated by Edmund L. King. Princeton, N. J.: Princeton University Press, 1954. Reedited and updated as *The Spaniards: An Introduction to Their History.* Berkeley and Los Angeles: University of California Press, 1971.

Caxton, William. *Dialogues in French and English.* London: Early English Text Society Reprint, 1900.

Chailley, J. *Histoire musicale du moyen âge.* Paris: Rieder, 1950.

Chazelas, J. "Les livrets de prières privées du IXe siècle." In *Positions de thèses de l'école de chartes.* Paris: 1959.

Chellini, J. "La pratique dominicale des laïcs dans l'église franque sous le règne de Pépin." In *Revue d'histoire de l'église de France* (1956), pp. 161–74.

Chevalier, Ulysse. *Poésie liturgique du moyen âge.* Lyon: E. Vitte, 1892.

Cohen, G. *L'anthologie du drame liturgique en France au moyen âge.* Paris: Cerf, 1955.

———. *Le théâtre en France au moyen âge.* Paris: Rieder, 1928.

Conant, Kenneth T. *Carolingian and Romanesque Architecture, 800–1200.* Harmondsworth and Baltimore: Penguin, 1959.

———. *The Early Architectural History of The Cathedral of Santiago de Compostela.* Cambridge, Mass.: Harvard University Press, 1926.

Correas, Gonzalo de. *Vocabulario de refranes*. Madrid: Rates, 1924.

Coussemaker, E. de. *Drames Liturgiques du moyen âge*. Paris: Didron, 1861.

————. *La Madelaine, maison de lépreux*. Lille: Lefebvre & Ducrocq, 1898.

Craplet, Bernard. *Auvergne romane*. 3d ed. Yonne: Zodiaque, 1972.

Cross, F. L., ed. *The Oxford Dictionary of the Christian Church*. London: Oxford University Press, 1963.

Cullman, Oscar. *Peter: Disciple-Apostle-Martyr*. Rev. ed. Philadelphia: Westminister Press, 1962.

Daras, Charles. *Angoumois roman*. Yonne: Zodiaque, 1961.

David, Pierre. *Etudes sur le livre de saint Jacques attribué au pape Calixte II*. 4 vols. Lisbon: Institut français des études portugaises, 1946–49.

Davy, M. M. *Essai sur la symbolique romane (XIIe siècle)*. Paris: Flammarion, 1955.

de Boussac, G. *L'église d'Issoire, st. Austremoine*. Clermont-Ferrand: Guide du visiteur, 1971.

de Champeaux, G.; and Sterckx, S. *Introduction au monde des symboles*. Yonne: Zodiaque, 1966.

Delaruelle, E. "La piété populaire à la fin du moyen âge." In *Relazioni del Xe Congresso de Science storiche* 3 (Rome, 1956).

————. "La piété populaire au Xe siècle." In *Relazioni di Xe Congresso di Science storiche* 3 (Rome, 1956).

————. "La spiritualité des pèlerinages à Saint Martin de Tours du Ve au Xe siècle." In *Pellegrinàggi e culto dei santi in Europa fino alla Ia Crociata*. Todi: Centro di Studi sulla Spiritualita Medievale, 1963.

de Lasteyrie, Charles. *L'abbaye de saint Martial de Limoges*. Paris: Colin, 1901.

————. *L'architecture religieuse en France à l'époque romane*. Paris: A. Picard, 1929.

Demus, Otto. *Romanesque Mural Paintings*. London: Thames & Hudson, 1970.

Deyermond, A. D. *Epic Poetry and the Clergy: Studies on the "Mocedades de Rodrigo."* London: Tamesis, 1968.

————. *A Literary History of Spain: The Middle Ages*. London: Benn, 1971.

D'Herbecourt, P.; and Porcher, J. *Anjou roman*. Yonne: Zodiaque, 1969.

Didier. "La dévotion à l'humanité du Christ et saint Bernard." In *Vie spirituelle, ascétique et mystique* (August–September; October, 1930), pp. 1–19; 79–94.

Dodd, C. H. *The Apostolic Preaching and Its Developments*. New York: Willet, Clark, 1951.

Doncoeur, P. *Le Christ dans l'art français*. 2 vols. Paris: Plon, 1939.

Donovan, Richard B. *The Liturgical Drama in Medieval Spain*. Toronto: University of Toronto Press, 1958.

Duchesne, L. "Saint Jacques en Galice." In *Annales du Midi*, April 1900.

Dumoutet, E. *Le Christ selon la chair et la vie liturgique au moyen âge*. Paris: Beauchesne, 1932.

———. *Le désir de voir l'Hostie et les origines de la dévotion au sacré sacrament*. Paris: Beauchesne, 1926.

Duncan, Edmondstoune. *The Story of the Minstrelsy*. New York: Scribner's, 1907.

Durliat, L.; and Allègre. *Pyrénées romanes*. Yonne: Zodiaque, 1969.

Eliade, Mircea. *Image et symbole*. Paris: Gallimard, 1952.

España Sagrada. Madrid: Rodriguez, 1795.

Evans, Joan. *Art in Medieval France, 987–1498*. London: Phaidon, 1948.

———. *Cluniac Art of the Romanesque Period*. Cambridge: Cambridge University Press, 1950.

———. *Life in Medieval France*. London: Phaidon, 1957.

———. *Monastic Life at Cluny, 910–1157*. Oxford: Clarendon Press, 1931.

Eygun, F.; and Dupont, J. *Saintonge romane*. Yonne: Zodiaque, 1970.

Faral, Edmond. *Les jongleurs en France au moyen âge*. Paris: Champion, 1910.

Farrer, Austin. *The Brink of Mystery*. London: S.P.C.K., 1976.

Faux, A., ed. *Guide du visiteur de la cathédrale du Puy*. 3d ed. Le Puy-en-Velay, 1971.

Favière, Jean. *Berry roman*. Yonne: Zodiaque, 1970.

Ferrante, Joan M. *Guillaume d'Orange: Four Twelfth-Century Epics*. New York: Columbia University Press, 1974.

Focillon, Henri. *L'art des sculpteurs romans*. Paris: Leroux, 1931.

Forsyth, Ilene H. *The Throne of Wisdom: Wood Sculptures of the Madonna in Romanesque France*. Princeton, N.J.: Princeton University Press, 1972.

Fracard, M. L. "L'équipement hospitalier en Bas-Poitou sur les routes de Compostelle." In exhibition catalog: *Hôpitaux et confréries des pèlerins de saint Jacques*. Cadillac-sur-Garonne, May–September, 1967.

Furnivall, F. J., ed. *The Stacions of Rome and the Pilgrim's Sea Voyage*. London: Early English Text Society, 1867.

Gaillard, G. "Les commencements de l'art roman en Espagne." In *Bulletin Hispanique* 37 (1935): 272–308.

———. "Le Porche de la Gloire à st. Jacques de Compostelle et ses origines espagnoles." In *Les cahiers de civilisation médiévale*, 1958.

———; Gauthier, M.-M. S.; Balsan, L.; and Surchamp, A. *Rouergue roman*. Yonne: Zodiaque, 1963.

Gambacorta, A. "Culto e pellegrinàggi a San Nicola di Bari fino alla prima Crociata." In *Pellegrinàggi e culto dei santi in Europa fino alla I^a Crociata*. Todi: Centro di Studi sulla Spiritualita Medievale, 1963.

Gasnault, P. "Le tombeau de saint Martin et les invasions normandes." In *Revue de l'église de France,* 1961, pp. 51–66.

Gautier, Léon. *La poésie religieuse dans les cloîtres des IX–XIième siècles.* Paris: V. Palmé, 1887.

Geary, Patrick. *Furta Sacra: Thefts of Relics in the Central Middle Ages.* Princeton, N.J.: Princeton University Press, 1978.

Gimpel, Jean. *The Cathedral Builders.* New York: Grove Press, 1961.

Gonzáles, Antonio Vinayo. *L'ancien royaume de León roman.* Yonne: Zodiaque, 1972.,

Grabar, André. *Early Christian Iconography.* Princeton, N.J.: Princeton University Press, 1968.

———. *Martyrium: recherches sur le culte des reliques et l'art chrétien antique.* 2 vols. Paris: Collège de France, 1943–46.

Gregorovius, F. *History of the City of Rome in the Middle Ages.* London: Bell, 1895.

Grivot, D.; and Zarnecki, G. *Giselbertus, sculpteur d'Autun.* Paris: Editions Trianon, 1965.

Grodecki, L.; Mütherich, F.; Taleron, J.; and Wormald, F. *Le siècle de l'an mille.* Paris: Gallimard, 1973.

Guardini, Romano. *The Spirit of the Liturgy.* Translated by Ada Lang. New York: Sheed & Ward, 1940.

Hall, D. J. *English Medieval Pilgrimage.* London: Kegan Paul, 1966.

Hardison, O.B., Jr. *Christian Rite and Christian Drama in the Middle Ages.* Baltimore and London: Johns Hopkins University Press, 1965.

Hartley, G. G. *The Story of Santiago de Compostela.* New York, 1912.

Heard, Nigel. *International Fairs.* Lavenham: Dalton, 1973.

Heath, Sidney. *Pilgrim Life in the Middle Ages.* Boston and New York: Houghton Mifflin, 1912.

Heitz, Carol. *Recherches sur les rapports entre architecture et liturgie à l'époque carolingienne.* Paris: S.E.V.E.N., 1963.

Hell, Vera and Hellmut. *The Great Pilgrimage of the Middle Ages.* German original, Tübingen: Wasmuth, 1964; English translation, London: Barrie & Rockliff, 1966.

Hubert, J.; Porcher, J.; and Volbach, W. F. *L'empire carolingien.* Paris: Gallimard, 1968.

Jiménez de Rada, Rodrigo. *De rebus Hispaniae.* In *Opera.* Edited by M. D. Pecanes Pecourt. Valencia: Textes Medievales, 1968.

Jung, Carl. "Das Wandlungssymbol in der Messe." In *Eranos Jahrbuch,* 1970–71.

———. *Psychologische Typen.* Zurich: Lascher Verlag, 1946.

Jungmann, Josef A. *The Mass: An Historical, Theological and Pastoral Survey.*

Translated by Julian Fernandez. Collegeville, Minn.: The Liturgical Press, 1976.

———. *Missarum solemnia: Eine genetische Erklärung der römischen Messe*. 2 vols. 2d ed. Vienna: Herder, 1949.

Junyent, Edouard. *Catalogne romane*. 2 vols. Yonne: Zodiaque, 1969.

Jusserand, J. J. *English Wayfaring Life in the Middle Ages*. Rev. ed. London: Unwin, 1925.

Kajava, O. *Etude sur deux poèmes relatifs à l'abbaye de Fécamp*. Helsinki: Imprimerie de la société de littérature finnoise, 1928.

Kantorowicz, E. *Laudes Regiae: A Study in Liturgical Acclamations and Medieval Ruler Worship*. Berkeley and Los Angeles: University of California Press, 1946.

Keet, C. C. *A Study of the Psalms of Ascent*. London: Mitre, 1969.

Kendall, Alan. *Medieval Pilgrims*. New York: Putnam, 1970.

King, Georgiana Goddard. *The Way of Saint James*. 3 vols. New York: Putnam, 1920.

Klauser, Theodor. "Die liturgischen Austauschbeziehungen zwischen der römischen und der fränkisch-deutschen Kirche vom 8. bis zum 11. Jh." In *Historiches Jahrbuch* 53 (1933): 169–89.

———. *A Short History of the Western Liturgy*. Translated by John Halliburton. London: Oxford University Press, 1969.

Kötting, Bernhard. *Peregrinatio Religiosa: Wallfahrten in der Antike und das Pilgerwesen in der alten Kirche*. Regensburg, Münster, 1950.

Kraft, Heinz. *Kaiser Konstantins religiöse Entwicklung*. Tübingen: Mohr, 1955.

Künstler, G. *Romanesque Art in Europe*. Greenwich, Conn.: New York Graphic Society, 1968.

Labande, E.-R. "Recherches sur les pèlerins dans l'Europe des XIe et XIIe siècles." In *Les cahiers de civilisation médiévale*, January–March, 1959.

———. *Spiritualité et vie littéraire de l'occident, Xe–XIVe siècles*. London: Variorum Reprints, 1974.

———. *Spiritualité et vie littéraire des XIe et XIIe siècles*. London: Variorum Reprints, 1974.

Labande-Mailfert, Y. *Poitou roman*. 2d ed. Yonne: Zodiaque, 1962.

Lacarra, J. M. "Espiritualidad del culto y de la peregrinación a Santiago antes de la primera cruzada." In *Pellegrinàggi e culto dei santi in Europa fino alla Iª Crociata*. Todi: Centro di Studi sulla Spiritualita Medievale, 1963.

Ladner, Gerhart B. "*Homo viator*: Medieval Ideas on Alienation and Order." In *Speculum* 12 (April 1967): 233–59.

Ladurie, Emmanuel. *Montaillou*. Harmondsworth and Baltimore: Penguin Books, 1980.

Lafont, Robert. *Nouvelle histoire de la littérature occitane.* Paris: P.U.F., 1970.

Lamas, M. C.; Gonzalez, V.; and Regal, B. *Galice romane.* Yonne: Zodiaque, 1973.

Lambert, Elie. *Etudes médiévales.* 4 vols. Toulouse: Privat, 1956–57.

———. "La peregrinación a Compostela." In *Archivo español de arte,* 1943, pp. 273–309.

Leclercq, Jean; Vandenbrouke, F.; and Bouyer, L. *La spiritualité du moyen âge.* Paris: Auber, 1961. English edition: *The Spirituality of the Middle Ages.* London and New York: Burns, Oates, 1968.

le Goff, Jacques. *Marchands et banquiers du moyen âge.* Paris: P.U.F., 1969.

Lelong, Charles. *Touraine romane.* Yonne: Zodiaque, 1977.

———. *La vie quotidienne en Gaule à l'époque mérovingienne.* Paris: Hachette, 1963.

Lightfoot, J. B., ed. *The Apostolic Fathers.* New York: Macmillan, 1885.

Lopez, Ferreiro, A. *Historia de la iglesia de Santiago de Compostela.* 11 vols. Santiago: Imp. del Seminario conciliar central, 1898–1909.

Lot, Ferdinand. *Etudes sur les légendes épiques françaises.* Paris: Champion, 1958.

Louillo, José Guerrero. *Las cantigas: estudio arqueologico de sus miniaturas.* Madrid: Consejo Superior de Investigaciones Científicas, 1958.

Loyola, Marqués de. "De Santiago peregrino a Santiago matamoros." In *Cuadernos hispanoamericanos,* nos. 238–40, 1969.

Luc, Brigitte. "Un pèlerinage type: Saint Jacques de Compostelle." In Madaule, J.; Luc, B.; Gaillard, G.; and Abbé Branthomme. *Pèlerins comme nos pères: retour à saint Jacques.* Saint-Mandé: La Tourelle, 1950.

Madaule, J.: Luc, B.; Gaillard, G.; and Abbé Branthomme. *Pèlerins comme nos pères: retour à saint Jacques.* Saint-Mandé: La Tourelle, 1950.

Mâle, Emile. *L'art religieux du XIIe siècle en France.* 3d ed. Paris: Colin, 1924.

———. *L'art religieux du XIe siècle en France.* Paris: Colin, 1924.

———. *Religious Art from the Twelfth to the Eighteenth Century.* New York: Farrar, Straus, 1958.

———. *Religious Art in France: The Twelfth Century.* Princeton, N.J.: Princeton University Press, 1978.

Mansi, J. D. *Sacrorum conciliarum nova et amplissima collectio.* 53 vols. in 58. Paris: Welter, 1901–27.

Masson, A. "Existe-t-il une architecture de saint Jacques?" In *Revue historique de Bordeaux et du département de la Gironde* 35 (1942): 5–17.

Maury, J.; Gauthier, M.-M. S.; and Porcher, J. *Limousin roman.* Yonne: Zodiaque, 1960.

Menéndez Pidal, R. *Cantar de Mio Cid.* 3 vols. Madrid: Bailly-Ballière, 1964–69.

――――. *Historia y epopeya.* Madrid: Hernando, 1934.

――――. *Poésia juglaresca y origenes de las literaturas romanticas.* Madrid: Instituto de estudios Politicos, 1957.

――――, ed. *Primera crónica general de España.* 2 vols. Madrid: Nueva Biblioteca de Autores Españoles, 1955.

Meredith-Jones, C. *Historia Karoli et Rhotolandi ou chronique de pseudo-Turpin.* 2 vols. Paris: Droz, 1970–71.

Mone, F. J., ed. *Hymni Latini medii aevii.* 3 vols. Freiburg im Breisgau: Herder, 1853–55.

Moreno, Gómez. *El arte románico español.* Madrid: Centro de Estudios historicos, 1934.

Morison, Samuel Eliot. *Admiral of the Ocean Sea.* Boston: Little, Brown, 1942.

――――. *The European Discovery of America: The Southern Voyages,* A.D. *1492–1616.* New York: Oxford University Press, 1974.

Mudroch, V.; and Couse, G. S. *Essays on the Reconstruction of Medieval History.* Montreal and London: McGill–Queen's University Press, 1974.

Mullins, E. B. *The Pilgrimage to Santiago.* London: Taplinger, 1974.

Nagler, A. M. *The Medieval Religious Stage—Shapes and Phantoms.* New Haven, Conn.: Yale University Press, 1976.

Netzer, H. *L'introduction de la messe romaine en France.* Paris: A. Picard, 1910.

Nichols, J. G., trans. *Peregrinatio religionis ergo.* In Erasmus. *Pilgrimages to Saint Mary of Walsingham and Saint Thomas of Canterbury.* London: J. B. Nichols and Son, 1849.

Oursel, Raymond. *Bourgogne romane.* 5th ed. Yonne: Zodiaque, 1968.

――――. *Evocation de la chrétienté romane.* Yonne: Zodiaque, 1968.

――――. *Living Architecture: Romanesque.* New York: Grosset & Dunlap, 1967.

――――. *Les pèlerins du moyen âge: les hommes, les chemins, les sanctuaires.* Paris: A. Fayard, 1963.

Owst, G. R. *Literature and Pulpit in Medieval England.* 2d rev. ed. Oxford: Blackwells, 1961.

Ozinga, M. D. *De romaanse kerkelijke boukunst.* Amsterdam: Contact, 1941.

Panofksy, E. *The Gothic Image: Religious Art in France in the Thirteenth Century.* New York: Harper's, 1938.

Pauphilet, A. *Jeux et sapiences du moyen âge.* Paris: Gallimard, 1951.

Pelikan, Jaroslav. *The Christian Tradition: A History of the Development of Doctrine.* Vol. 3. *The Growth of Medieval Theology.* Chicago: University of Chicago Press, 1978.

Pellegrinàggi e culto dei santi in Europa fino alla I^a Crociata. Todi: Centro di Studi sulla Spiritualita Medievale, 1963.

Penicault, Michel. *Eglises de la Creuse.* Paris: Nouvelles éditions latines, 1977.

Pirenne, Henri. *Histoire de l'Europe.* Paris: Alcan, 1934.

Pollard, A. W., ed. *Fifteenth Century Prose and Verse.* London: Constable, 1903.

Porter, A. K. *Romanesque Sculpture of the Pilgrimage Roads.* 10 vols. Boston: Marshall Jones, 1923. New edition: 10 vols. in 3. New York: Hacker Art Books, 1966–69.

———. *Spanish Romanesque Sculpture.* 2 vols. Florence: Pantheon, 1928.

Puig y Cadafalch, J. *Le premier art roman.* Paris: Laurens, 1928.

Quadralo, J. M. *Asturias y León.* Barcelona: D. Cortez, 1885.

Raby, F. J. E. *A History of Christian Latin Poetry from the Beginning to the Close of the Middle Ages.* 2d ed. Oxford: Clarendon Press, 1953.

Regueiro, J. M. "El *Auto de los Reyes Magos* y teatro liturgico medieval." In *Hispanic Review* 45 (1977): 139–64.

Riant, Paul. *Expéditions et pèlerinages des scandinaves en Terre Sainte.* Paris: Lainé & Havard, 1865.

Ricard, José Gudiol. "Les peintres itinérants de l'époque romane." In *Les cahiers de civilisation médiévale*, 1958.

Riché, Pierre. *La vie quotidienne dans l'empire carolingien.* Paris: Hachette, 1974.

———; and Tate, G. *Textes et documents d'histoire du moyen âge.* 2 vols. Paris: Sedes, 1974.

Riquier, M. *Los cantares de gesta frances.* Madrid: Gredos, 1952.

Rossiter, A. P. *English Drama from Early Times to the Elizabethans.* London: Hutchinson, 1956.

Rouquette, J. M. *Provence romane.* 2 vols. Yonne: Zodiaque, 1971.

Rousset, Paul. "L'émotivité romane." In *Les cahiers de civilisation médiévale* 2 (1959).

Sadea and Sansoni, eds. *I primitivi catalani.* Florence: Forma e Colori, 1965.

Salvatorelli, Luigi. *L'Italia medioevale.* Milan: A. Mondadori, 1938.

Salvini, R. *La scultura romanica in Europa.* Milan, 1956.

Salzman, L. F. *English Life in the Middle Ages.* London: Oxford University Press, 1926.

Sánchez Romeralo, A. *El villancico.* Madrid: Gredos, 1969.

Schmidt, Hermanus A. P. *Introductio in liturgiam occidentalem.* Rome: Herder, 1960.

Secret, Jean. *Périgord roman.* Yonne: Zodiaque, 1968.

———. *Saint Jacques et les chemins de Compostelle.* Paris: Horizons de France, 1957.

Seward, Desmond. *The Monks of War: The Military Religious Orders.* Hamden, Conn.: Archon Books, 1972.

Sigal, P. A. *Les marcheurs de Dieu.* Paris: Colin, 1974.

Smalley, Beryl. *The Study of the Bible in the Middle Ages.* Oxford: Clarendon Press, 1941.

Smith, J. Toulmin. *English Guilds.* London: Trübner, 1870.

Soares, Torquato de Sousa. "Les bourgs dans le nord-ouest de la pénisule ibérique." In *Bulletin des études portugaises* 9 (1943).

Stanley, A. P. *Historical Memorials of Canterbury.* 5th rev. ed. London: Murray, 1882.

Stoddard, W. S. *The Façade of Saint-Gilles-du-Gard: Its Influence on French Sculpture.* Middletown, Conn.: Wesleyan University Press, 1973.

Stokstad, Marilyn. *Santiago de Compostela in the Age of the Great Pilgrimages.* Norman: University of Oklahoma Press, 1978.

Stone, J. S. *The Cult of Santiago.* New York: Longmans, 1927.

Stummer, F. "Monumenta historiam et geographicam Terrae Sanctae illustrantia." In *Florilegum patristicum* 41 (1935): 27–49.

Sturdevant, W. *The Misterio de los Reyes Magos: Its Position in the Development of the Mediaeval Legend of the Three Kings.* Baltimore: Johns Hopkins University Press; Paris: P.U.F., 1927.

Sumption, Jonathan. *Pilgrimage: An Image of Mediaeval Religion.* London: Faber & Faber, 1975.

Thorpe, B. *Ancient Laws.* London: English Record Commission, 1840.

Thompson, James Westfall. *The Literacy of the Laity in the Middle Ages.* Berkeley: University of California Press, 1939.

Timmers, J. M. *A Handbook of Romanesque Art.* London: Nelson, 1969.

Turner, Victor. "The Center Out There: The Pilgrims' Goal." In *History of Religions* 12 (1973): 191–230.

———; and Turner, Edith. *Image and Pilgrimage in Christian Culture.* New York: Columbia University Press, 1978.

Vacandard, E. "Les origines de l'hérésie albigeoise." In *Revue des questions historiques* 55 (1896): 50–83.

Vázquez de Parga, L.; Lacarra, J. M.; and Riú, J. U. *Las peregrinaciónes a Santiago de Compostela.* 3 vols. Madrid: Escuela de Estudios Medievales, 1948–49.

Vidal, M.; Maury, J.; and Porcher, J. *Quercy roman.* 2d ed. Yonne: Zodiaque, 1969.

Villada, García. *Historia eclesiástica de España.* 3 vols. in 4. Madrid: Compañía Ibero-Americana de Publicaciones, 1929–36.

Vogel, Cyril. "Le pèlerinage pénitentiel." In *Pellegrinàggi e culto dei santi in Europa fino alla Iª Crociata.* Todi: Centro di Studi sulla Spiritualita Medievale, 1963, pp. 37–94.

———. "La réforme liturgique sous Charlemagne." In *Karl der Grosse.* 4 vols. Düsseldorf, 1965.

Vogüé, Melchior de. *Glossaire.* Yonne: Zodiaque, 1965.

Weiser, Francis X. *Handbook of Christian Feasts and Customs.* New York: Harcourt Brace, 1958.

Weitzmann, Kurt, ed. *Age of Spirituality: Late Antique and Early Christian Art, 3rd to 7th Centuries.* New York: Metropolitan Museum of Art, 1978.

Wilkinson, John. *Jerusalem Pilgrims before the Crusades.* Warminster: Aris & Phillips, 1978.

Wilmart, A. *Auteurs spirituels et textes dévots du moyen âge latin.* Paris: Bloud, 1932.

Young, Karl. *The Drama of the Medieval Church.* 2 vols. Oxford: Clarendon Press, 1933.

Index

245